Hedly Hodkin
March 1951

D1458954

WITHDRAWN

227.6
M621e

The
MOFFATT
NEW TESTAMENT COMMENTARY
Based on *The New Translation* by the
REV. PROFESSOR JAMES MOFFATT, D.D.
and under his Editorship

THE EPISTLE OF PAUL
TO THE
PHILIPPIANS

227.6
M621e

THE
EPISTLE OF PAUL
TO THE
PHILIPPIANS

BY THE REV.

J. HUGH MICHAEL
D.D.

*Professor of New Testament Exegesis and Literature
Emmanuel College and Victoria College, in the
University of Toronto*

2360

LONDON: HODDER AND STOUGHTON LIMITED

FIRST PUBLISHED . . . OCTOBER 1928
FIFTH IMPRESSION . . . MARCH 1948

BRITISH ISLES NAZARENE COLLEGE LIBRARY

WITHDRAWN

Made and Printed in Great Britain.
Hazell, Watson & Viney, Ltd., London and Aylesbury

EDITOR'S PREFACE

MOFFATT'S NEW TESTAMENT COMMENTARY

THE aim of this commentary is to bring out the religious meaning and message of the New Testament writings. To do this, it is needful to explain what they originally meant for the communities to which they were addressed in the first century, and this involves literary and historical criticism ; otherwise, our reading becomes unintelligent. But the New Testament was the literature of the early Church, written out of faith and for faith, and no study of it is intelligent unless this aim is kept in mind. It is literature written for a religious purpose. ' These are written that ye might believe that Jesus is the Christ, the Son of God.' This is the real object of the New Testament, that Christians might believe it better, in the light of contemporary life with its intellectual and moral problems. So with any commentary upon it. Everything ought to be subordinated to the aim of elucidating the religious content, of showing how the faith was held in such and such a way by the first Christians, and of making clear what that faith was and is.

The idea of the commentary arose from a repeated demand to have my New Testament translation explained ; which accounts for the fact that this translation has been adopted as a convenient basis for the commentary. But the contributors have been left free to take their own way. If they interpret the text differently, they have been at liberty to say so. Only, as a translation is in itself a partial commentary, it has often saved space to print the commentary and start from it.

As everyman has not Greek, the commentary has been written, as far as possible, for the Greekless. But it is based

v

upon a first-hand study of the Greek original, and readers
may rest assured that it represents a close reproduction of
the original writers' meaning, or at anyrate of what we
consider that to have been. Our common aim has been to
enable everyman to-day to sit where these first Christians sat,
to feel the impetus and inspiration of the Christian faith as
it dawned upon the minds of the communities in the first
century, and thereby to realize more vividly how new and
lasting is the message which prompted these New Testament
writings to take shape as they did. Sometimes people
inside as well as outside the church make mistakes about
the New Testament. They think it means this or that,
whereas its words frequently mean something very different
from what traditional associations suggest. The saving thing
is to let the New Testament speak for itself. This is our desire
and plan in the present commentary, to place each writing
or group of writings in its original setting and allow their
words to come home thus to the imagination and conscience
of everyman to-day.

The general form of the commentary is to provide a running
comment on the text, instead of one broken up into separate
verses. But within these limits, each contributor has been
left free. Thus, to comment on a gospel requires a method
which is not precisely the same as that necessitated by
commenting on an epistle. Still, the variety of treatment
ought not to interfere with the uniformity of aim and form.
Our principle has been that nothing mattered, so long as the
reader could understand what he was reading in the text of
the New Testament.

JAMES MOFFATT.

PREFACE

THERE were within my reach as I wrote this exposition of Philippians the Commentaries of Lipsius and Dibelius, the majority of recent English works on the epistle, Bengel's *Gnomon*, the quaint Commentary of John Trapp, as well as the Welsh Commentary of T. Isfryn Hughes. The articles on the epistle in the various Bible Dictionaries and in the *Encyclopaedia Britannica* have been consulted, as have also the Introductions of Zahn, Moffatt, and Goguel. I do not suppose there is one of these works to which I am not in some measure beholden.

I have not been able to resist the force of the arguments that have been adduced in recent years in favour of Ephesus as the place in which the epistle was written. These arguments have been collected and well set forth by Professor Clayton R. Bowen in two articles in the *American Journal of Theology*, vol. xxiv, nos. 1 and 2 (January and April 1920). I desire to acknowledge my special obligation to these articles in Section 5 of the *Introduction*.

J. H. M.

May 17th, 1927.

INTRODUCTION

§ 1. PAUL AND PHILIPPI

THERE is no more vivid passage in the Acts of the Apostles than the brief paragraph in chap. 16 which describes how Paul came to enter Macedonia for the first time (vers. 6–10). It is here—at ver. 10—that the first of the ' we '-sections of Acts begins. Accompanied by Silas, Timotheus, and the diarist (who is also in all probability the historian), Paul makes his way to Philippi. The city is described as ' the Roman colony of Philippi, which is the foremost town of the district of Macedonia ' (ver. 12). The story of the events that occurred during the Apostle's stay in the city is told with great vividness. Here Lydia, ' a dealer in purple, who belonged to the town of Thyatira,' was converted, and baptized ' along with her household ' (vers. 13–15) ; here, too, the slave-girl ' possessed by a spirit of ventriloquism ' lost the power which made her a source of gain to her owners when Paul ordered the spirit out of her in the name of Jesus Christ (vers. 16–18). The outcome of this was that Paul and Silas were arrested, flogged, and put into prison. There follows a graphic account of the earthquake ' which shook the very foundations of the prison,' of the conversion of the jailer, who was baptized with all his family, of the release of the apostles and their refusal to leave the city until the praetors, alarmed by the discovery that they had flogged and imprisoned Roman citizens, had come in person entreating them to depart, and, finally, of their departure after they had encouraged the brethren assembled in the house of Lydia (vers. 19–40).

Some five years later, at the close of his ministry in Ephesus, Paul ' went his way to Macedonia ' (Acts 20 : 1). We may assume that Philippi was visited on this occasion, for we read that the Apostle passed ' through the districts of Macedonia, . . . encouraging the people at length.' From Macedonia he went to Greece, where he spent three months. He returned through Macedonia on his last journey to Jerusalem. We are told that he sailed from Philippi ' after the days of unleavened bread ' (Acts 20 : 2–6).

§ 2. THE CITY OF PHILIPPI

The history of the city in which Christianity first took root in Europe stretches far back beyond the time when it received the name of ' Philippi ' from Philip of Macedon, the father of Alexander the Great. Influenced by its strategic position and by the gold-mines in its vicinity, Philip refounded the city. It was in the neighbourhood of Philippi that Octavian and Antony in 42 B.C. defeated the Republican forces under Brutus and Cassius. Octavian made it a military colony, bestowing upon it the *Ius Italicum*, which conferred various privileges on its citizens. The narrative of Acts 16 reflects the pride of the inhabitants in their Roman citizenship. Their duumviri are styled ' praetors ' (vers. 20, 22, 35, 36, 38), and the attendants are ' lictors ' (vers. 35, 38). Their pride reveals itself also in the words spoken by the owners of the slave-girl when they bring Paul and Silas before the praetors. ' These fellows,' they say, ' are Jews who are making an agitation in our town ; they are proclaiming customs which as Romans we are not allowed to accept or observe ! ' (vers. 20, 21). When in 31 B.C. Octavian defeated Antony at the battle of Actium, the victor refounded the city of Philippi, settling there some of the defeated followers of Antony. The number of Jews in the city appears to have been small.

§ 3. THE GENUINENESS OF THE EPISTLE TO THE PHILIPPIANS

The genuineness of our epistle is taken for granted by almost all modern scholars. From time to time, however, its claim has been disputed on various grounds ; but even to enumerate these grounds is no longer necessary. The letter exhibits all the tokens of Pauline authorship, and no apparent motive for fabrication suggests itself. Allusions to it are to be found in several second-century writers, and the influence of its thought and language is seen even in the early letter of Clement of Rome to the Church in Corinth.

§ 4. DOES THE EPISTLE CONTAIN AN INTERPOLATION ?

In the middle of the first verse of chap. 3 there occurs a sudden and unexpected change of tone and subject. This change has given rise to much discussion. Some scholars would divide our epistle at this point into two distinct letters. One writer—Heinrichs—has suggested that 3 : 1-4 : 19 is a letter addressed to the leaders of the Philippian Church, and 1 : 1-2 : 30, 4 : 21-23, a letter addressed to the Church as a whole ; but this suggestion has little to commend it.

Among those who think the epistle contains an interpolated passage is Kirsopp Lake. In an article on the ' Critical Problems of the Epistle to the Philippians ' in the *Expositor* (June 1914) he argues for the presence of an interpolation extending from 3 : 1*b* to 4 : 3. The majority of scholars, however, see no necessity for postulating an interpolation at all. They think the sudden change at the beginning of chap. 3 may be adequately accounted for by the effect on Paul either of some disturbing occurrence at the place at which he was writing, or else of some happening at Philippi news of which had just reached him. Of these two suggestions the latter is much the more probable, for it is in the highest degree unlikely that the Apostle would break out into the passionate invective of chap. 3 because of some occurrence in his own vicinity and not say one word regarding the cause of the sudden outburst.

The sudden change, however, is difficult to account for except on the hypothesis of interpolation. The main cause of the general reluctance to recognize the presence of an interpolation is the difficulty felt by many of discovering a place at which the interpolation manifestly comes to an end. But is not the close of ver. 19 a place at which it naturally ends ? Beyond all doubt ver. 20 in the true text opens with ' for,' not with ' but,' as in our translation. When ' for ' is read, ver. 20 does not follow at all easily after ver. 19, whereas it follows most naturally after ver. 1*a*. It is true that attempts have been made to attach ver. 20 in its true and original form to ver. 19, but they cannot be said to be convincing. The appropriateness of the sequence is immediately evident when ver. 20 follows ver. 1*a* : ' Well then, my brothers, rejoice in the Lord, for we are a colony of heaven.' This new arrangement reminds us of the words of Jesus spoken on the return of the Seventy : ' Rejoice because your names are enrolled in heaven ' (Luke 10 : 20) ; and there are other hints discernible in Paul's words that the Lucan passage was in his mind as he wrote. All this helps to confirm the suggestion that the section of chap. 3 extending from ver. 1*b* to ver. 19 is an interpolation. (See the article entitled ' The Philippian Interpolation : Where does it End ? ' in the *Expositor* for January 1920.) In the present commentary the section is treated as an interpolation. It is undoubtedly from the pen of Paul, but for whom it was first written and how it came to be embedded in our epistle are questions which may never be answered. Perhaps it originally formed part of another letter sent to Philippi. The hypothesis that the interpolation ends at 3 : 19 is much more probable than the theory of Kirsopp Lake, according to which, as we have seen, it extends as far as 4 : 3 ; for surely the first three verses of chap. 4 attest themselves unmistakably as belonging not to the interpolation but to *Philippians* proper. Attempts have been made to discover points of connexion between the verses which we regard as interpolated and the rest of the epistle, with the object of discrediting the theory of inter- polation, but the attempts are not convincing.

§ 5. WHERE WAS PAUL WHEN HE WROTE THE EPISTLE ?

From the epistle itself we learn that the Apostle was a prisoner when he wrote it. The Acts of the Apostles records imprisonments at Philippi, Caesarea, and Rome. Philippi, of course, is ruled out, and until quite recent times the discussion of the place of origin resolved itself into an examination of the rival claims of Caesarea and Rome.

(*a*) The claims of Rome are much stronger than those of

Caesarea, and are looked upon as conclusive by most scholars. They may be summarized as follows :—

(1) It is known that Paul was imprisoned in Rome.

(2) Reference is made in 1 : 13 to the praetorian guard, whose headquarters were in Rome.

(3) In 4 : 22 greetings are sent from the saints among the Imperial slaves.

(4) The general situation reflected in the epistle is said to suit Rome. The Church in the place at which Paul is imprisoned is strong and energetic, and the Apostle is facing the possibility of execution.

(5) Paul associates Timotheus with himself in the salutation, as he does in the salutations of Colossians and Philemon, which are presumed to have been written in Rome.

(6) There is a certain amount of early tradition in favour of Rome, such as that of the Monarchian Prologue to the epistle.

Until quite recent times these reasons were regarded by most writers as establishing the Roman hypothesis beyond the possibility of contradiction.

(b) Now, however, the claims of another city are being advanced by an influential group of scholars. This city is Ephesus, and the scholars who recognize its claims include Lisco, Albertz, Feine, Lake, Goguel, C. R. Bowen, and A. H. McNeile. Deissmann (*Light from the Ancient East*, pp. 229, 230) and E. W. Winstanley (*Expositor*, June 1915, pp. 495, 496) both incline to the view that Philippians comes from an Ephesian imprisonment, though they are less certain in its case than in the case of the other prison epistles. A full and exhaustive statement of the case for Ephesus is given by Bowen in two articles entitled ' Are Paul's Prison Letters from Ephesus ? ' which appeared in the *American Journal of Theology* for January and April 1920 (vol. xxiv, nos. 1 and 2).

Of the six reasons enumerated above in favour of Rome, the last-mentioned is not of much moment, for the early tradition is meagre, and may only be an example of ' the guesswork which is honoured as " tradition " ' (Moffatt, *Hebrews*, p. ix). Of the remaining five, there is not one that is not as applicable to Ephesus as it is to Rome. Let us consider them from this point of view.

(1) It can be shown beyond the possibility of reasonable doubt that Paul was imprisoned at Ephesus. See Bowen, as above, and also B. W. Robinson in the *Journal of Biblical Literature* for 1910, pp. 181-9. Not much importance need be attached to the fact that a building at Ephesus is called ' Paul's Prison,' though the absence from the New Testament of any definite mention of an Ephesian imprisonment lessens the probability that the name of the building is an attempt to provide support for a mere inference. Of more account is the reference to an imprisonment at Ephesus in the Apocryphal *Acts of Paul* (see M. R. James, *Apocryphal New Testament*, pp. 291, 292). The Monarchian Prologue to Colossians tells in so many words that that epistle was written when Paul was a prisoner in Ephesus; and the suggestion of Corssen and Moffatt that the meaning of the statement is that Paul was in Ephesus as a prisoner on his way to Rome is not convincing in view of the detailed story of the voyage to Rome in the Acts of the Apostles.

If Rom. 16 was sent to Ephesus, as may well have been the case, it is by no means far-fetched to see in vers. 4 and 7 allusions to an imprisonment of Paul in that city. The First Epistle to the Corinthians was written at Ephesus, and in it Paul speaks of ' fighting with wild beasts at Ephesus ' (15 : 32). If, as is quite possible, his words mean that he had literally faced wild beasts at Ephesus, that would place the question of an imprisonment in that city beyond all doubt. It is very probable that chaps. 10-13 of 2 Corinthians originally formed part of the painful letter which Paul sent to the Corinthians from Ephesus (see 2 Cor. 2 : 3, 4, 9, and 7 : 8, 12). Now, in 2 Cor. 11 : 23 he speaks of being much ' in prisons '—and the words were written before the imprisonments at Caesarea and Rome. They do not prove that the Apostle was imprisoned in Ephesus, but they strengthen the probability that he was. The testimony of 2 Cor. 1 : 8-10 is more explicit. ' Now I would like you to know,' writes the Apostle, ' about the distress which befell me in Asia, brothers. I was crushed, crushed

far more than I could stand, so much so that I despaired
even of life ; in fact I told myself it was the sentence of death.
But that was to make me rely not on myself but on the God
who raises the dead ; he rescued me from so terrible a death,
he rescues still, and I rely upon him for the hope that he will
continue to rescue me.' The reference is probably to some
experience that befell the Apostle in the city of Ephesus, and
the words are most naturally understood of an actual condemnation to death and of an unexpected rescue when all hope
had been abandoned.

Goguel interprets 1 : 12 ff. of our epistle to mean that the
preaching of the Gospel was temporarily checked by the arrest
of the Apostle at the place in which he was imprisoned when
he was writing (*Introduction au Nouveau Testament*, p. 376,
especially note[1]).   He does not think Paul came to the place
as a prisoner, and it must be admitted that this is a natural
interpretation of Paul's words ; and if it is the correct interpretation, it tells strongly in favour of Ephesus as against
Caesarea and Rome.

The silence of Luke in the Acts of the Apostles regarding
an imprisonment at Ephesus may at first sight seem to constitute a strong argument against the view that the Apostle
was imprisoned there—until we remind ourselves that Paul
in his epistles makes mention of several experiences about
which Luke is utterly silent. In 2 Cor. 11 : 25, for example, he
says he was three times shipwrecked—and that was before the
shipwreck on the voyage to Rome—but Acts does not mention
any one of the three occasions.

Other arguments have been brought forward against the
view that Paul was imprisoned in Ephesus, but they fall far
short of nullifying the cumulative force of the arguments that
support the view.

(2) The word translated ' praetorian guard ' in 1 : 13 often
denotes the official residence of the governor of a province ;
and as Ephesus was the virtual capital of the province of Asia,
it follows that if Paul was writing from Ephesus the reference
might be to the palace of the Proconsul. At the same time
the rendering ' praetorian guard ' may be correct even if the

letter was sent from Ephesus, for detachments of the praetorian guard were often sent to the provincial capitals, and as a matter of fact we possess inscriptional evidence of the presence of *praetoriani* at Ephesus (see, for example, McNeile, *St. Paul*, p. 229, note [1]). Clearly there is nothing in 1 : 13 to preclude an Ephesian origin for our epistle.

(3) The same may be said of 4 : 22. Rome was not the only place at which Imperial slaves were to be found. There is extant in this case also inscriptional evidence that favours the Ephesian hypothesis. We know that there existed in Ephesus associations of Imperial freedmen and slaves (see McNeile, *loc. cit.*, note [2], and Dibelius on 4 : 22).

(4) As to the general situation reflected in our epistle, it cannot be said to be less compatible with Ephesus than with Rome. We know from Acts 19 : 10 that the new faith prospered greatly in Ephesus as the result of Paul's ministry. Nothing is said or implied in our epistle regarding the Church at the place where Paul was writing but would suit the Church in Ephesus quite as well as it suits the Church in Rome. Nor is the fact that Paul is expecting his execution out of harmony with the situation at Ephesus. We have seen already that the words of 2 Cor. 1 : 8–10 speak of an occasion on which the Apostle, as it seems, was condemned, and rescued from the very jaws of death. Moreover, in 2 Cor. 11 : 23 he writes : ' I have been often at the point of death ' ; and if that chapter was written at Ephesus, some of the episodes to which Paul refers may well have occurred in that city. If, again, Rom. 16 was sent to Ephesus, it is natural to see in ver. 4 a reference to some experience in that city from which the Apostle was rescued through the intervention of Prisca and Aquila. It may be the same experience as the distress of 2 Cor. 1 : 8.

(5) The association of Timotheus with Paul in the salutation of our epistle cannot be used as an argument for Rome as against Ephesus. Even if Colossians and Philemon, in each of which Timotheus's name appears in the opening salutation, were written at Rome, we are not bound to conclude that Philippians must have been written there just because it also

has his name in the salutation ; and, furthermore, there is much to be said for the view, now held by many scholars, that Colossians and Philemon were written at Ephesus.

We know that Timotheus was with Paul in Ephesus, whereas we have no knowledge, apart from that furnished by the prison epistles on the supposition of their Roman origin, of his being in Rome ; although, as Kennedy says, ' there is nothing to oppose the hypothesis that Timothy visited Rome ; in fact, it would be surprising if he had never seen his beloved master during so long a period of suspense ' (*Philippians*, p. 405). We also know that Paul did send Timotheus from Ephesus to Macedonia (Acts 19 : 22), which harmonizes with the intention expressed in Phil. 2 : 19–23, and that he went himself soon after, which accords with the confidence expressed in Phil. 2 : 24.

(*c*) The evidence furnished by the arguments considered so far is too evenly balanced to enable us to decide with any confidence either for Rome or for Ephesus. Are there, then, any considerations which will make it possible for us to reach a definite conclusion ? Some arguments that favour Ephesus may be mentioned first.

(1) At the time of his last journey to Jerusalem, Paul was minded to turn his face towards Italy and the West. His determination to visit Rome after he had been to Jerusalem is recorded in Acts 19 : 21, and his words to the Ephesian elders reported in Acts 20 : 25 point to his intention of leaving the eastern sphere in which he had so far been labouring. He gives expression to the same desires and determinations in Rom. 1 : 10–15 and 15 : 19*b*–29. Vers. 23 and 24 of chap. 15 contain an unequivocal statement of his determination to change the scene of his toil : ' But now, as I have no further scope for work in these parts, and as for a number of years I have had a longing to visit you whenever I went to Spain, I am hoping to see you on my way there, and to be sped forward by you after I have enjoyed your company for a while.' In view of all this, is it in the least degree probable that in his prison in Rome he should contemplate paying the Philippians a visit immediately upon his liberation ? That is what he is

contemplating in Phil. 1 : 25 and 2 : 24. This is a strong argument against Rome, and it tells with equal force against the Roman origin of Philemon, in which (ver. 22) the Apostle is hopeful of paying Colossae an early visit.

(2) Although not without some slender hope of release, it is clear that when he wrote Philippians the Apostle in his inmost heart was expecting sentence of death. This also tells strongly for Ephesus and against Rome ; for whatever may have been the actual issue of his Roman imprisonment, it is not likely that Paul at Rome expected a verdict of execution. Lightfoot (*Philippians*, pp. 3, 4) remarks that Paul's accusers had every reason for not hastening his trial, because ' they must have foreseen plainly enough the acquittal of a person whom the provincial governor himself had declared to be innocent.' But if the Apostle had no anticipation of death in Rome, he himself tells us that in Asia, which in all probability means in Ephesus, he at one time despaired even of life (2 Cor. 1 : 8, 9).

(3) The resemblances between Philippians and the earlier epistles of Paul should also be considered in this connexion. They supply Lightfoot with one of his main arguments in his contention that Philippians was written earlier in the Roman imprisonment than were Colossians, Ephesians, and Philemon (*op. cit.*, pp. 42–4). The resemblances are set forth fully and minutely by Bowen in the interests of the theory of Ephesian origin (*American Journal of Theology*, April 1920, pp. 277–84). He takes cognizance of similarities in the writer's moods and situations as well as of resemblances in words and expressions. The use of similar words and expressions does not prove much, for we cannot think that only at one period of his life is a writer able to employ certain words and phrases. Similarities in mood and situation may, however, be used as evidence that two writings belong to the same period ; and such similarities are discernible between our epistle and some of Paul's earlier writings. The mood that lies behind the words of 2 Cor. 5 : 1–9 is similar to that which led to the writing of Phil. 1 : 21–23, and Bowen suggests that the warmth of the Apostle's statement of his gratitude to the Macedonians in 2 Cor. 8 : 1–5 may

not unnaturally be supposed to be due in part to their personal kindness to himself.

Then there are similar situations. Some of the afflictions chronicled in 2 Cor. 6 : 4, 5 must surely have belonged to the Ephesus period; and if so, the Apostle while in Ephesus must have been in just the condition that would move the Philippians to send him aid. We have already seen that Timotheus was as a matter of fact sent from Ephesus to Macedonia (see Acts 19 : 22, and compare Phil. 2 : 19–23). We also know from Acts 19 : 21, 1 Cor. 16 : 5, 2 Cor. 1 : 16, that Paul was minded to go from Ephesus to Macedonia (compare Phil. 1 : 25, 2 : 24). Acts 20 : 1, 2 Cor. 2 : 13, 7 : 5, show that the intention was carried out.

(4) We have argued in an earlier section of this Introduction that 3 : 1*b*–19 of our epistle is an interpolation. If, however, these verses were a part of the original letter, that would strongly support the earlier date, inasmuch as the period of keen Judaistic controversy, to which it manifestly belongs, was past when the Apostle was taken to Rome. The paragraph exhibits some striking resemblances to 2 Cor. 11, a chapter that probably formed part, as we have seen, of the painful letter sent from Ephesus to Corinth. Compare especially Phil. 3 : 2 with 2 Cor. 11 : 13, Phil. 3 : 3 with 2 Cor. 11 : 18, and Phil. 3 : 4 ff. with 2 Cor. 11 : 21 ff.

(5) The journeyings implied in our epistle between Philippi and the place of Paul's imprisonment would be more intelligible if that place was Ephesus. The route of travel between Philippi and Rome is about 840 miles, and at that time the single journey took a whole month. Particularly significant is Paul's expectation that he will be enheartened by news sent to him from Philippi after Timotheus has arrived there (2 : 19) ; and yet Timotheus was not to leave the Apostle until he knew whether his imprisonment was to issue in release or in condemnation ! Is it at all probable that, in the event of an adverse verdict, the Apostle would expect the round trip between Rome and Philippi to be completed in the time that would elapse between the giving of the verdict and the execution ? Even if we place the imprisonment at

Ephesus, it is not easy to see how the double journey could
be accomplished in the interval between the Apostle's condemnation and execution ; but the difficulty is much increased
if he was in Rome. It may be that we are taking his words
too literally : perhaps it was only in the event of his release
that he expected news to reach him. Be that as it may, the
manner in which the Apostle expresses himself in 2 : 24 shows
that he was not without hope of being with the Philippians
soon ; and it is difficult to believe that he would have expressed
himself just as he does if the long double journey between
Rome and Philippi had to be undertaken before he himself
could set out. It must be admitted, however, that whereas
the Ephesian hypothesis renders less acute the problems
raised by this paragraph concerning the sending of Timotheus
(2 : 19–24), it does not solve them altogether and thereby
remove the grounds for suspecting its genuineness which are
set forth in the notes on the passage.

(*d*) Let us now look at the arguments that have been
brought against the hypothesis of Ephesian origin.

(1) It has been urged that if Philippians was written from
Ephesus it would inevitably have contained some reference
to the collection for the Jerusalem saints which the Apostle
was at that time so strenuously promoting. See Maurice
Jones, *Philippians*, p. xxxiv, and Moffatt, *Introduction to the
Literature of the N.T.*, third edition, Appendix C, p. 622. But
there is not much force in this argument from silence, for we
cannot decide what Paul must have said in any particular
letter ; and there are considerations in the present case which
make the omission appear less strange than it otherwise
would have been. Paul had already, as we shall see presently,
sent a letter to the Philippians after receiving the gift which
they had sent by the hand of Epaphroditus ; and Epaphroditus
was just about to leave for Philippi with the present letter.
Moreover, Timotheus (if we can accept the testimony of
2 : 19–23) would be going soon, and the Apostle had some
hope of going himself (2 : 24). Under these circumstances it
is not surprising that our epistle should make no mention of
the collection.

(2) Jones (on pp. xxxiv, xxxv) employs another argument. He urges that inasmuch as the Corinthian epistles were written in a stormy and turbulent period of the Apostle's life, the agitation would of necessity have been reflected in our epistle had it been written in the same period. But surely we may think that, with death staring him in the face, the Apostle could write to his friends at Philippi just such a note as we find in our epistle.

(e) What conclusion are we to draw in regard to the place of origin ? The arguments that have been adduced against the Ephesian hypothesis seem to us to have much less force than those that have been urged in its favour. The epistle, we conclude, was composed when Paul was a prisoner at Ephesus.

§ 6. The Date of the Epistle

Paul spent over two years in Ephesus, leaving, as it seems, in the year 55. Whether our epistle was written early or late in the Ephesian period it is impossible to say. Feine places it after 1 Corinthians, about half-way through the stay at Ephesus. Goguel places it before 1 Corinthians, but late in the Ephesian period—' towards the end of the year 55.'

Of those who maintain the Roman origin of our epistle there is scarce one who does not reject the view of Lightfoot, by whom it is placed early in the Roman imprisonment. If it was written in Rome, it is almost certain that it should be assigned to the closing period of the imprisonment.

§ 7. Previous Correspondence with the Philippians, and the Occasion of the Present Letter

Paul had received from Philippi a gift brought by Epaphroditus (4 : 18). With the gift would come a letter, just as a letter—the present epistle—went to Philippi when Epaphroditus was sent back. There are several indications that Paul had replied to the letter that came with the gift before he dispatched our epistle, and that the Philippians had written again, expressing their displeasure at something the Apostle had said in his last letter to them. They seem to have suspected a lack of adequate appreciation on his part. It is to this second letter from Philippi that Paul is replying in our epistle. The evidence on which these conclusions are based is to be found in the main in vers. 10–20 of chap. 4, and is set forth in detail in the notes on that paragraph. This reading of the situation finds support in other places in the epistle, as is shown by the fact that Zahn arrives at these conclusions with but little help from 4 : 10–20.

It was the intention of the Philippians that Epaphroditus should remain with Paul so long as the Apostle had need of him. And right worthily had he played his part. His devotion to Paul brought on an illness that was all but mortal. As he recovered, he yearned to be back in Philippi. Paul was quick to discern his longing, and resolved to send him back. This was the more immediate occasion of the writing of our epistle. Paul explains why he is sending him back, and bespeaks for him a cordial welcome (2 : 25–30).

Besides this he had other objects in writing :

(*a*) To tell the Philippians of his intention to send Timotheus (2 : 19–23), and of his hope that he may be able himself to visit them soon (2 : 24).

(*b*) To answer their inquiries about his welfare and his prospects, and to assuage their concern regarding the effect of his imprisonment on the fortunes of the Gospel.

(*c*) To urge them to be united, steadfast, and even joyful in the face of pagan persecution.

(*d*) To disabuse their minds regarding the lack of appreciation with which they had wrongly charged him.

Written as it was under the shadow of a dark and ominous cloud, the epistle resounds with the note of joy. It is one of the priceless treasures of the Christian Church. To countless pilgrims on the way of life it has brought comfort and strength, and it will continue so to do so long as time shall last.

CHAPTER I

THE OPENING SALUTATION (I. 1, 2)

Paul and Timotheus, servants of Christ Jesus, to all the saints 1
in Christ Jesus who are at Philippi, as well as to the bishops
and deacons : grace and peace to you from God our Father 2
and the Lord Jesus Christ.

Paul cannot even write a brief salutation without revealing
the great commanding passion of his life—his devotion to the
Saviour whose name occurs three times in these two verses.
The three occurrences of the name of Christ are the pivots of
the present salutation : they speak of a relation *to* Christ
(**servants of Christ Jesus**), of a state *in* Christ (**saints in Christ
Jesus**), and of a blessing *from* Christ and from the Father
(**grace and peace to you from God our Father and the Lord
Jesus Christ**).

Paul associates Timotheus with himself, as he also does in 1
the salutations of 2 Corinthians, Colossians, 1 and 2 Thessalonians, and Philemon. **Timotheus,** which is the Latin form of
the name, is used uniformly in our translation throughout the
New Testament. The R.V. as uniformly has the form
' Timothy.' The A.V. inconsistently uses both forms, having
Timotheus seventeen times and Timothy seven times. In the
present passage it has Timotheus. In 2 Cor. 1 both forms occur
in the same chapter, Timothy in ver. 1 and Timotheus in
ver. 19 !

Although Timotheus is brought into the salutation, he is not
joint-author with Paul, for the letter is written in the first
person singular from 1 : 3 to the end, and in 2 : 19–23 Timotheus
is spoken of in the third person. Why, then, is his name introduced into the salutation at all ? Some see in the mention of
his name a mere act of courtesy on the part of Paul. But **it**

B   1

was not the habit of the Apostle to show this courtesy to all those who happened to be with him when he was writing a letter. The presence of the name is sometimes explained on the ground that Timotheus must have acted as amanuensis. Others find the explanation in Paul's desire to impress upon the Philippians that they should receive Timotheus with due respect when he should come to them ; but surely the words of 2 : 19–23 would suffice to ensure for Timotheus the right kind of welcome, if the Philippians needed any reminder of the respect due to him. There must be some other explanation. There can be detected in one place in the epistle, as we shall see, a gentle though quite distinct note of censure, and it is not impossible that Paul introduces the name of Timotheus into the opening greeting in order to intimate to his readers that the censure has the sanction of his concurrence.

Paul does not in the present salutation describe himself as an ' apostle,' as he does in the salutations of Romans, 1 and 2 Corinthians, Galatians, Ephesians, and Colossians, and as he is styled in the salutations of 1 and 2 Timotheus and Titus. Only in the Macedonian epistles (that is, 1 and 2 Thessalonians, and Philippians) and in the private letter to Philemon is that designation wanting. In 2 Corinthians and Colossians, the only two letters in which Paul both calls himself an apostle and also associates Timotheus with himself, he is careful to apply the title to himself alone. The description **servants of Christ Jesus,** which is used in our salutation, is applicable to both alike. In the greetings of Romans and Titus both terms, apostle and servant, are used.

In the Macedonian epistles and Philemon, Paul abstains from calling himself an apostle presumably because his relation with his correspondents rendered unnecessary any emphasis on the authority pertaining to him as an apostle.

The word rendered **servants** is the ordinary Greek word for ' slaves.' Servants is too weak a rendering, and yet ' slaves ' would err in the opposite direction, as it would connote an absence of freedom utterly alien to the conception. In the Old Testament the prophets are often spoken of as the servants

2

of the Lord, and it may well be that Paul has here in mind the idea of a call and a service analogous to those of the prophets. Just as the prophets were the servants of Yahweh, so he and Timotheus are the **servants of Christ Jesus.** The term betokens utter self-surrender. Christ Jesus is their owner and master : they are his for life. Cf. Gal. 6 : 17. What more honourable and authoritative title than this, after all, could Paul have employed ? Others since his day, with a humility akin to his own, have in their letters spoken of themselves in similar fashion ; Savonarola, for example, begins his letters after this manner : ' Brother Jerome, by the mercy of God a servant of Jesus Christ,' or ' Brother Jerome, an unworthy servant of Jesus Christ.'

The salutation is addressed **to all the saints in Christ Jesus who are at Philippi.** The word **saints** comes also in the salutations of Romans, 1 and 2 Corinthians, Ephesians, and Colossians. The word ' ecclesia,' or church, which occurs in the salutations of 1 and 2 Corinthians, Galatians, 1 and 2 Thessalonians, and Philemon, belongs to the same circle of ideas. Both terms embody the conception of the Christian Church as the successor of Israel. The nation of Israel was holy unto the Lord, and of this holy nation the early Christian community regarded itself as the successor and heir. It is as members of the new ecclesia that the Philippians are addressed as saints. The compellation does not mean that each member was of necessity characterized by a faultless perfection, but it must have implied a responsibility to strive after a life in harmony with the character of the God whose ' saints ' they were.

They are **saints in Christ Jesus.** It is in him that the new order consists. He is the sphere of all its operations. It was lack of faith in him that removed the nation of Israel from its privileged position, and it is faith in him that bestows membership in the ecclesia that has taken its place. ' In Christ ' or ' in Christ Jesus ' is Paul's great phrase to denote the close union subsisting between the believer and his Lord ; he never once says ' in Jesus Christ,' the reason being that the reference is always to the glorified Christ. Slight though their present

3

achievement may have been, the Philippians were saints in the glorified Christ ; in him was the pledge of what they were destined to become. ' 'Twas glorious to me,' says Bunyan in *Grace Abounding*, ' to see His Exaltation, and the Worth and Prevalency of all His Benefits, and that because now I could look from myself to Him, and should reckon that all those graces of God that now were green on me, were yet but like those crack-groats and fourpence-halfpennies that rich men carry in their Purses, when their Gold is in their Trunks at home ! Oh, I saw my Gold was in my Trunk at home ! In Christ, my Lord and Saviour ! '

Paul addresses **all** the saints. The word **all** comes with great frequency in the verses that follow the salutation, as if Paul were anxious to make it clear to his readers at the outset that he does not countenance their dissensions. It may be that the same reason prompted him to address his opening greeting to **all the saints,** though the presence of **all** in the salutations of Romans and 1 and 2 Corinthians makes this doubtful.

The saints addressed are **at Philippi.** The juxtaposition of **in Christ Jesus** and **at Philippi** is arresting. It is because they are *in him* that they remain faithful even **at Philippi.** We gather from our epistle that the malevolence that had caused Paul and his associates to depart from Philippi at the first was still harassing the company of believers. They were, however, rooted in Christ Jesus and so able to stand firm even at Philippi.

No words in our epistle have occasioned more discussion than has the clause **as well as to the bishops and deacons.** Doubt has frequently been cast upon its genuineness, and the doubt is by no means unreasonable. Officials are not mentioned in any other Pauline salutation, and here the clause does not attach itself at all naturally to the context, for the bishops and deacons would be included in **all the saints.** This last difficulty may, however, be overcome by taking the clause as an afterthought, the Apostle suddenly deciding to emphasize the fact that the bishops and deacons are included within the scope of his greeting. **In** that case the meaning intended would be

4

' not omitting the bishops and deacons '; but that is not the sense of the Greek as it stands.

Again, one is forced to admit that the words give the impression of belonging to a later date than that of Paul. The combination ' bishops and deacons ' meets us in Clement of Rome, who wrote at the very end of the first century, and in the *Didaché*, or *Teaching of the Twelve Apostles*, which probably belongs to the second century. It is not altogether easy to think that in Paul's lifetime there existed at Philippi two distinct orders of officials. Some authorities, foremost among whom is Hort, do not give to the words bishops and deacons here their technical, official meaning. As they think, the words refer respectively to those who exercised oversight and to those who served in the Christian community at Philippi. If in this interpretation these two classes are meant to comprise all the Christians at Philippi, the awkwardness with which the clause attaches itself to the context is more marked than in the case of the usual interpretation. But apart from this, the view that the words do not refer to two classes of officials is not satisfactory and has met with but scant favour with scholars.

There are reasons enough, it must be admitted, to warrant the reluctance of those who hesitate to regard the clause as a part of the original salutation. On the other hand, it is by no means impossible that Paul may have written the words. The terms ' bishop ' and ' deacon ' are both found elsewhere in the New Testament denoting local church officials—the ministry attached to a church in a particular locality with functions administrative and pastoral. The New Testament and other early Christian documents make it clear that there existed also an itinerant or missionary ministry whose functions were mainly evangelistic. Apostles, prophets, evangelists, are the terms most commonly employed to denote the itinerant ministers.

In the New Testament the word ' bishop ' is used only in connexion with Gentile Churches—those at Philippi, at Ephesus, and in Crete (Phil. 1 : 1, Acts 20 : 28, 1 Tim. 3 : 1–7, Titus 1 : 7–9). It is now generally recognized that in the New

Testament the terms 'bishop' and 'presbyter' refer to the same office (see Lightfoot, *Philippians*, pp. 95 ff.). The terms are synonymous also in Clement of Rome, while in the letter of Polycarp we have presbyters and deacons, but no mention of bishops. The words 'presbyter' (which means 'elder') and 'bishop' (which means 'overseer') are seemingly descriptive of status and function respectively.

The need for officials would soon be felt in the Christian communities, and it would be unreasonable to maintain that the Gentile Churches from the earliest days could not have had officials answering to the presbyters, or could not have called them 'bishops,' for the term was common in the guilds and associations then so numerous, and was employed, as we know, even in 'the technical religious diction of pre-Christian times' (Deissmann, *Bible Studies*, p. 231). The Philippian Christians may well have had church-officers whom they called 'bishops,' and Paul may well have addressed them by that title.

The word 'deacon' (*diakonos*) is of frequent occurrence in the New Testament in its ordinary, non-technical sense of servant; but apart from the present passage it occurs in its official sense only in 1 Tim. 3 : 8–12, a passage which does not belong to Paul. Proof exists that the term was used of religious officials in pre-Christian times (see Moulton and Milligan, *Vocabulary of the Greek Testament, sub verbo*; and Milligan's note on 1 Thess. 3 : 2). Improbable as it may seem, there is no a priori reason why the Christians at Philippi should not have had a second class of officials whom they called 'deacons.'

If the clause is from Paul, why does he introduce the bishops and deacons into the salutation? The special mention of them in the greeting may have had some relation to the dissensions prevailing in the Church. Were the members wanting in due respect to the officials? Is Paul desirous of showing that he, at any rate, regards them as worthy of respect?

It is frequently assumed that they are mentioned because of their special connexion with the gift which had come to Paul from Philippi. Paul was most eager to remove the impression which the Philippians seem to have formed that he was not

6

duly appreciative of their kindness (see on 4 : 10–20). We learn from the *Apostolic Constitutions* (third century) and from other sources that the deacons had the care of the Churches' money, and it may be that this part of the work devolved on them early. It is possible that the deacons were the assistants of the bishops in money matters, both classes being concerned in the control of the finances, and that may account for the special reference to them in the greeting of our epistle.

Grace and peace to you from God our Father and the Lord **2** **Jesus Christ**—these words appear in precisely the same order in the salutations of Romans, 1 and 2 Corinthians, Ephesians, and Philemon ; and we find virtually the same words in the salutations of Galatians, 2 Thessalonians, and Titus. The words **and the Lord Jesus Christ** are wanting in Colossians. ' Mercy ' comes between grace and peace in 1 and 2 Timotheus. 1 Thessalonians has simply ' Grace and peace to you.'

In the conventional epistolary salutations of the time the commonest form is the simple word ' greeting.' In Greek this is *chairein*, and we may well suppose that Paul was consciously enriching this everyday greeting when in his salutations he employed the word **grace**, which in Greek is *charis*. The change from *chairein* to *charis* is a parable of the enrichment of the commonplace by the new faith of Christ, which elevates a salutation into a benediction. The grace which the Apostle desires for his readers is the Divine favour—the love of God as it comes to man, in and through Christ, in redeeming and sanctifying potency.

' Peace be to you ' was the customary Hebrew formula of salutation (cf. Gen. 43 : 23). This also is enriched and ennobled in the hands of Paul, becoming much more than a conventional greeting. He desires for his readers peace in the deepest, fullest, and most comprehensive sense.

The grace and peace are to come **from God our Father and the Lord Jesus Christ.** God the Father is the ultimate source of all blessing. It was He who conferred on Jesus the Lordship (see 2 : 9) in virtue of which he is here ranked with the Father as giver of grace and peace.

7

JOYFUL THANKSGIVING AND CONFIDENT EXPECTATION OF PROGRESS (I. 3–7)

3, 4   I thank my God for all your remembrance of me ; in all my prayers for you all I always pray with a sense of joy
5   for what you have contributed to the gospel from the very
6   first day down to this moment ; of this I am confident, that he who has begun the good work in you will go on
7   completing it until the day of Jesus Christ. It is only natural for me to be thinking of you all in this way, for alike in my prison and as I defend and vindicate the gospel, I bear in mind how you all share with me in the grace divine.

Not often do we find in so short a passage so many ambiguities of grammar as are to be found in the Greek of these five verses.

In secular letters of the days of Paul it was the common practice to introduce, immediately after the opening salutation, some reference to prayer. A second-century letter discovered in Egypt opens thus : ' Antoni(u)s Longus to Nilous, his mother many greetings. Continually I pray for your health. Supplication on your behalf I direct each day to the lord Serapis ' (see Milligan, *Selections from the Greek Papyri*, p. 93).

Here again, as in his opening greeting, Paul uplifts and vivifies the conventional and the commonplace. In the paragraph now before us, even though some of its sentences are couched in the language of epistolary convention, the Apostle strikes the keynote of the whole epistle. He makes it evident at the outset how thorough is his appreciation of the Philippians and their doings, how firm his confidence in their future prospects ; and this wealth of esteem and trust goes out to them all. The frequency with which the word ' all ' occurs in these opening sentences is remarkable. ' There is,' says Lightfoot, ' a studied repetition of the word " all " in this epistle, when the Philippian Church is mentioned. It is impossible not to connect this recurrence of the word with the strong and repeated exhortations to unity which the epistle contains. The Apostle seems to say, " I make no difference between man and man, or between party and party : my heart is open to all ; my prayers, my thanksgivings, my hopes, my obligations, extend to all." '

But there can be detected throughout the letter also a faint note of dissatisfaction. Paul's joy in his readers is not complete (see 2 : 2). It is possible that this note is to be heard even in this opening paragraph. The Apostle tells his readers that it is his wont to pray for them with a sense of joy for what they had contributed to the gospel, and then adds words which affirm that this sense of joy is reinforced by his confidence that the good work already begun in them will be brought to completion. May we not think that he makes mention of this confidence in their future progress in part at least in order to convey the hint that his cup of joy is not yet full to the brim ? He does not say in so many words that the Philippians are not all he desires them to be ; rather, with unsurpassable delicacy, he tells them of his confidence that God will make them better !

Vers. 3–5 may be entitled ' A Joyful Thanksgiving,' and vers. 6 and 7 ' Confident Expectation of Progress.'

In spite of the association of Timotheus with himself in 3 the opening greeting, Paul at once starts off in the first person singular, which is maintained to the very end of the letter. A few ancient authorities read ' I indeed thank my God,' instead of the simpler **I thank my God** ; and Zahn argues for the originality of that reading, believing that here in Philippians the less usual form of expression has been assimilated to the simpler and more usual form found in 1 Cor. 1 : 4, Col. 1 : 3, Philem. 4. Paul may well have laid emphasis on the personal pronoun, for he was aware that the Philippians suspected a lack of cordiality in his appreciation of the gift which they had sent to him. ' Whatever others may think or say,' he seems to imply, ' I for my part fully appreciate all that you have done.'

My God occurs also in 4 : 19, as well as in Rom. 1 : 8, 1 Cor. 1 : 4(?), and Philem. 4. The expression bespeaks a clear and certain consciousness of a personal relation to God. In

9

Acts 27 : 23, where Paul speaks of ' the God I belong to,' we have the converse conception.

The clause **for all your remembrance of me** presents one of the ambiguities to which reference has been made. The R.V. renders ' upon all my remembrance of you.' Now, the translation in our text may well be the correct rendering. The preposition translated **for** may quite naturally bear the meaning ' on the basis of,' and according to this rendering Paul says that all the remembrance of him on the part of the Philippians forms a basis for his thanksgiving. This interpretation, which is accepted by Zahn, Harnack, Kennedy, and others, gives excellent sense. Nevertheless, we do not think it represents Paul's meaning. For one thing, the words **of me** are not in the Greek, as we should have expected them to be if the meaning were **for all your remembrance of me.** Again, the word translated **remembrance** is of frequent occurrence in the opening sentences of the Pauline letters in the sense of ' mention in prayer.' It is so used in Rom. 1 : 9, Eph. 1 : 16, 1 Thess. 1 : 2, 2 Tim. 1 : 3, Philem. 4, and in each case it is closely associated with thanksgiving. It would be contrary to all analogy to give the word a different meaning in the present passage. Indeed, the word seems to have come to be used as a technical term in this sense long before the days of Paul. For an early example see Milligan, *Selections*, p. 9. Moreover, one of the uses of the preposition translated **for** (even with the case by which it is here followed) is to mark a point of time in the sense of ' at ' or ' on ' (see Moulton and Milligan, *Vocabulary*, p. 234). So we take Paul's meaning here to be, ' I thank my God on every mention of you in my prayers.' ' Every time,' he says, ' I mention you in my prayers I give thanks to my God.'

4 The opening words of ver. 4, **always in all my prayers for you all** (that is the order in which they come in the Greek), should, we think, be taken closely with ver. 3 ; they show how comprehensive is the statement made in the latter verse. **Always**—there are no periods during which he desists ; **in all my prayers**—no single prayer of his fails to include them in its embrace ; **for you all**—not one of his readers is outside

10

the circle of his interest. The R.V. rendering, ' in every supplication of mine,' is more literal than in all my prayers,
inasmuch as the noun used by Paul is not the word meaning
prayer in general, but the word denoting prayer in one of
its aspects—prayer as entreaty or supplication.

There follows in the Greek a participial clause, ' making
my supplication with a sense of joy,' which in our rendering
appears as an independent clause, I pray with a sense of joy.
Paul supplicates with joy ! Even his entreaties are suffused
with joy ! He has not to force himself to pray for the Philippians ; their attitude to him makes the task easy and grateful.
' Those who grieve their faithful ministers,' says Trapp in his
comment on this verse, ' and quench the spirit in them, do
it to their own singular disadvantage.'

The clause **for what you have contributed to the gospel** is 5
dependent on **with a sense of joy.** Lightfoot and others connect it with **I thank my God** in ver. 3, taking ver. 4 as a parenthesis. The first-mentioned connexion, however, is more
natural, though of course it is true that ver. 5, just because it
states the ground of the joy, at the same time gives the reason
for the thanksgiving which springs out of it.

A more literal rendering than **for what you have contributed
to the gospel** would be ' on the ground of your fellowship
(*koinōnia*) for the gospel.' ' *Koinōnia* ' is the common word
in the New Testament for fellowship ; but it is used several
times for gifts or contributions of money. See Rom. 15 : 26,
2 Cor. 8 : 4 ; 9 : 13, Heb. 13 : 16. The same preposition that
is here rendered **to** (in the phrase **to the gospel**) follows the
word *koinōnia* also in Rom. 15 : 26 and 2 Cor. 9 : 13, and is of
frequent occurrence in the papyri in connexion with contributions and payments in such phrases as ' for the rent.' All this
goes to show that the rendering **for what you have contributed
to the gospel** is fully justified. The money gifts of the Philippians are in Paul's thoughts. At the same time we hesitate to
think that this exhausts the meaning of his words. The word
koinōnia embraces also the sympathy of which the gifts were
the outward expression, and all the various ministrations by
means of which the Philippians in fellowship with the Apostle

had helped to spread the good news. The sending of the gifts was but one aspect of their fellowship—an aspect which showed that, to quote Trapp again, ' the communion of saints was with them a point of practice as well as an article of belief.'

This fellowship had existed **from the very first day,** that is, from the very beginning of their acquaintance with Paul and his gospel. Gifts had come to the Apostle from the Philippians immediately after his first departure from their midst. Even while he was in Thessalonica, which place he must have reached soon after leaving Philippi, more than one gift came to him from them (4 : 16) ; and we learn from 2 Cor. 11 : 9 that help came from the same quarter when he reached Corinth, for ' the brothers who came from Macedonia ' must have come from Philippi, since we know that in those early days no other Church had any ' financial dealings ' with him (4 : 15).

And the sympathy had continued **down to this moment.** Not long before the writing of the present letter a gift had come, borne by Epaphroditus, bearing evidence of the abiding goodwill of the Philippians (4 : 18).

6   In vers. 6 and 7 the Apostle gives expression to his feeling of confidence in their future progress. **Of this,** he says, **I am confident that he who has begun the good work in you will go on completing it.** The joy of his supplications is due in part to his confidence that his supplications will not be in vain. It was the God to whom his entreaties on their behalf were addressed that had begun in them the good work, and surely He would not leave it unfinished. ' Not even a man,' says Bengel, ' begins anything without design.' God must have had a purpose in view when He began the work, and that purpose will not be abandoned.

The word ' begin ' in classical Greek often bears a ritual sense ' to begin the offering ' ; so also the word ' complete ' sometimes means ' to discharge a religious service,' or ' to perform a sacrifice,' a meaning found in the papyri as well. Both verbs, however, are frequent in the papyri with the ordinary meanings of ' begin ' and ' complete.' See Moulton and Milligan, *Vocabulary,* pp. 211, 247, 248. Whether the words are intended to bear a sacrificial sense in the present

12

passage is very doubtful. To assume a ritual significance would not effect any evident enrichment of the meaning. Yet when we find the same two verbs coupled together again in Gal. 3 : 3 and (virtually) in 2 Cor. 8 : 6, we begin to wonder whether the fact that they were both used in a technical sense in the same circle of ideas explains this triple conjunction of them in the writings of Paul. Would the sacrificial meaning if present in our passage help to deepen the readers' sense of the dignity of the divine work ? Perhaps it would.

And what is the **good work** of which the Apostle speaks ? Is it the inward operation of God's grace in the hearts of the Philippians ? Or is it their co-operation with the Apostle in the furthering of the gospel ? The words **in you** do not decide the question, for the words so translated may mean 'among you.' The former view is, we think, the more natural, and it receives support from the reference to the divine grace in ver. 7. The outward co-operation is, of course, the outcome and expression of the inward work of grace. Note the rendering **will go on completing**: there is a reference to the process as well as to the final issue. Commencement, continuance, and consummation—all three are of God.

The process is to continue **until the day of Jesus Christ.** **The day of Jesus Christ** is the day of his Parousia, for the coming of which Paul never ceased to hope. The main idea in the expression which Paul here uses is the temporal one. The preposition employed is the same as that used in the phrase **down to this moment** in ver. 5. In the corresponding expression in 1 : 10 and 2 : 16 a different preposition is used, whereby the thought of preparation for the scrutiny of the great day is more unmistakably suggested. It is possible, however, that this thought, as well as the kindred thought of a consummation worthy of the great day, is not utterly absent from the present passage.

It is difficult not to find in this verse ground for the inference that the Apostle expected the Parousia to come in the lifetime of his readers, for it is of *their* progress that he speaks. The thought of the progress of the Church at Philippi after the present generation had passed away does not seem to be in his

13

mind ; nor yet the thought of the progress of his readers after their death.

The long story of the erection of Cologne Cathedral has been used to illustrate the persistence of the work of divine grace in the heart of man. See the *Expository Times* for May 1914, p. 346. The first stone was laid in 1248, and the cathedral was completed in 1880. Though the building of it was spread over more than half a millennium, it was finished according to the original plan.

7   **It is only natural,** adds the Apostle, **for me to be thinking of you all in this way, for alike in my prison and as I defend and vindicate the gospel, I bear in mind how you all share with me in the grace divine.** This rendering brings out exactly the meaning of Paul, and at the same time it does the reader the service of concealing the somewhat obscure and complicated character of the Apostle's language at this point. In the Greek, vers. 3–7 consist of one long sentence, and ver. 7 is closely connected with ver. 6. The opening words of ver. 7 may be literally rendered thus : ' even as it is your due for me to be thinking of you all in this way,' the meaning being that Paul's confident expectation of his readers' progress is in accordance with the fact that it is their due that he should be thinking thus of them all. What the Greek says in a somewhat periphrastic manner is more succinctly expressed in our translation.

There is emphasis on the words **for me.** His readers would surely not expect anything else from *him*—from one who knows them so well, and sees at work in them (as he proceeds to tell them) the same grace whose operations he discerns in his own heart.

The word rendered **to be thinking** connotes much more than mere thought. It signifies sympathetic interest and concern, expressing as it does the action of the heart as well as the intellect ; it is one of Paul's favourite words, occurring more than twenty times in his epistles, half of the occurrences being in Philippians. In 4 : 10 Paul employs this word to denote the Philippians' care for him as shown in the gift which they had sent to him. His concern for them has perforce to find expression in another way. ' He cannot and need not send them money in return, but he can cherish great and good hopes of their religious prospects ' (Moffatt, in the *Expositor*, VIII. xii, p. 340). Note the word **all** : once again he makes it clear that he excludes no one of them. **In this way** means in the way described in ver. 6.

The remainder of ver. 7—**for alike in my prison . . . in the grace divine**—is a statement of the ground on which he regards his hopes of their progress as no more than their due.

Several ambiguities in meaning and arrangement meet us in the Greek that underlies these words.

(*a*) Where our translation has **I bear in mind how you,** it is possible to reverse the pronouns and render ' you bear me in mind ' or ' you have me in your heart ' (so R.V. margin). The context, however, as well as the order of the Greek, is decidedly against the latter rendering.

(*b*) It is permissible to take the words rendered **alike in my prison and as I defend and vindicate the gospel** closely with **you all share with me in the grace divine.** In that case the meaning would be that Paul thought of the Philippians, in virtue of their sharing with him in the divine grace, as co-partners with him in his imprisonment, and as co-operating with him in his defence and vindication of the gospel.

(*c*) Again, it is possible to understand the clause **as I defend and vindicate the gospel** either of Paul's indirect service to the cause of the new faith through his defence of himself when on trial, or else of his direct service through his teaching and influence. Literally the Apostle's words may be rendered, as in the R.V., ' in the defence and confirmation of the gospel.' In the Greek there is only one article for the two nouns, which shows that they are to be taken closely together. Lightfoot, who holds that our epistle was written early in Paul's Roman imprisonment, and that consequently it cannot contain any reference to his trial as actually in process, takes these two nouns to stand respectively for ' the negative or defensive side of the Apostle's preaching, the preparatory process of removing obstacles and prejudices,' and ' the positive or aggressive side, the direct advancement and establishment of the Gospel.' But the words are more naturally taken as referring to his trial. The former of the two nouns is the ordinary word for defence in a court of law, and of the latter also the technical sense has been empha- sized by Deissmann. Speaking of the use by Paul of this second term in our present passage, Deissmann says : ' He is indeed in bonds, but he is standing on his defence, and this defence before the court will be at the same time an evictio or con- victio of the Gospel' (*Bible Studies*, p. 108). Moulton and Milligan remark that ' the papyri discovered since Deissmann's pioneer work was published support with numerous examples his thesis that the word must always be read with the tech- nical sense in mind ' (*Vocabulary*, p. 108). The translation given in our text is, we think, correct both in rendering and arrangement. Whether he be in prison or standing before his judges, the Apostle thinks of the Philippians, and he thinks of them as sharing with him in the grace divine.

I bear in mind is the true meaning of the words which in the R.V. are rendered ' I have in my heart,' for in the present context, as often in the New Testament, the word which the Revisers render by ' heart ' stands for the mind. The reason for Paul's confidence regarding the prospects of the Philippians is that he is able to think of them in a certain way (namely, as sharing with him in the grace divine), not that he has them as objects of affection in his heart ; so that the homiletical use that is sometimes made of this verse—for example, by Jordan and Jowett—is wholly unjustifiable. These and other writers base upon this verse a homily on the thought that love engenders confidence—that we have faith in those whom we love. However true this may be in fact, it is not what Paul is saying here.

In the grace divine surely represents Paul's meaning. There is in the Greek no epithet with the word **grace**, but the reference must be to the divine grace, just as in Rom. 12 : 19 ' the wrath ' is the wrath of God. Paul knows from his own experience what the grace of God can achieve—that is why he is confident regarding those who share with him in **that grace**. And once again he includes them all !

Affectionate Yearning and Prayer for the Enrichment of Love (i. 8–11)

(God is my witness that I yearn for you all with the affection of 8
Christ Jesus himself!) And it is my prayer that your love 9
may be more and more rich in knowledge and all manner
of insight, enabling you to have a sense of what is vital,
so that you may be transparent and no harm to anyone in 10
view of the day of Christ, your life covered with that 11
harvest of righteousness which Jesus Christ produces to
the glory and the praise of God.

The twofold attitude towards the Philippians which we saw
revealing itself in the last paragraph is seen here again. The
present passage contains a statement of the Apostle's boundless
affection for them, followed by a detailed statement of the
burden of his prayer on their behalf, designed in part, as we
think, to remind them that they have not yet reached that
perfection which he desires them to attain.

It is for an enrichment of their love that he prays, mindful,
we may be sure, of the dissensions which, springing from
poverty of love, mar their life, like some disfiguring ailment
that springs from poverty of blood. The Philippians were not
without love, but their love was not sufficiently rich in certain
qualities.

God is my witness, says the Apostle, **that I yearn for you all** 8
with the affection of Christ Jesus himself! In varying phraseology Paul invokes the witness of God also in Rom. 1 : 9,
2 Cor. 1 : 23, 11 : 31, Gal. 1 : 20, 1 Thess. 2 : 5, 10. Compare
also Rom. 9 : 1. In all these cases his object is to certify or
authenticate the truth of some statement he is making. Here
and in Rom. 1 : 9 it is a declaration of affectionate interest
that is verified by means of the adjuration. As a rule, when
the Apostle invokes the witness of God he seems to be conscious of a disposition to doubt the truth of his affirmation,
so that there is justification for the view of Zahn and others
who find in this verse an indication of the existence among

c   17

the Philippians of a suspicion of a lack of cordiality on Paul's part.

Instead of **God is my witness** *that,* the A.V. and the R.V. both have 'God is my witness *how.*' Either rendering is possible, but the former is much the more probable ; for, seeing that the depth of the Apostle's yearning is set forth in the phrase **with the affection of Christ Jesus himself,** there is no need to call the witness of God to anything but the *fact* that he so yearns.

What precisely is it that Paul is yearning for ? Is Ellicott justified when he says that ' the longing and yearning of the Apostle was for something more than mere earthly reunion, it was for their eternal welfare and blessedness ' ? It is true, as we shall see presently, that it was not merely because fellowship with his readers would be agreeable to him that he yearned for them ; but at the same time the meaning of the clause with which we are now dealing is that Paul was longing to be with them. The same verb, with the same construction, is used in 2 : 26 of Epaphroditus, and there the evident meaning is that Epaphroditus is longing to be back with his friends at Philippi. The use of the cognate adjective in 4 : 1 describing the readers as greatly longed-for points in the same direction. Paul yearns for them **all :** he is still anxious that no one should imagine himself to be excluded.

He yearns for them **with the affection of Christ Jesus himself !** The affection with which he longs for them is something more than his own unaided affection, for that has been ennobled and sanctified by his union with Christ. The form of expression used points to the consciousness of a union with him of the closest kind. Lightfoot paraphrases the words of Paul thus : ' " Did I speak of having you in my own heart ? I should rather have said that in the heart of Christ Jesus I long for you," ' and adds : ' A powerful metaphor describing perfect union. The believer has no yearnings apart from his Lord ; his pulse beats with the pulse of Christ ; his heart throbs with the heart of Christ.' The striking way in which Paul speaks of his longing for the Philippians shows that he means something more than a mere desire to enjoy their fellowship ; his yearn-

ing is a yearning to be with them, it is true, but he longs to be
with them to help, to guide, to bless.

The rendering of the A.V.—'in the bowels of Jesus Christ '—
is as inexact as it is inelegant. It goes back to Wyclif, whose
translation of this verse (A.D. 1382) is the earliest passage
quoted in the *Oxford New English Dictionary* showing the
use of the word ' bowels ' in this metaphorical sense. The
Greek word used by Paul denoted the nobler viscera, the
heart, lungs, liver, and not the lower viscera, the intestines or
bowels. Wyclif's rendering would come from the Vulgate, *in
visceribus Iesu Christi*, for the Latin *viscera* can mean the
bowels or intestines as well as the nobler vitals. For this
metaphorical use Hebrew selected the less noble parts, and in
the LXX the Greek word found in our passage (which stands
for the nobler organs) is used to render Hebrew words which
ordinarily signify the lower organs when these are used meta-
phorically for the feelings.

Paul now proceeds to give the substance of his supplica- 9
tions on behalf of the Philippians of which he has already
spoken in ver. 4. Whatever forms his entreaties assumed,
they were all in essence petitions for the enrichment of their
love. **And it is my prayer, he says, that your love may be
more and more rich in knowledge and all manner of insight.**
He assumes that there is love in their hearts; unless the
divine love had found *some* response in them, kindling a love
akin to itself, he could not have addressed them as ' saints in
Christ Jesus,' or regarded them as members of the new
ecclesia; nor could he have spoken of the ' good work '
which God had already begun in them.

Kennedy holds that **your love** in the present clause ' can
scarcely mean anything else than your love towards one
another.' Lightfoot and Ellicott, on the other hand, refuse to
restrict the love spoken of here in any such way ; and in this
refusal the majority of expositors rightly concur. ' Love
absolutely,' is Lightfoot's comment, ' the inward state of the
soul.' At the same time it is possible—the context indeed
makes it very probable—that it was something reprehensible
in the behaviour of the Philippians towards each other, and

it may be towards the surrounding pagan population as well, that led the Apostle to conclude that their love was in need of enrichment ; but this is not the same thing as to say that **your love** in this clause should be restricted to their love towards one another.

The words **may be more and more rich** imply that their love was not wholly deficient in those qualities in which the Apostle desires it to be enriched. Paul is not wanting in appreciation of their present attainment, but he is not satisfied with it. The love that burns in his own heart sets the standard high. 'Ignis in apostolo nunquam dicit, Sufficit,' says Bengel. Paul's prayer is not that some fresh elements should be introduced into their love. Knowledge and insight are essential elements in Christian love, and in these qualities the love of the Philippians was deficient.

The word here used by Paul for **knowledge** invariably stands in the New Testament for ethical or spiritual knowledge. It is not the simple word for knowledge (*gnosis*), but a compound (*epignosis*). In 3 : 8 it is the simple *gnosis* that is used. Does *epignosis* in the present passage mean more than *gnosis* would have meant ? When a distinction is drawn between the two words, *epignosis* is taken to mean full, thorough, clear, or accurate knowledge. So the word is often interpreted here ; and the question arises whether our translation is justified in using the simple **knowledge**. In 1 Cor. 13 : 12 Paul, using the cognate verbs, suddenly changes from the simple to the compound. ' It is difficult to believe,' remark Robertson and Plummer in their note on that passage, ' that here the compound is not meant to indicate more complete knowledge than the simple verb ; but,' they add, ' it does not follow from this that the compound always does so.' Still less is it a necessary corollary from the Corinthian passage that the compound *noun* always indicates fuller knowledge than the simple noun. The use of the compound verb in the papyri leads Moulton and Milligan (*Vocabulary*, p. 236) to endorse the conclusion reached by Armitage Robinson in his *Ephesians* (pp. 248 ff.) that it does not denote more complete or perfect knowledge. They are also very doubtful whether the compound noun signifies fuller or more accurate knowledge. The probability is that the simple **knowledge** states all that the noun *epignosis* would convey to Paul's readers. In all the ' prison letters ' the Apostle uses the word *epignosis* when telling his readers of his prayers on their behalf. See Eph. 1 : 17, Col. 1 : 9, 10, Philem. 6. The word occurs also in Eph. 4 : 13 and Col. 2 : 2, 3 : 10.

This is the solitary New Testament occurrence of the word translated **insight**. The word was first used of bodily sense perception, and then by a natural development came to be used of spiritual perception. The distinction commonly drawn between **knowledge** and **insight** in the present passage is that the former signifies acquaintance with general principles, whereas the latter signifies a sense of what is right in concrete situations ; and this would seem to be the natural distinction to draw. Words from the same root as the word **knowledge** are abundant in Plato, Aristotle, and other writers for pure knowledge, acquaintance with principles, while the word **insight,** having originally meant sense perception, comes easily to be used of the tact or moral instinct which perceives the right course of action to be pursued in a given situation. Insight, as Lightfoot puts it, ' is concerned with practical applications.'

All manner of insight means insight for all kinds of situations as they may arise. This rendering is better than ' all discernment ' (R.V.), which might be understood to mean full power of discernment. The adjective used with the word insight here is the ordinary word **all** ; it is, however, as Ellicott says, ' not *intensive*, but, as apparently always in St. Paul's Epistles, *extensive*, every form of.' Paul prays that the love of the Philippians may not only be rich in its grasp of the great fundamental principles of the spiritual life, but also richly endowed with that spiritual insight which would enable them instinctively to size up all manner of concrete situations as they arose. ' The fundamental choice, arrived at in believing, has to be reiterated continually, in a just application of it to a world of varying and sometimes perplexing cases ' (Rainy, *Expositor's Bible*, p. 37).

10   The clause **enabling you to have a sense of what is vital** sets
forth the purpose that would be achieved by the enrichment of
their love in knowledge and insight.   Two verbs are employed
in this clause, one of them being a participle, which is represented in our translation by the words **what is vital.**   Now,
each of these two verbs has two meanings.   The first means
either ' to prove ' or ' to approve,' and both of these meanings are common in Paul and in the papyri.   The second verb
means either ' to differ ' or ' to excel '; and each of these
meanings, again, is found in the papyri.   In the New Testament ' to excel ' is the prevalent meaning.   The same two
verbs are found in Rom. 2 : 18 in a similar construction.   In
both passages—Rom. 2 : 18 and our present clause—two renderings are possible :   (*a*) ' to prove the things that differ ' (so
R.V. margin in both places), and (*b*) ' to approve the things
that are excellent ' (so R.V. text in both places).   Among
those who adopt the former of these meanings there is no
agreement with respect to the interpretation of the phrase
' the things that differ.'   Some understand Paul to be speaking of proving, or distinguishing between, things that are good
and things that are bad, whereas others take him to be referring to things that are good and things that are better.   The
latter would seem to be the more commonly adopted of these
two views.   It is the view adopted by Sanday and Headlam
in their note on Rom. 2 : 18.   Bengel, in his comment on our
present passage, in which occur his oft-quoted words *non modo
prae malis bona, sed in bonis optima*, combines the two views.
Lightfoot thinks Paul has in mind things that are good and
things that are better inasmuch as ' it requires no keen moral
sense to discriminate between ' things that are opposed as
good and bad ; to which Kennedy replies by asking, ' But
was not this precisely the great difficulty for heathen-
Christians ? '

Between the two renderings (*a*) and (*b*), each of which is
based upon normal meanings of the two verbs as they are used
in the papyri, scholars are divided.   If we regard ' to prove
the things that differ ' as expressing the precise meaning of
Paul's words, we must of course at the same time believe that

22

the other meaning—' to approve the things that are excellent '
—is implied ; for to distinguish between things that differ
would not avail anything unless it led to approval of the things
found to be most worthy of approval.

To these two renderings Ellicott adds a third, namely, ' to
prove, bring to the test, things that are excellent,' and this is
the rendering in favour of which he decides. The words
would thus mean ' to discover, by testing, the value of the
things that are excellent,' or ' to arrive at a valuation of that
which excels.' It will be seen that the rendering in our translation—**to have a sense of what is vital**—comes very near to
this. It differs from it in having **what is vital** instead of ' things
that are excellent.' The former is fully justified by the
specific use of our participle in one of the papyri in the sense
of ' essential.' Moulton and Milligan (*Vocabulary*, p. 157)
remark that the use in the papyrus ' may be taken as sup-
porting Moffatt's translation ' in Rom. 2 : 18 and our present
passage. The remainder of the verse shows that the Apostle
takes for granted that his readers will order their lives in a
manner befitting their sense of what is vital. It would appear
that the dissensions at Philippi were due to the lack of a proper
sense of what was vital on the part of some members of the
Church.

The outcome of their having a sense of what is vital is
described in the clause **so that you may be transparent and no
harm to anyone in view of the day of Christ.** The adjective
rendered **transparent** occurs elsewhere in the New Testament
only in 2 Pet. 3 : 1, but the cognate noun is found in 1 Cor. 5 : 8,
2 Cor. 1 : 12, 2 : 17. The word means unmixed, unalloyed,
pure. In our passage the A.V. and the R.V. both have
' sincere,' a word which when the A.V. was made was used
in the sense of ' unadulterated.' All was not pure gold at
Philippi. The lack of a sense of what was vital had caused
the lives of some members of the Christian community to
become tainted. It is possible that the adjective **transparent**
refers especially to the scrutiny of God : the Philippians were
not transparent in His sight ! Maurice Jones suggests that
the meaning in our passage *may* be ' uncontaminated by the

pagan atmosphere in which the Philippians are compelled to live.' The suggestion is by no means improbable, for it may be that the trouble at Philippi was due to the inability of some members of the Christian community to distinguish between what was vital and what was not vital in that region in which their lives came into contact with the heathen life around them. Paul may here be warning his readers not to allow themselves to be contaminated by the evil things in pagan life, just as in 4 : 8, 9 he may be commending what is noble in pagan life.

No harm to anyone represents a single word in the Greek, an adjective. Three times only does it occur in the New Testament—in Acts 24 : 16, 1 Cor. 10 : 32, and the present passage. It may mean either (1) not stumbling (as in Acts 24 : 16), or (2) not causing to stumble (as in 1 Cor. 10 : 32). Which of these meanings does it bear in our passage? Authorities are not agreed, as either meaning gives good sense, and there is nothing to turn the scale definitely in favour of one or the other. Lightfoot adopts the former—the intransitive—sense, on the ground that ' it is a question solely of the fitness of the Philippians to appear before the tribunal of Christ, and any reference to their influence on others would be out of place.' But we have only to read the description of the judgment scene in Matt. 25 : 31–46 to see how vital in the eyes of the early Christians as a preparation for the judgment was one's behaviour towards others. To be harmful to others would bespeak a low spiritual state and gross unfitness to stand before the judgment-seat of Christ.

The transitive meaning ' not causing harm to anyone ' is, to say the least, quite as probable in the present passage as the intransitive. Perhaps 2 Cor. 6 : 3 may be said to give it some support, for there the Apostle employs a cognate noun when he says ' I put no obstacle in the path of any.' Moulton and Milligan, it is true, while they give instances of the meaning ' free from hurt ' and the metaphorical sense ' blameless,' give no example of the exact meaning ' not causing harm.' Still, here that meaning suits the context well and is, we think, the meaning intended by the Apostle.

24

Paul does not here say ' until ' the day of Christ, as he does in ver. 6, but **in view of** or ' against ' that day. The ideas of preparation for the scrutiny of the great day and ability to stand its test are suggested by the preposition used here. If the Philippians have a sense of what is vital, enabling them instinctively to test each suggested course of action as it presents itself, they need not fear to be themselves tested of God. The great day was never long absent from the thoughts of Paul.

A literal rendering of the opening words of ver. 11 would 11 be ' filled with the fruit of righteousness,' but as the fruit stands for the outward manifestation of their inward life, our translation—**your life covered with that harvest of righteousness**—expresses the meaning with accuracy. **Harvest** brings out well the force of the collective singular ' fruit.' What is this **harvest of righteousness** ? Some take it to mean the harvest that consists of righteousness. But it is more consonant with Paul's habitual way of thinking and speaking to regard **righteousness** not as the outward fruit, but rather as the inward state out of which the fruit proceeds. The very phrase ' fruit of righteousness ' is found in the LXX (see Prov. 11 : 30 and 13 : 2 ; Amos 6 : 12), but we cannot gain from a study of its use in the LXX any certain light on its exact significance in our passage. It probably refers to the graces and actions which are the inevitable outcome of an inward state of harmony with God. We are reminded of the description of Tabitha in Acts 9 : 36—' a woman whose life was full of good actions and of charitable practices.'

The present clause does not (as Moule, for example, seems to think) primarily describe the Philippians as Paul desires them to appear in the day of Christ. Grammatically the words are parallel with **transparent and no harm to anyone**, and as the Philippians are to be **transparent and no harm to anyone** *in view of* **the day of Christ**, it follows that their life is to be covered with the **harvest of righteousness** also in view of that day. The harvest is to reveal itself in their dealings with one another and with their neighbours in Philippi.

In the clause which Jesus Christ produces the relative refers to harvest, not to righteousness. The righteousness, it is true, is produced by him ; but here it is the harvest springing from righteousness that is spoken of as his handiwork. The graces which emanate from the inward state are produced by him no less than the inward state itself. No amount of exertion apart from him can cause the harvest to appear. ' Just as a branch cannot bear fruit by itself, without remaining on the vine, neither can you, unless you remain in me ' (John 15 : 4).

The words **to the glory and the praise of God** should not be taken closely with the words **which Jesus Christ produces.** They go with the words **your life covered with that harvest of righteousness.** It is the life thus adorned that Paul thinks of as conducing to the glory and the praise of God. God's **glory** is the manifestation of His character ; His **praise** is the recognition of His character by men. How can the character of God be truly revealed save in His handiwork in man ? The love for whose enrichment the Apostle prays is kindled by His love ; the enrichment also comes from Him —else why should Paul pray for it ? And the outward harvest is produced by Jesus Christ. All is of God in Christ, and all redounds to His glory. ' As you bear rich fruit and prove yourselves my disciples, my Father is glorified ' (John 15 : 8). And the harvest conduces to His praise as well as to His glory. ' So your light is to shine before men, that they may see the good you do and glorify your Father in heaven ' (Matt. 5 : 16). The glory and the praise of God is with Paul the ultimate end of all things. Compare 2 : 11.

The Influence of Paul's Imprisonment (i. 12–14)

12 I would have you understand, my brothers, that my affairs
13 have really tended to advance the gospel ; throughout the whole of the praetorian guard and everywhere else it is recognized that I am imprisoned on account of my
14 connexion with Christ, and my imprisonment has given the majority of the brotherhood greater confidence in the Lord to venture on speaking the word of God without being afraid.

Paul here suddenly turns to speak of his own affairs. It is not improbable that he is now answering inquiries which have been addressed to him by the Philippians. How would his arrest and imprisonment in Ephesus affect the prospects of the new faith? There would also be concern for the Apostle himself. The anxiety of the Philippians is mirrored in Paul's evident desire to reassure them. Compare Eph. 3 : 13 and Col. 1 : 24.

The phrase **I would have you understand** is one form of a 12 common epistolary formula. This exact form is not found elsewhere in the New Testament, but is of frequent occurrence in the papyri. A less emphatic form is also common in the papyri, in which a verb expressing the mere fact of desire or volition is used, whereas in our present passage the verb employed expresses volition as guided by purpose (see Hort on Jas. 1 : 18 and 4 : 4). The weaker verb is used in a slightly different form of the formula in 1 Cor. 11 : 3 and Col. 2 : 1, and also in yet another form which Paul uses more often than any other, namely, ' I do not wish you to be ignorant ' (Rom. 1 : 13, 11 : 25, 1 Cor. 10 : 1, 12 : 1, 2 Cor. 1 : 8, 1 Thess. 4 : 13). In each of these six last-mentioned passages he addresses his readers as ' brothers,' as he does in our present passage.

Six times in our epistle the Philippians are addressed as ' brothers.' In the papyri the term is used of members of the same religious community, and in one papyrus ' the same designation is applied to the " fellows " of a religious corporation established in the Serapeum of Memphis ' (Moulton and Milligan, *Vocabulary*, p. 9). ' Brother ' is also in the papyri a frequent title of epistolary address. In ver. 14 Paul speaks of the Ephesian Christians as brothers, or a brotherhood.

The phrase here rendered **my affairs** is found also in Eph. 6 : 21 and Col. 4 : 7 in the same sense. The **affairs** will be the imprisonment spoken of in the next verse and the attendant circumstances. ' My sufferings and restraints ' is Lightfoot's paraphrase.

The word **really** would seem to imply two things: (*a*) that the Philippians had expressed a fear that the contrary would have been the case, and (*b*) that such fear was natural and reasonable. Paul assures them that so far from having had the effect apprehended by them, his affairs had actually tended to advance the gospel. 'Rumours to the contrary,' says Bengel, 'may have circulated in the Churches'; and Calvin suggests that Paul's enemies may have been making capital out of his imprisonment. Trapp likens the troubles of Luther, which also tended to advance the gospel. 'For whatsoever the pope and the emperor attempted against the gospel, Christ turned it all to the furtherance of the gospel. The pope's bull, the emperor's thunderbolt, amazed not men, but animated them to embrace the truth ; weakened them not, but wakened them rather.'

13   In this and the next verse Paul shows how the gospel has been advanced. The results of his imprisonment are portrayed in order to prove that it has helped the gospel. He speaks of the influence of his imprisonment in two spheres : (*a*) outside the Christian community (ver. 13), and (*b*) within the Christian community (ver. 14).

The influence exerted outside the Christian community comes first. The clause that in our translation opens ver. 13 is rendered quite literally in the margin of the R.V. 'in the whole Praetorium,' while the text of the R.V. interprets it— as does our translation—to mean 'throughout the whole praetorian guard.' The A.V. renders 'in all the palace,' and in its margin explains that the palace is 'Caesar's court.' What does Paul mean by the Praetorium ? This is the only occurrence of the word in his epistles. It is used in Matt. 27 : 27, Mark 15 : 16, John 18 : 28, 33 ; 19 : 9, of the residence of the Roman procurator in Jerusalem, and in Acts 23 : 35 we are told that Felix the procurator gave orders that Paul ' was to be kept in the Praetorium of Herod,' that is, in the palace-fortress in Caesarea built by Herod the Great and used as the residence of the procurator.

The Latin word *praetorium* (of which the Greek word is but a transliteration) originally meant the tent of the praetor. The praetor was the leader or general of a Roman army, so that the *Praetorium* would be the headquarters of the camp.

By and by the word came to be used for a council of war from the fact that the council was held in the praetor's tent. By a natural development the word came to signify the residence of the governor of a province ; this is the meaning it bears in the passages from the Gospels and Acts to which reference has just been made. In late Latin it stands for any palace or stately building.

On the assumption that the epistle was written from Rome it is not impossible that the A.V. is right in taking it in the present passage of the Emperor's palace, which was situated on the Palatine Hill. If the word was used in Paul's time— we have evidence that it was used not long afterwards—in the general sense of palace, it is not inconceivable that he should have used it of the palace *par excellence* in Rome. Perhaps it would be easy for a provincial to do this, for the reason that the word was used of the official residence of the governor of a province, and of the residence of the Emperor when away from Rome. Still, there is more to be said against this inter- pretation than can be said in its favour. There does not seem to be even a solitary example of the application of the term to the Imperial residence in Rome ; and, moreover, as Lightfoot has pointed out (p. 100), such an application would in itself be highly improbable.

Two other explanations which regard the word as denoting a place rather than persons are suggested by expositors who maintain the Roman origin of our epistle. One of these is that the reference is to the large permanent camp constructed by Tiberius for the praetorian guards outside the eastern walls of the city near the Porta Viminalis. This camp, however, was not known as the Praetorium. The other explanation is that the word denotes the praetorian barracks attached to the Imperial palace, where a small detachment of the praetorian guards was wont to be stationed. But there is no authority for the use of the term to denote these barracks, and in any case the space was too limited to warrant the use of the phrase ' in the whole Praetorium.'

But if no certain evidence exists of the use of the term in the aforementioned senses, there is abundant evidence that it was employed of the praetorian guards. This is the meaning given to the word in our passage by most modern scholars, and it is, we think, the right meaning, whether the letter was written at Ephesus or at Rome. This is the view for which Lightfoot argues in his famous note (*Philippians*, pp. 99–104). He demonstrates that this was the common meaning of the term, adducing evidence not only from inscriptions, but also from the pages of Tacitus, Pliny, Suetonius, and Josephus.

The praetorian guards were organized by Augustus in 2 B.C. They were the Imperial life-guards. The idea was suggested by, and the name derived from, the *cohors praetoria*, the body-guard of a praetor of a Roman army. At first the praetorian guards consisted of nine or ten thousand picked men, but the number was increased by Vitellius to sixteen thousand. They were reorganized by Septimius Severus, and finally disbanded by Constantine the Great in 312 after an existence of just over three hundred years.

It has been pointed out in the Introduction that the reference to the Praetorium suits Ephesus quite as well as it suits Rome. The Proconsul of Asia would have a residence in Ephesus, and to that residence the Apostle may be referring. But if we take the word of the praetorian guards, even so it suits Ephesus, for it was no uncommon thing for detachments of *praetoriani* to be sent to the provincial capitals ; and we possess inscriptional evidence of the presence of members of the guards at Ephesus. Whether Paul is referring to the guards or to the palace remains an open question.

The literal meaning of the words rendered **and everywhere else** is ' and to all the rest ' (so R.V.). Exactly the same phrase occurs in 2 Cor. 13 : 2, and there it evidently refers to persons, not places. The A.V. having taken the word ' Praetorium ' of the Imperial Palace is obliged to render the present clause ' and in all other places,' giving however in the margin the personal interpretation ' to all others.' Chrysostom, Theodoret, and Calvin give to the words a local meaning, but this is contrary to the usage of the New Testament elsewhere ; and Lightfoot declares of the translation of the text of the A.V. that it ' will not stand.' In view of the rendering of the word Prætorium in our translation, the rendering of the present clause is probably a paraphrase of the personal interpretation. In any case, the expression must not, of course, be taken too literally. It is, as Lightfoot says, ' a comprehensive expression, which must not be rigorously interpreted.'

The exact meaning of the words rendered **it is recognized that I am imprisoned on account of my connexion with Christ** is uncertain. It will help us to decide upon the probable meaning if we note that it is possible to render the words literally in three different ways : (*a*) ' my bonds-in-Christ have become manifest ' (so, virtually, the A.V.) ; (*b*) ' my bonds have become manifest-in-Christ ' (so, virtually, the R.V.) ; and (*c*) ' in Christ my bonds have become manifest.' The variation, it will be seen, is due to the fact that ' in Christ ' may be taken closely either with ' my bonds ' or with ' manifest,' or be regarded as qualifying the whole statement ' my bonds have become manifest.' Our translation implies the second of these as the correct literal rendering. The first of the three— that of the A.V.—may safely be set aside, inasmuch as it is put out of court by the order of the Greek. There remain, then, the other two—(*b*) and (*c*). Does Paul speak of his bonds as having become ' manifest-in-Christ ' ? Or does he say that ' in Christ his bonds have become manifest ' ? Maurice Jones argues strongly against the former and for the latter. He gives three reasons for rejecting the former. He contends, in the first place, that the grammar of the Greek is ' decidedly opposed to it.' There is nothing, however, in the Greek to prevent us from taking ' in Christ ' closely with ' manifest ' ; and it is significant that both Lightfoot and Ellicott so construe the words. Jones's second reason is that it is doubtful whether the profession of Christianity was at this time a criminal offence. But surely this is not of necessity involved in the interpretation which Jones is combating. In the third place, Jones insists that the phrase ' in Christ ' should here be given the meaning which it always bears in Paul's epistles. But the significance of the phrase need not be precisely identical in every occurrence, and its force in the

31

translation deprecated by Jones cannot be said to be after all very far removed from its force in the interpretation which he advocates. And if we connect ' in Christ ' with the verb, as Jones would have us do, does not that leave the word ' manifest ' too undefined ? We feel that something is required to complete the predicate. As Jones interprets the words they cannot really mean more than that Christ has made Paul's imprisonment known. Surely that is not what Paul means. How could the mere knowledge that he was in bonds help the gospel ? ' In Christ ' must be taken, as it seems to us, closely with ' manifest,' and in this respect the rendering of our translation is accurate. Paul's imprisonment could advance the gospel only when it had come to be regarded in a particular way.

Nevertheless, though we regard our translation as based on the correct syntactical arrangement of Paul's words, we are not so sure that it exactly expresses the Apostle's meaning. What it makes Paul say is that the reason for his imprisonment has become known. But does he not mean rather that the spirit in which he is bearing his imprisonment has become a matter of common knowledge ? When he says that his bonds have become ' manifest in Christ,' he means, as Ellicott paraphrases, that they are ' manifestly borne in fellowship with him, and in his service.' He does not mean that men have come to see that his imprisonment is due to his connexion with Christ ; he means rather that men have become cognizant of the fact that he is bearing it ' in Christ.' In this interpretation the great phrase ' in Christ ' bears the meaning for which Jones contends. The cause of the gospel is helped because men mark the Christian spirit in which the Apostle endures his imprisonment. And how consistently conformable with the spirit of Christ must his demeanour have been to achieve the result which he claims for it ! Moule appositely compares the noble spirit manifested by Bishop Ridley (see *Philippian Studies*, pp. 48–50).

The transformation of the imprisonment into an opportunity reminds us of John Wesley's letter to his trusty helper, John Nelson, then imprisoned in York Castle. He writes ·

' Well, my brother, is the God whom you serve able to deliver you ; and do you still find Him faithful to His word ? Is His grace still sufficient for you ? I doubt it not. He will not suffer you to be weary or faint in your mind. But He had work for you to do that you knew not of, and thus His counsel was to be fulfilled. O lose no time ! Who knows how many souls God may by this means deliver into your hands ? Shall not all these things be for the furtherance of the gospel ? ' (see *Letters of John Wesley*, edited by George Eayrs, p. 147).

Paul now proceeds to speak of the influence of his imprison- **14** ment upon the Christian community : **and my imprisonment has given the majority of the brotherhood greater confidence in the Lord to venture on speaking the word of God without being afraid.** The major part of the believers at Ephesus were inspired with greater confidence, and stimulated to greater activity in the proclamation of the word of God. It is implied that a minority remained uninfluenced. It is worthy of note that Paul is speaking, not of the officials or ministers of the Church, but of the whole membership. Clearly, then, the proclamation of the word was looked upon as the duty and prerogative of each and all. This conception of the Church's responsibility is one which we are ever prone to overlook. 'I cannot do much more here,' writes Dr. Forsyth, ' than place myself on the side of the sound principle that it is the Church that is the great missionary to Humanity, and not apostles, prophets, and agents here and there. If a preacher is to act on the world he must, as a rule, do it through his Church ' (*Positive Preaching and the Modern Mind*, p. 77).

Greater confidence, be it noticed, suggesting that they had been doing already what they now do more worthily. Already they were venturing to speak the word of God.

What was it that made the Apostle's imprisonment **a** stimulus to the Christian community ? Two answers have been given to this question. According to some it was the favourable view of his case to which the authorities seemed to be inclining. This is the view favoured by Kennedy. The second, and the more commonly accepted, view is that his imprisonment gave Paul the opportunity of manifesting his

D 33

own confidence and intrepidity, and that this reacted upon those who observed his demeanour. The latter, we think, is the right view to take. At any rate, it makes the heightened boldness displayed by the community a nobler thing than does the other view ; and it is more consonant with the language of Paul which speaks of his imprisonment—and not of any view taken of it—as that which gives them greater confidence. Moreover, Paul speaks of their *venturing* to proclaim the word of God, as if it involved a risk, and the language is scarcely compatible with the view that their greater activity was inspired by the prospect of a favourable verdict. The impression produced by the epistle as a whole is that the Apostle hardly dared to hope for such a verdict, and this too favours the view that the Ephesian Christians were influenced by the spirit which he manifested rather than by any goodwill on the part of the authorities.

There is one consideration which seems to tell against the view for which we are arguing. The next paragraph of the epistle speaks of certain members of the community who preach ' from envy and rivalry,' intending to annoy the Apostle as he lies in his prison. As we shall see, it is probable that these are included in the **majority of the brotherhood** who are stimulated by Paul's imprisonment. Does not this show that the stimulation had its source, not in the nobility of his spirit, which would not be likely to affect them, but rather in the goodwill of the authorities ? No quite satisfactory solution of this problem presents itself, although, after all, it is not inconceivable that those whose spirit is condemned by Paul should be roused to greater exertion by his example. If he, in his circumstances, could show such confidence and courage, why should not they, even though they abhorred some of his views and were not unwilling to cause him annoyance, manifest a similar zeal for their own views and aims ?

In illustration of the encouraging influence of Paul's imprisonment, Trapp quotes the following from a letter sent by Bishop Ridley to John Bradford in which he tells of the effect produced on him by the death of John Rogers, the martyred prebendary of St. Paul's : ' I thank our Lord God that since I heard of our dear brother Rogers' departing, and stout confessing of Christ and his truth even unto death, my heart, blessed be God, rejoiced of it ; neither ever since that time I have felt any lumpish heaviness, as I grant I have felt sometimes before.'

The exact relation of the words **in the Lord** to the context is a matter of uncertainty. Bengel takes them closely with **to venture,** but the order of the Greek scarcely permits of that. Both the A.V. and the R.V. attach the words to **the brotherhood,** and this is the connexion adopted by Alford, Moule, Kennedy, and others. We are often told that the phrase **the brotherhood in the Lord** (to which no exact parallel is to be found in the New Testament) would be tautological, inasmuch as **the brotherhood,** without any addition, would be an adequate and perfectly intelligible designation for the Christian community. It is hardly credible, however, that Christian terminology had by this time become so fixed and stereotyped that the expression **the brotherhood in the Lord** could not have been used.

On the other hand, the words **in the Lord** may go closely with **greater confidence.** So taken they may express either the ground or the sphere of the confidence. In the former case the Lord is the personal object of the trust ; in the latter the confidence is exercised in that sphere in which Paul regards all true Christian activity as being exercised. Pauline usage would seem to point to the latter as the true interpretation. See 2 : 24 of our epistle, and also Rom. 14 : 14, Gal. 5 : 10, 2 Thess. 3 : 4, in all of which Paul seems to speak of his confidence, not as resting on the Lord, but as existing in the sphere of the Lord. Whatever be the correct grammatical construction, the phrase applies to those preachers whose spirit the Apostle condemns. We can only marvel at his magnanimity !

It is greater confidence **to venture on speaking the word of God without being afraid** that the Apostle's imprisonment inspires. Instead of **the word of God** the A.V. has ' the word ' simply ; but the fuller expression is strongly attested,

35

and doubtless is the correct reading. Compare Acts 4 : 31.
Lightfoot remarks that ' the Apostle accumulates words
expressive of courage.' It is clear that it required courage
to speak the word of God in Ephesus. The calm confidence
of the imprisoned Apostle, however, inspired the preachers.
' They were infected with the contagion of Paul's heroism.
The sources of Paul's consecration and of his comfort became
more real to them, and no discouragement arising from pain
or danger could hold its ground against these forces ' (Rainy
p. 52). What a welcome issue of his imprisonment was all
this ! But it is one of the commonplaces of Christian history
that trials and hardships redound to the progress of the
gospel and the glory of God.

DIFFERING MOTIVES AND A GENEROUS MAGNANIMITY (I. 15–18)

15 Some of them, it is true, are actually preaching Christ from
17   envy and rivalry, others from goodwill ; the latter do it
    from love to me, knowing that I am set here to defend the
16   gospel, but the former proclaim Christ for their own ends,
    with mixed motives, intending to annoy me as I lie in
18   prison. What does it matter? Anyhow, for ulterior ends
    or honestly, Christ is being proclaimed, and I rejoice over
    that ; yes and I will rejoice over it.

The Apostle now proceeds to speak of two classes of
preachers. Of the one class he approves and commends the
spirit and motives ; for the spirit and motives of the second
class he has only censure and dispraise. Even when he
condemns, however, he reveals his magnanimity.

In the previous paragraph Paul has told his readers that his
imprisonment has stimulated the majority of the local
Christians to a more daring and fearless proclamation of the
word of God. He implies, as we have seen, that a minority
has remained unmoved. The question inevitably arises
whether the two classes spoken of in the present paragraph
answer to the majority and the minority respectively, or
whether they are two subdivisions of the majority, which
alone is actually mentioned in ver. 14. Our translation, by

opening ver. 15 with **some of them,** makes it clear that it regards the two classes as two subsections of the majority. This, we think, is the meaning of Paul's words, even though the words **of them** are not actually represented in the Greek.

Ellicott adopts the other view, and in this he is followed by many recent expositors. ' The mention of " speaking the word," ' he writes, ' brings to the Apostle's mind *all* who were doing so ; he pauses then to allude to all.' There is nothing in Paul's language, however, to suggest that he has enlarged the field of his vision between ver. 14 and ver. 15. Having spoken of certain preachers in ver. 14, he immediately proceeds to say that some do one thing while others do some-thing else. Unless he means that these two classes are two sections of the preachers of ver. 14, his language is decidedly misleading. It would have been easy for Paul, had he so desired, to say, ' These indeed act in such and such a way, but there are other preachers who act in a different manner.' The words he wrote indicate that the class whose spirit he deprecates is included in the majority spoken of in ver. 14. This, as we have already seen (p. 34), creates a problem, to which we shall have occasion to return.

Some of them, it is true, are actually preaching Christ from 15 **envy and rivalry, others from goodwill.** So the Apostle states the motives of the two classes of preachers ; and the statement is amplified in vers. 17 and 16.

Some of them—there is nothing to show what proportion of the majority the ill-motived preachers formed. The word **actually** betokens Paul's amazement as he contemplates the incongruity between the subject and the motive of their preaching. In this verse he speaks of *preaching* Christ, whereas in vers. 16 and 18 he speaks of *proclaiming* him. For the difference between the two verbs see on ver. 16.

Envy and rivalry are combined also in Rom. 1 : 29, Gal. 5 : 20, 21, 1 Tim. 6 : 4. The words picture these preachers as forming a party that stood over against Paul and his adherents ; they are envious of the impetus which the imprison-ment of Paul has given to the others, and their prime desire is to outmatch and have the advantage of their rivals. The

37

very phrase **from envy** is found in Mark 15 : 10 = Matt. 27 : 18, where we read of Pilate's knowledge of the motive of the high-priests in handing Jesus over to him.

Envy of others and devotion to party—these are the things spoken of as motives for preaching Christ! Trapp quotes Luther's counsel to preachers 'that they should see that those three dogs did not follow them into the pulpit—pride, covetousness, and envy'; and Wesley in one of his letters urges his preachers 'by prayer, by exhortation, and by every possible means, to oppose a party spirit,' adding that 'this has always, so far as it has prevailed, been the bane of all true religion' (*Letters*, p. 252).

Others from goodwill : goodwill towards whom? Ellicott mentions and rejects the view of Estius, who takes it to be goodwill 'towards others in respect of their salvation.' Paul means goodwill towards himself. In vers. 17 and 16, where the motives of the two classes are more fully stated, it is of their attitude to himself that the Apostle speaks; but of course goodwill towards him presupposes and includes good-will towards the gospel which he proclaims.

17, 16   In these verses the order of the two classes is reversed. The A.V. follows a number of inferior authorities in placing ver. 16 before ver. 17, an arrangement obviously born of a desire to make the order tally with that of the clauses of ver. 15.

Before we examine these two verses in detail we may notice the translation found in the margin of the American R.V., and advocated by Ellicott and Vincent. According to this translation the phrases **from love** (ver. 17) and **for their own ends** (ver. 16) are construed adjectivally to describe the two classes, and not adverbially as in our rendering. The translation runs as follows : ' they that are moved by love *do it,* knowing,' etc., and ' but they that are factious proclaim Christ, not,' etc. Ellicott and Vincent favour this way of translating the verses on the ground that the phrases **from love** and **for their own ends,** if taken adverbially, only repeat what has been said already in ver. 15. Beet is diametrically opposed to them on this point, preferring the rendering which they reject, ' since the words *out of love* add definitely to the sense already conveyed by the word " goodwill " in ver. 15, noting that this goodwill is the central Christian virtue of *love.*' Ellicott gives another reason for rejecting the rendering adopted in our translation, namely, that in it the force of the participial clause ' knowing that I am set here to defend the gospel ' (and the same would apply to the participial clause in ver. 16) is impaired, ' for the object of the Apostle is rather to specify the motives which caused this difference of behaviour in the two classes than merely to reiterate the nature of it.' But surely in the translation rejected by Ellicott these participial clauses form a part of the statement of motive ; they tell us *why* the two classes behaved as they did : they do more than tell us *how* they behaved. Furthermore, in the rendering advocated by Ellicott the parallelism of the two verses is strangely disturbed by the introduction of the words **with mixed motives** in ver. 16. So, even though Rom. 2 : 8 and Gal. 3 : 7 may be cited as giving some support to Ellicott's rendering, we prefer to adhere to the other rendering—that of the A.V., the R.V., and our own translation—which (as Ellicott admits) is that of apparently all the ancient versions and the one adopted by nearly all the older expositors.

The latter do it from love to me, knowing that I am set here 17 to defend the gospel. The words **to me** are not represented in the Greek ; still, **love to me** is probably the correct interpretation, for the Apostle is dealing with the influence of his imprisonment on the preaching of the word. See the note on **others from goodwill** in ver. 15. He does not mean, however, mere personal attachment to himself, but (as the next clause shows) love to him as the representative and defender of the gospel. From this point of view there is justification for Bengel's comment : ' erga Christum et me.'

Nor is the word **here** directly represented in the Greek. It would be possible to interpret the words **I am set** of Paul's appointment to the apostleship, but the context justifies and requires the interpretation adopted in our translation. Paul is concerned with the influence of his imprisonment, and it was of it that some of the preachers had perceived the divine

intention. The phrase **I am set** suggests that the Apostle
thinks of himself as a soldier posted for duty. The use of the
same verb in Luke 2 : 34 and 1 Thess. 3 : 3 should be compared.

The words rendered **to defend the gospel** literally mean ' for
the defence of the gospel,' the same noun being used for
' defence ' as in the clause ' as I defend the gospel ' in ver. 7.
See the note there. Paul sees the hand of God in the events
which have brought him to his present position, in which
while he defends himself he is really defending the gospel.
The preachers whom he commends share with him the knowledge of the divine purpose in the strange march of events,
and it is love to him as God's instrument based upon this
knowledge that inspires them. To them his imprisonment is
not a sign of God's displeasure ; rather they regard it as a divine
appointment to a great and responsible task.

16   The motives of the other class are now stated. They
**proclaim Christ for their own ends, with mixed motives, intend-
ing to annoy me as I lie in prison.** The verb rendered **proclaim**
here and in ver. 18 is not the same as the verb rendered
' preach ' in ver. 15 ; but there is no substantial difference of
meaning. We may with Ellicott regard the verb **proclaim**
as ' perhaps presenting a little more distinctly the idea of
promulgation, " making fully known." ' The introduction
of the words **proclaim Christ,** after the practically identical
expression in ver. 15, would seem to be an almost needless
repetition. The sentence would have run smoothly and the
meaning would have been perfectly clear had they been
omitted. Why then are they introduced ? It is difficult not
to agree with Lightfoot when he says that they ' seem to be
added to bring out the contrast between the character of their
motives and the subject of their preaching.'

For their own ends is an excellent rendering of two Greek
words—a preposition and a noun—which in the A.V. are rendered ' of contention,' and in the R.V. ' of faction.' The noun
occurs also in 2 : 3, where our translation has ' for private
ends,' as well as in Rom. 2 : 8, 2 Cor. 12 : 20, Gal. 5 : 20,
and Jas. 3 : 14 and 16. Hort (on Jas. 3 : 14) describes it as
' a curious word with an obscure history.' In the time of

Homer a cognate noun stands for a hired labourer, and the earliest meaning of the noun used in our text would seem to be 'labour for hire.' From this beginning it developed a number of meanings, of which one is 'scheming for office.' It came to stand for ambition, rivalry, factiousness, selfishness. Its exact force must in each occurrence be determined by the context. Moulton and Milligan (*Vocabulary*, p. 254) hold that 'the meaning of "selfish" rather than "factious" ambition perhaps suits best all the N.T. occurrences.' Still, in our passage, seeing that these preachers are spoken of as if they constituted a faction opposed to the Apostle, the ends which they sought would probably not be altogether personal. The advantage of the party would be their supreme concern.

With mixed motives expresses Paul's meaning exactly. Literally his words mean 'not purely,' that is, 'not with motives that are all worthy.' This is the only New Testament occurrence of the adverb, but the cognate adjective occurs several times. It is used in 4 : 8 of our epistle. The adverb is common in honorific inscriptions in the sense which it bears in our passage (see Moulton and Milligan, *Vocabulary*, p. 5). The words of Paul imply that the motives of these preachers were not wholly reprehensible.

The Apostle adds that they intended to annoy him as he lay in his prison. What result did they anticipate from their preaching that would cause him annoyance? Was it some outward hurt or some inward vexation that they hoped to effect? Some think it was their hope by exasperating the authorities to intensify the rigours of his imprisonment. But to this it has been pertinently replied that 'if they had irritated the authorities by their preaching they would themselves have been the first sufferers' (Gibb, in Hastings' *D.B.*, vol. iii, p. 841). Ellicott holds that they intended by their false teaching to call forth ill-treatment for Paul at the hands of Jews and Judaizing Christians. It is more probable, however, that it was some inward annoyance, some trouble of spirit, they hoped to cause. Paul's declaration in ver. 18 that he will not cease to rejoice is in harmony with this view. The precise nature of the intended annoyance must remain a

2360

BRITISH ISLES NAZARENE LIBRARY COLLEGE

matter of conjecture. Calvin remarks that there would be many ways of annoying the Apostle which do not occur to us owing to our ignorance of the circumstances. Many are the suggestions which have been offered. Moule thinks they hoped to cause him annoyance by preventing inquirers from having access to him. Bengel suggests that the spread of the gospel among the Jews would cause the Gentile Christians to be indignant with Paul. Webster and Wilkinson think these preachers hoped to worry the Apostle by exciting the opposition of the Jews to the gospel which he proclaimed. Kennedy opines that, misreading his heart in the light of their own jealous feelings, they hoped to make him jealous of their success. Perhaps it was their desire, as Gibb suggests, to bring home to him the limitations and restraints of his condition as contrasted with their own unfettered freedom.

Vincent does not think that these preachers deliberately set themselves to aggravate the sufferings of the Apostle. Whether that was so in fact or not will be considered presently. In any case, Paul distinctly attributes to them the intention of annoying him. The rendering **intending to annoy me** is fully justified, for the participle employed by Paul unmistakably conveys the idea of purpose.

18 In this verse the Apostle's amazing magnanimity reveals itself. Whether the preaching be done **for ulterior ends or honestly,** something happens in which he can rejoice.

For ulterior ends renders one Greek word, a noun whose meaning is ' *ostensible* reason for which a thing is done (that is, commonly, the false reason), *pretence, excuse, pretext* ' (Souter). ' In pretence ' is the literal rendering of the A.V. and the R.V. The very same expression is found in Mark 12 : 40 = (Matt. 23 : 14) = Luke 20 : 47, where it describes the unreal praying of the scribes, and also in Acts 27 : 30. The noun occurs, but not in this identical construction, also in John 15 : 22 and 1 Thess. 2 : 5. In our passage the phrase furnishes an additional description of the way in which the preachers whom Paul condemns do their work. They pretend to preach for a certain reason, whereas the real reason is something quite different. Their ostensible reason is to spread the knowledge of the name of Christ ; their real reason, according to Paul, is to advance their own selfish ends and to annoy him. They are working **for ulterior ends** which are totally different from their avowed ends.

Honestly means the exact opposite of all this. When the preaching is done **honestly,** the real motives coincide with the ostensible motives, and these would be none other than to glorify the name of Christ and to advance his cause.

Christ is being proclaimed, declares the Apostle, whatever be the motives of the preachers or the spirit in which their propaganda is carried on. It is difficult to think that the gospel proclaimed by the preachers whom Paul censures can be the same as the gospel proclaimed by the Judaizers—that ' other sort of gospel, which is not another '—of which the Apostle speaks in Gal. 1 : 6, 7. Would Paul admit that the Judaizers proclaimed Christ in any sense that could cause him to rejoice ?

Over that, that is, over the fact that Christ is being proclaimed, the Apostle rejoices. It is implied that he is far from finding any ground for joy in the spirit of those whom he condemns. ' I blame all even that speak the truth otherwise than in love,' writes Wesley to some Irish friends. ' Keenness of spirit,' he adds, ' and tartness of language are never to be commended ' (*Letters*, p. 231). Paul's attitude manifests his wisdom as well as his magnanimity. ' To my humble apprehension,' wrote Cobden, ' it is as unwise as it is unjust in any kind of political warfare to assail those who are disposed to co-operate, however slightly, in the attempt to overthrow a formidable and uncompromising enemy (quoted by Moffatt, *Expositor,* November 1914, p. 474). So Paul thought with respect to the warfare against evil.

Lightfoot is insistent that we should render, not ' I will rejoice,' but ' I shall rejoice,' on the ground that the former of these two renderings ' brings out the idea of *determination* more strongly than the original justifies.' But surely the future tense, following as it does upon the present, signifies the Apostle's determination not to allow his rejoicing to cease. Why does he give expression to this determination ? Is he

43

showing in advance that he would set but little store by any objection that might be raised on the ground that the proclamation in which he rejoices springs in part from so unworthy a motive? Or is he curbing his fretful spirit and reassuring his own heart that his joy is justified? Lightfoot remarks that the abruptness of the language reflects the conflict that is going on in the Apostle's mind.

Who are these preachers whose motives and spirit the Apostle condemns? Many interpreters maintain that they are his old foes the Judaizers. The obvious objection to this view is that he deals so mildly with them. Some have found in the discrepancy between his attitude in the present passage and his attitude, for example, in the epistle to the Galatians a reason for denying the genuineness of our epistle.

Attempts have been made to weaken the force of the objection we have just mentioned. Lightfoot points out that the circumstances reflected in the epistle to the Galatians are not analogous to those reflected in the present paragraph. There it was a case of imposing a false Christianity upon persons who had known the true, whereas here it is a case of evangelizing a heathen population. Better a false Christianity than no Christianity at all. Hence the tolerance of Paul. But can we think that the Apostle who has waged so strenuous a warfare against the Judaizers would so submissively permit the poisonous teaching to be spread even among a heathen population? It is sometimes suggested that the Apostle himself had changed, and was now less intolerant of the teaching which he had once so scathingly denounced. But the suggestion has little to commend it.

The gospel proclaimed by these preachers must have been, we think, substantially identical with Paul's own gospel. One feels—though it is not possible to adduce any proof—that they were Jews. They bore some ill-will towards the Apostle, which seemingly was personal. We have already drawn from Paul's words the conclusion that they are included in the majority spoken of in ver. 14, and that it was Paul's spirit and demeanour, and not any lenient view of his case on the part of the authorities, that gave them greater confidence to preach. All this creates a problem, for we are conscious of a contradiction. How could men who were moved by the example of Paul's fortitude be capable of motives so unworthy ?

Can it be that their motives were not as deserving of censure as the Apostle's words would lead us to suppose ? It is generally admitted that in 2 : 21 he employs extravagant language of his fellow-workers ; and if the language is extravagant there, it may be so in the present passage as well. His spirit was fretful as he wrote. The splendid magnanimity of ver. 18 has blinded us to the signs of annoyance in vers. 15 and 16. The statement in ver. 18 of his determination to rejoice may well be a deliberate attempt on his part to curb his agitated spirit. Thus viewed, his magnanimity is no whit less magnificent ; it is even more amazing. These preachers were doubtless sincere and earnest men. Paul knew that it was ' in the Lord ' that they were inspired by his example. But they were resentful of something, and, it may be, had manifested some pettiness of spirit. Paul is hurt. Words escape him which in a calmer mood he would scarcely have uttered. He charges them with a deliberate desire to annoy him ! He closes the paragraph, however, on a note of victory. His indignation is mastered. He rejoices, and he will rejoice ! The irritation has produced a pearl !

CONFIDENCE OF VINDICATION, AND SERENITY IN FACE OF LIFE OR DEATH (I. 19-26)

The outcome of all this, I know, *will be my release,* as you 19 continue to pray for me, and as I am provided with the Spirit of Jesus Christ—my eager desire and hope being 20 that I may never feel ashamed but that now as ever I may do honour to Christ in my own person by fearless courage. Whether that means life or death, no matter ! As life means Christ to me, so death means gain. But 21 22 then, if it is to be life here below, that means fruitful work. So—well, I cannot tell which to choose ; I am 23 in a dilemma between the two. My strong desire is to depart and be with Christ, for that is far the best. But 24

for your sakes it is necessary I should live on here below.
25   I am sure it is, and so I know I shall remain alive and
serve you all by forwarding your progress and fostering
26   the joy of your faith. Thus you will have ample cause
to glory in Christ Jesus over me—over my return to you.

19   The words **the outcome of all this will be my** release are
printed in italics to show that they are quoted from the Old
Testament. They are taken from Job 13 : 16. References
to the book of Job are few and far between in the New Testament, and several scholars seem reluctant to see a quotation
in the present passage. There are, however, in the Greek five
words in exactly the same order as they occur in the LXX
rendering of Job 13 : 16 ; so that it is gratuitous to say there
is no quotation. So far from there being no quotation from
Job, it seems to us that the only way of arriving at the true
meaning of Paul is through a study of the context in Job.
Paul's meaning at this point is not easy to determine, and
has been the subject of much discussion. It is strange that
but few of the commentators make any use of Job in the
endeavour to elucidate the meaning of Paul. Kennedy is
one of the exceptions, and his words are not many. He finds
in Job corroboration for his view that Paul is here referring
to his release from captivity. Mackenzie, in the article on
Philippians in the *Dictionary of the Apostolic Church*, remarks
that the words of Job are quoted ' with the original context
clearly in view,' but he makes no further mention of the context
in Job.

What does Paul mean by **this** ?   Some think it stands for his
present situation in its entirety ; others find in it a reference
to his afflictions ; others still understand him to mean the
fact that Christ is being proclaimed. Whatever the Apostle
means by **this**, he declares that he knows it will turn out to
his ' salvation ' (R.V.). What meaning are we to give to
' salvation ' here ?   Our translation interprets it as release from
captivity. By some it is taken to mean the bracing of Paul's
spiritual life to face his trial or the remaining stages of his
trial ; by others his salvation in the fullest sense, including

final glory in heaven. Not one of these interpretations of the word 'salvation' can be described as in all respects satisfactory. In particular we find it hard to think that Paul means his release from imprisonment, for in the next verse he says that the 'salvation' will ensue whether he lives or whether he dies. If we were forced to select an interpretation from among these various meanings given to the words this and 'salvation,' we should prefer to understand Paul to mean that out of his present circumstances, in some ways so distressing, there would issue such a bracing of his spiritual life as would enable him to face with equanimity all that the future might have in store. We do not think, however, that this is what the words mean.

It appears to us that the Apostle recognized certain points of resemblance between the situation of Job as reflected in Job 13 and his own circumstances, and that he makes the words of Job his own in what is essentially their original meaning. This accounts for the fact that Paul's meaning is not immediately evident.

Job 13 : 16 is thus rendered by Driver in the *International Critical Commentary*:

> 'Even that is to me (an omen of) salvation ;
> For not before him doth a godless man come';

and Buchanan Gray, who writes the commentary on this chapter, explains 'that' to mean 'the fact that Job can and does maintain his integrity before God,' and 'salvation' to signify 'success or victory in his argument with God.' The words of Job, then, in their original context would seem to state his conviction, based upon his ability and willingness to plead his cause before God, that he will have victory in his argument with the Almighty. In other words, his consciousness of innocence makes him confident of vindication. Paul, we think, makes use of the words of Job to state that his own consciousness of integrity—the feeling that he has been in the right in all that has brought him to his present situation—justifies his hope of vindication. Whether or not death be his fate, he will be vindicated. His certainty of vindication reminds us of the words of Newman in his *Apologia* : ' I have never doubted, that in my hour, in God's hour, my avenger will appear, and the world will acquit me of untruthfulness, even though it be not while I live.'

Attention will be drawn in the notes on the remainder of this verse and on ver. 20 to some points of contact with the context in Job which will support our contention that Paul is quoting Job 13 : 16 with the original context in view. See the paper on ' Paul and Job : a Neglected Analogy ' in the *Expository Times* for November 1924.

It may be asked whether the reference to Job is not too casual and vague to convey to Paul's readers the meaning we have given to the words. Would the Philippians recognize a reference to Job at all ? What knowledge would such Gentile converts have of the Old Testament ? Did the Apostle's words always convey to his first readers all that was in his mind ? After his release from his imprisonment *at Philippi* it is possible that he may have spoken to the brothers whom he saw and encouraged in Lydia's house (Acts 16 : 40) of his vindication on that occasion ; and for all we know he may then have made use of the passage from Job which he here quotes, thus making it familiar to the Philippians. The possibility must be borne in mind, too, that the Philippians themselves had used the words of Job in a letter sent to the Apostle. Note that he takes for granted that they are praying that ' this may turn to his salvation.' Had they informed him that that was a subject of prayer at Philippi ? If they had, it is not impossible that they had used the very words which Paul employs when he gives expression to his certainty that their prayer will be answered.

We shall see when we come to examine 2 : 12 ff. that Paul there compares and contrasts himself with Moses when he gave his parting injunctions to the children of Israel. If that suggestion is well founded, and if we are right in our view that in the present passage he is noting the points of resemblance between himself and Job, then it would appear that as he lay in prison the Apostle solaced his soul by dwelling upon the analogies between his own lot and the circumstances of the saints of God of whom he read in the Scriptures.

His vindication will come, he says, **as you continue to pray for me, and as I am provided with the Spirit of Jesus Christ.** Paul has said much about his prayers on behalf of the Philippians ; now he refers to their prayers on his behalf, and to the rich bestowment of the Spirit of Jesus Christ which he expects therefrom. Compare 2 Cor. 1 : 11. It is clear that he sets great store by the ministry of intercession. So Ignatius says to the Philadelphians : ' Your prayer will make me perfect for God ' (*Philad.* 5).

The Greek makes it clear that the clause **and as I am provided with the Spirit of Jesus Christ** is to be construed in close connexion with the preceding clause. Paul thinks of the Spirit of Jesus Christ as coming to him in answer to the prayers of the Philippians. It is possible to interpret his words to mean ' as I am provided with the aid which the Spirit of Jesus Christ supplies ' ; but it is better (as in our translation) to regard the Spirit as that which is supplied. The Spirit is here the gift, not the giver. Lightfoot needlessly finds both ideas in the words.

This is the only place in the New Testament where the exact phrase **the Spirit of Jesus Christ** occurs, although equivalent expressions are not uncommon. Some take the phrase to mean ' the Spirit which is Jesus Christ ' ; and it must be admitted that in several passages Paul seems to be identifying the Spirit with the Risen Lord. Here, however, the meaning probably is the Spirit which Jesus bestows. The Spirit given by him would produce in Paul a spirit akin to that manifested by him in the days of his flesh. The order of the names **Jesus Christ** suggests that Paul is thinking mainly of the disposition of his Master. The manifestation of the same spirit by the Apostle would constitute his vindication. Whether he lived or died, he could and would show the same spirit that Jesus showed.

A noun used by Paul in the present clause indicates that he expects to receive an *abundant* supply of the Spirit. Elsewhere in the New Testament it occurs only in Eph. 4 : 16 ; but the

E
49

cognate verb is found in 2 Pet. 1 : 5 and 11. Moulton and Milligan (*Vocabulary*, p. 251) quote from a first-century papyrus in which the verb is used by a man who is lodging a complaint against his wife. ' I for my part,' says the man, ' provided for my wife in a manner that exceeded my resources.' The same scholars add that ' the passage may perhaps be taken as illustrating the " generous " connotation underlying the corresponding substantive, as in Phil. 1 : 19.'

20   Literally rendered, the opening words of this verse would run : ' in accordance with my eager desire and hope that I may never feel ashamed.' Paul's expectation of vindication accords with a desire and a hope that tenant his heart. The feeling of his heart affords ground for the expectation. This clause lends support to the view we have taken of the opening words of ver. 19, for in the case of Job, as we have seen, it was his inner consciousness—his sense of integrity, and his willingness to maintain that integrity before God—that furnished the ground of his hope that he would ultimately be vindicated.

Eager desire translates one word in the Greek—a noun found also in Rom. 8 : 19, and apparently nowhere else. Moulton and Milligan endorse the view that the word may have been Paul's own formation. It is a strong word, implying a stretching-out of the head in eager longing to catch sight of the object of desire, and a turning away from all things else. The cognate verb (in simple form) is used in an ' interesting sixth-century papyrus from Aphrodite in Egypt in which certain oppressed peasants petition a high official whose parousia they have been expecting, assuring him that they await him " as those in Hades watch eagerly for the parousia of Christ the everlasting God " ' (Moulton and Milligan, *Vocabulary*, p. 63. See also Deissmann, *Light from the Ancient East*, pp. 377, 378). ' St. Paul,' says Trapp, ' stood as it were on tip-toes to see which way he might best glorify God by life or by death.'

There is in the Apostle's heart more even than this eager desire ; there is hope as well. The two nouns are in the Greek bound together by one article.

50

The negative side of this double feeling is expressed in the words **that I may never feel ashamed.** The Apostle desires and hopes that he will never do anything unworthy of his Lord or of his own convictions, anything that will cause him to hang down his head in shame. Is it at all surprising that the feeling of his soul engendered a conviction that sooner or later, whether by life or by death, he would be vindicated? The heart that cherished the desire and hope of which Paul was conscious surely would not for ever remain a subject of suspicion and obloquy.

But that now as ever I may do honour to Christ in my own person by fearless courage—that is the positive side of his desire and hope. The translation here paraphrases the language of Paul in some measure. What he actually says is not **that I may do honour to Christ,** but ' that Christ may be honoured.' The paraphrase obscures the significant fact that the Apostle deliberately changes from the first person to the third, and employs a passive instead of an active construction. He seems to be on the point of saying ' that I may honour Christ,' when he suddenly pulls himself up and says ' that Christ may be honoured,' as though he felt that the construction which he had originally intended to use would have given too great prominence to himself. **Now** implies that the time of crisis was not far distant. And how eloquent are the words **as ever** ! His conscience was clear that he had always honoured his Saviour ; and this would fortify his conviction that he would not fail to do so now. To honour or magnify Christ is to show forth and enhance his glory before men.

The literal meaning of the words rendered **in my own person** is ' in my body.' Paul thinks of his body as the scene or sphere in which his Saviour would be honoured. Whether he lived or whether he died, Christ would be honoured in his body : if he lived, he would be honoured through the toil, the drudgery, the suffering which his body would undergo ; if he were condemned to die, by the spirit in which he would surrender his body to its fate.

The noun used in the phrase **by fearless courage** means

literally ' freedom or plainness of speech ' ; and from that developed the meaning of courage—the freedom from fear which ordinarily accompanies plainness of speech. As Paul may be thinking of his coming trial, it is quite possible that he is using the word in its original sense of boldness of utterance ; though, on the other hand, it is equally possible that it bears here its more general sense of courage. Whichever meaning was uppermost in Paul's mind, there is here another point of contact with Job, for in the verses which immediately precede the one quoted by Paul in ver. 19 Job in memorable words declares his intention of approaching the Almighty fearlessly and with boldness of speech. This is how Driver renders Job 13 : 13–15 :

> ' Hold your peace, let me alone, that *I* may speak,
>   And let come on me what will.
> I will take my flesh in my teeth,
>   And put my life in my hand !
> Behold, he will slay me ; I have no hope ;
>   Nevertheless I will maintain my ways before him.'

The words **Whether that means life or death, no matter!** do not mean, as our translation might perhaps suggest, that Paul is indifferent whether his fate is to be life or death ; they mean rather that, be his fate life or be it death, he is confident that Christ will be honoured in his person. So far as the magnifying of his Master goes, it matters not whether it be his destiny to live or to die. It is clear that he does not yet know what the issue of his imprisonment will be (compare 2 : 23), and the passages in which he speaks of again visiting Philippi must be interpreted in the light of this uncertainty.

Here again we are reminded of Job, who was determined to be vindicated, even though vindication should entail his death. In the passage just quoted from the book of Job, Driver is at one with the margin of the R.V. in representing the patriarch not merely as willing to face all hazards, but also as convinced that death would be his lot. We believe that Paul also in his **inmost heart anticipated for himself no other fate than death.**

In the Greek this verse consists of two separate and distinct 21 clauses—joined together by a simple ' and '—in neither of which is the copula expressed : ' For to me to live—Christ, and to die—gain.' Our translation—**as life means Christ to me, so death means gain**—omits the ' for,' and also co-ordinates the two clauses by means of **as** and **so.**

The mention of life and death in the last verse leads the Apostle to state what each of the two means to him. If we are to take cognizance of the ' for,' the logical connexion implied is not quite clear. Paul has just declared that whether his fate be life or death, Christ will be honoured. Now the clause ' for life means Christ to me ' comes in naturally as an explanation of his confidence that he would honour Christ by his life ; but it is not so evident how the clause **death means gain** provides an explanation of, or a reason for, the statement that he would honour him also by his death. Does Paul mean that inasmuch as death to him means gain he will be able to face it with a courage and a serenity which will be an honouring of his Master ? Perhaps, however, our translation is justified in refusing to find any very close logical connexion between ver. 20 and ver. 21.

Life means Christ to me, says the Apostle. If he is destined to live, life will mean—as it has meant ever since his conversion—Christ ! Life to him has no meaning apart from Christ. Christ is the object, the motive, the inspiration, the goal of all he does. ' Quicquid vivo (vita naturali), Christum vivo,' is Bengel's paraphrase.

Death means gain—just because life means Christ. Death here, of course, is not the act of dying, but the condition into which the Apostle would be ushered when his life here below should end. That condition too will be a life that means Christ, only with the limitations and restrictions of this earthly life removed That is why death means gain. Some scholars have thought that the words of Wisd. of Sol. 3 : 1–3 were in Paul's mind as he wrote. His view of death stands in strong contrast to the notion of ' the foolish ' as set forth in that passage. When life means Christ, the prospect of closer fellowship with him, and of nobler, more unfettered service

53

rendered to him, creates a serenity in the face of death unknown under any other circumstances.

There is emphasis on the words **to me**—a stronger emphasis than our translation would lead one to think. What is the explanation of this emphasis? Is the Apostle contrasting himself with the heathen thousands by whom he is surrounded, to whom Christ is unknown, and who would regard death as anything but gain? Or is he contrasting himself with his readers, to whom his death would be a loss? Is the emphasis an attempt to assuage their grief at the prospect of his death? Howsoever they may view his death, let them rest assured that *for him* it could only mean gain. Or can it be that the contrast implied in the emphasis is between Paul and Job, who has been in the Apostle's mind, as we have seen, when he was writing vers. 19 and 20? Death for Job was not something desirable in itself, but an untoward experience he was prepared to risk in order to maintain his integrity before God. In an earlier passage than the one from which Paul quotes in ver. 19—namely, in 10 : 20–22, which we quote from Driver's rendering—Job says :

> ' Are not the days of my life few ?
>   Look away from me, that I may brighten up a little,
> Before I go whence I shall not return,
>   Unto the land of darkness and dense darkness,
> A land of gloom, like blackness,
>   A land of dense darkness and disorder,
>   And where the shining is as blackness.'

How different the prospect of the Apostle ! Because life to him means Christ, death means gain.

22   **But then,** continues the Apostle, **if it is to be life here below, that means fruitful work. So—well, I cannot tell which to choose.** The interpretation of this verse is a well-known difficulty. It will help us here again if we start with the bald, literal rendering of Paul's words. Literally translated, the verse runs : ' But if to live in flesh this to me fruit of work and what I shall choose I do not make known.' What are we to make of this? Lightfoot would regard the verse as an interrogation with the apodosis suppressed. He renders :

54

'But what if my living in the flesh will bear fruit, etc. ? In fact what to choose I know not.' This interpretation, however, has not met with much acceptance, and is probably to be set aside. Taking the opening words as a conditional clause, we may render in two ways :

(*a*) 'But if to live in the flesh,—*if* this is the fruit of my work, then what I shall choose I wot not ' (R.V., text).

(*b*) 'But if to live in the flesh *be my lot,* this is the fruit of my work: and what I shall choose I wot not '' (R.V., margin).

On these two methods of construing the words different interpretations have been based :

(1) Some, adopting the former method, understand the words to mean : 'But if to live is going to mean for me fruitful toil, then I cannot tell which to choose.'

This interpretation is accepted by a large number of scholars.

(2) Others, adopting the second method of construing the words, take them to mean : 'But if I am destined to live, that will mean fruitful toil on my part—and which of the two to choose I cannot tell.'

This interpretation also can boast a long array of sponsors, though some scholars find the ellipsis which necessitates the insertion of the words *be my lot* in the margin of the R.V. too awkward to be admissible.

It will be seen that this second interpretation is the one adopted in our text, and it is, we think, the most satisfactory if the whole verse as it stands is original. The reflection embodied in the words as thus understood is prompted seemingly by a fear that the Philippians might draw a mistaken inference from the Apostle's statement that death means gain for him. He will not let them think that he is tired of life and pining for death ; so he says : **but then, if it is to be life here below, that means fruitful work.**

(3) A third interpretation is possible, and is advocated by Maurice Jones. He adopts the text of the R.V. as the literal rendering, but he objects to the commonly accepted interpretation of the words ' fruit of work.' His paraphrase will show the meaning he attaches to this phrase and to the

verse as a whole : ' If my work in the past, with all its rich results in the mission-field and the plenteous harvest garnered for Christ, makes it desirable or necessary that I should go on living and working—then when I measure this against the rest and peace I gain in death, what to choose I dare not venture to declare.' We do not think, however, that this interpretation is as probable as the one adopted in our translation.

Not one of these interpretations can claim to be quite satisfactory ; and we are disposed to think that the major part of the verse—all except the last clause—is an interpolation in the text. The last clause would come quite naturally after ver. 21 : ' As life means Christ to me, so death means gain ; and which to choose I cannot tell.' We suggest that two short marginal comments have worked their way into the text at this point. Apart from the introductory words **but if** (which may have been added by someone who was endeavouring to form an intelligible sentence out of the interpolated words), the part of the verse which we take to be an interpolation, when literally rendered, runs as follows : ' to live in flesh this to me fruit of work.' Our suggestion is that originally these words formed two distinct marginal comments, thus : (1) ' to live : in flesh,' and (2) ' this to me : fruit of work.' ' To live ' comes in ver. 21, and someone in a marginal note added to this the words ' in flesh ' as an explanation of it. Similarly ' this to me ' occurs in ver. 19, and ' fruit of work ' was in this case added in the marginal note as the explanation of ' this.' This suggestion is stated somewhat more fully in a note in the *Expository Times* for December 1923.

Whatever be the right view to take of the first part of ver. 22, in the last clause Paul declares his inability to tell whether he would choose life or death if the choice were left to him. **I cannot tell** is a decided improvement on the ' I wot not ' (i.e. ' I know not ') of the R.V. as being a more exact rendering of the Greek. Moulton and Milligan (*Vocabulary*, p. 129) give it as their opinion that the verb used by Paul has the meaning to make known ' in all its N.T. occurrences, ' even Phil. 1 : 22.' Why does Paul say he cannot tell ?

Surely not because, as Vincent suggests, ' he felt that under the strong pressure of his desire to depart, he might be tempted to express himself too strongly in favour of his own wish.' He was, as a matter of fact, in a dilemma. This is how Trapp quaintly puts it : ' As a loving wife sent for by her husband far from home, and yet loth to leave her children, is in a muse and doubt what to do, so was the Apostle.' How free from all worry and agitation Paul must have been to be able in this calm fashion to balance the contending attractions of life and death !

In the words **I am in a dilemma between the two** the Apostle 23 seems to picture himself as standing between life and death ; each attracts him ; but the attraction exerted upon him by either is so strong that it does not permit him to approach the other. Our translation scarcely does justice to the strength of the pressure brought to bear upon him by the alternatives. It will help us to realize how powerful that pressure is if we note that the verb used here is used also in Luke 12 : 50 (' How I am distressed till it is all over ! '), in Acts 18 : 5 (' Paul was engrossed in this preaching of the word '), and in 2 Cor. 5 : 14 (' I am controlled by the love of Christ ').

So far as personal predilection goes, Paul is not in any doubt. **My strong desire is to depart and be with Christ, for that is far the best.** The word here used for **strong desire** is not the same as that rendered ' eager desire ' in ver. 20. The verb translated **to depart** occurs in one other place only in the New Testament, namely in Luke 12 : 36, where it means ' to return.' Moulton and Milligan quote a papyrus passage in which it bears the latter meaning (*Vocabulary*, p. 36) ; and they also cite a memorial inscription in which it means ' to die.' The cognate noun is used in 2 Tim. 4 : 6—in a passage which is probably from Paul himself—in the sense of ' death.' The metaphor in these words is drawn either from loosing the moorings of a ship or from breaking up a camp. Whether either of these metaphors was actually in Paul's mind as he wrote the present verse is more than we can tell. Vincent remarks that his circumstances ' would more naturally suggest the military than the nautical metaphor,' and adds that ' singularly enough,

57

nautical expressions and metaphors are very rare in his writings.' But there is nothing singular in a Jew making but scant use of nautical terms and metaphors.

It is a natural and legitimate inference to draw from the words we are now considering that the Apostle expected to find himself in the presence of Christ immediately after death ; for surely had he contemplated being ensepulchred in unconsciousness and inactivity during the interval between his death and the parousia of his Lord, he would not have hesitated to choose to remain in the flesh. It is often said that his conception of the intermediate state must have changed, since in 1 Thessalonians and 1 Corinthians he had spoken of death as a sleep. See 1 Thess. 4 : 13–15, 5 : 10, and 1 Cor. 15 : 51. We know too little about the Apostle's conception of the intermediate state to be dogmatic ; but it may be doubted whether there is any difference between his thought of that state as reflected in 1 Thessalonians and 1 Corinthians and the conception implied in our epistle. Although in the former epistles he speaks of the dead being wakened for the judgment by the trumpet of God, we must not be too certain that he does not think of the spirits of those who sleep as being all the time in communion with Christ. In his note on 1 Thess. 5 : 10 Findlay draws from that passage the inference that even during the sleep of death those who die in Christ are living somewhere with and in him. ' Just as our natural life,' he says, ' holds its course unbroken through waking or sleeping hours, so our spiritual life in Christ continues whether we are awake to this world or the body lies asleep in the grave.' The same conception of the intermediate state as involving communion with Christ underlies 2 Cor. 5 : 8, where the Apostle tells us that he ' would fain get away from the body and reside with the Lord ' ; and we cannot fail to be reminded of the words of Jesus spoken on the cross to the dying criminal : ' I tell you truly, you will be in paradise with me this very day ' (Luke 23 : 43).

If we are right in thinking that in the present passage the Apostle is entertaining the expectation that immediately after death he will go into the presence of Christ, that would not of necessity imply, as Maurice Jones thinks, that he had discarded the conceptions of a visible advent of Christ and a resurrection. The references to these events in other parts of the epistle are by no means incompatible with the view we have taken of the present verse.

When the Apostle adds **for that is far the best,** he uses a phrase of triple force, so desirous is he of expressing fully his sense of the superior excellence of being with Christ, even as compared with living in the flesh a life that means **Christ.** The Vulgate literally renders the phrase by *multo magis melius.*

But, continues the Apostle, **for your sakes it is necessary I 24 should live on here below.** What he actually says is ' more necessary ' ; and although we admit that the positive adjective is all that an English rendering demands, we cannot forbear wondering why Paul should employ the comparative. Perhaps the force of the comparative may be stated thus : if the alternatives were set before him, he would feel some obligation to choose both ; but he declares that the obligation to stay is greater than the obligation to depart. The form of expression used for ' living here below ' shows that the Apostle is thinking of the limitations, the difficulties, the toil, that will be entailed in remaining in this life ; but, however eager he may be to escape from them, however mighty his desire to be with his Lord, his personal longing weighs but little in comparison with the opportunity of being of service to the Philippians and his other converts, so deeply has he drunk of the spirit of him of whom he says in another place that ' rich though he was, he became poor for the sake of you, that by his poverty you might be rich ' (2 Cor. 8 : 9).

I am sure it is, he adds. He has no doubt whatsoever that **25** to remain here for their sakes would be his duty if the choice were left to him, because he is convinced that his remaining would be for their good. No mock modesty blinds him to their need of him or to his value for them. This clause is eloquent of his sense of his worth as a servant of Christ.

Lightfoot objects to the manner of construing this clause adopted in our translation ; he refuses to refer the **it** to what Paul has just said, namely, that the continuance of his life

59

would be advantageous to his readers. He prefers to take the present clause closely with the words that follow, thus getting the meaning : ' I am confidently persuaded that I shall remain.' There is, however, no cogent reason for thus departing from the more obvious meaning of the words.

His sense of his readers' need of him kindles within him a momentary assurance of acquittal : **and so I know I shall remain alive and serve you all.** The closing words of ver. 20 show, as we have seen, that the Apostle does not yet know whether life or death is to be his lot ; and his words in the present verse must be interpreted in the light of this uncertainty regarding the issue of his imprisonment. He is merely giving expression to a personal conviction based on his sense of the Philippians' need of him. The future with all the details of its happenings does not lie open to his gaze. But just at the moment the need of his converts comes so vividly before him that he expresses, in words more definite than the hard facts of the situation warrant, the impression that he will be spared for their sakes.

The verb rendered **serve** is a compound of the simple verb rendered **remain alive.** The compound means ' to remain beside, to stand by one,' and so to serve. Paul's impression is not merely that he will remain alive ; he might conceivably so remain and yet be of no service to his readers. He anticipates that he will be again in their midst to serve them ; he sees himself once more at Philippi, in happy, helpful fellowship with the Philippians. And his ministry will extend to them **all.** Once again he lets them see that he does not countenance their divisions.

By forwarding your progress and fostering the joy of your faith—that is how he would serve them. The same noun is used here for progress as is used in ver. 12 of the advance of the gospel. Elsewhere in the New Testament it occurs only in 1 Tim. 4 : 15. Some expositors hold that **progress** (as well as **joy**) should be taken closely with **faith** ; but Paul's language is not decisive on the point. In either case the meaning is the same ; for the only progress Paul would be concerned to forward would be the progress of their faith.

Faith seems here to stand for the experience that is based upon trust in God and Christ. Paul assumes that joy is an element in that experience ; the joy of the first Christians meets us at every turn in the New Testament ; and whenever in the history of the Church there has been a deepening of faith, there has also been an increase of joy. That the Apostle should specify the fostering of his readers' joy as one of the means by which he would serve them shows that his imprisonment and the uncertainty of his present condition had not succeeded in beclouding the joy of his own heart.

Thus you will have ample cause to glory in Christ Jesus 26 over me—over my return to you. That would be the result of his ministry among them. **To glory** means to exult with joy. They would have ample cause to exult, and that cause would be found in Paul himself—but it would all be in the sphere of Christ Jesus ! Christ is the sphere of the glorying of the Christian as of all else that he does ; and when he is the sphere the glorying is no vain boasting. Some writers have thought that the Philippians may themselves have spoken of the Apostle as the ground of their glorying, which would account for the manner of Paul's reference to himself in this verse.

The words **over my return to you** expand and explain the preceding **over me.** The noun used by Paul of his return is the word ' parousia,' on which see Deissmann, *Light from the Ancient East,* pp. 372-8. The ground of the Philippians' exultation would be the Apostle, not imprisoned in a distant cell, but back with them, present again as in days gone by to help and to inspire.

AN EXHORTATION TO LIVE A LIFE WORTHY OF THE GOSPEL
OF CHRIST (I. 27-30)

Only, do lead a life that is worthy of the gospel of Christ. 27 Whether I come and see you or only hear of you in absence, let me know you are standing firm in a common spirit, fighting side by side like one man for the faith of the gospel. Never be scared for a second by your oppo- 28

nents ; your fearlessness is a clear omen of ruin for them
29   and of your own salvation—at the hands of God. For
on behalf of Christ you have the favour of suffering no
30   less than of believing in him, by waging the same conflict
that, as once you saw and now you hear, I wage myself.

At this point there begins a well-marked section of the
epistle, extending from 1 : 27 to 2 : 18, in which the Apostle
manifests his concern about a tendency to disunion that was
revealing itself in the Church at Philippi. The whole section
is a closely-woven unit in which Paul endeavours to impress
upon the Philippians the duty of their forming one compact,
harmonious body free from all disputes and dissensions, each
member sacrificing personal desires and ambitions in order
to promote the good of the whole.

In the present paragraph (1 : 27–30) Paul urges his readers
to manifest a united firmness on behalf of the gospel, and a
self-control based upon an appreciation of the meaning of
suffering.

27   The word **only** is not infrequently used by Paul in the
manner in which he employs it here ; see, e.g., 1 Cor. 7 : 39,
Gal. 2 : 10, 5 : 13, 2 Thess. 2 : 7. Whether the Apostle comes
to Philippi or not, there is one thing his readers must not
fail to do. If he does not come to them, it is no less their
duty to **lead a life worthy of the gospel of Christ,** for their life
in Christ is not to be dependent upon the stimulus provided
by his presence with them. He seems to be preparing them
for the possibility that they may see him no more. ' Now,
therefore, dear brothers,' writes Savonarola to the Brethren
of his convent, ' detach yourselves from all human affection,
aye, even from your affection for myself. . . . Of a truth
your love for me were, then, indeed, a pure love if any one
of you from the time that I left you took care to cleave more
closely unto God. . . . But if, sorrowing beyond measure,
ye so lament me absent as to think that without me ye cannot
live, then, indeed, not yet is your love for me pure and true,
and, therefore, surely God hath willed that I should be withdrawn from you in order that ye may know that for the future

ye must not trust in man' (*Spiritual and Ascetic Letters*, edited by B. W. Randolph, pp. 45, 46, 47).

The words **do lead a life** translate one word in the Greek, and that word sets the keynote for the whole section extending to 2 : 18. Elsewhere in the New Testament it is found only in Acts 23 : 1. Originally it meant 'to live the life of a citizen, or a member of a community'; but eventually it lost this original sense and came to mean simply 'to live.' At the time when Paul was writing, however, some trace at least of the original meaning seems to survive whenever the word is used. In our present passage the verb probably bears its full original sense, which would accord well with the context. See 3 : 20, where the cognate noun is used. Polycarp, in his letter to the Philippians, combines the expression here used by Paul with an expression from 2 Tim. 2 : 12 to form a sentence which Lightfoot renders thus : 'If we perform our duties under him as simple citizens, he will promote us to a share of his sovereignty.'

The Apostle urges them to live a life **that is worthy of the gospel of Christ.** The **gospel of Christ** is the good news concerning him by believing which the Philippians had become members of the Christian commonwealth. It also sets a standard for them now that they have entered into the commonwealth ; and Paul urges them to live in a manner that is consistent with this standard, some of the requirements of which he sets forth in this paragraph. There are inscriptions extant which, using language similar to that employed here by the Apostle, speak of the persons commemorated in them as living lives worthy of their city or of their country.

The rendering **whether I come and see you or only hear of you in absence, let me know,** etc., while it sets forth Paul's meaning exactly, hides a striking irregularity in his method of expression. Quite literally what he says is : 'in order that, whether having come and seen you or else remaining absent, I may hear the things concerning you.' We should have expected him to say : 'in order that, whether having come and seen you or else remaining absent and hearing about you, I may learn the things concerning you.' We may, it is true, regard the sentence as quite regular if we make the 'hearing' apply to either contingency, interpreting it in one case to mean 'to hear from you in person,' and in the other case 'to hear from others about you.' So Meyer interprets. But, as Ellicott points out, this explanation is precluded by the opposition between 'having seen you' and 'I may hear the things concerning you,' which 'seems too distinct to have been otherwise than specially intended.' The irregularity is certainly present, but the meaning is not obscure. The turn which Paul gives to the sentence would seem to indicate that in his inmost heart he expected that in actual fact it would be a case of hearing about them rather than of seeing them face to face. To say the least, the words make it clear that he was far from being certain that acquittal would be his lot. There is revealed in them also his keen interest in his converts: he will learn all about the Philippians whether he comes to them or not. As Beet puts it, he 'adds to his exhortation a motive, namely, his own attentive interest in them.'

Paul desires and expects to learn that they **are standing firm in a common spirit**; and in some participial clauses which follow these words he expands and defines this initial statement of his expectation. Lightfoot remarks that the idea of *firmness* or *uprightness* is prominent in the very verb here used; but seeing that the same verb is used in other places in the New Testament meaning simply 'to stand,' it is more correct to say, as Ellicott, Vincent, and others do, that the idea of firmness comes from the context, though it must be admitted that the thought of firmness seems to be present every time Paul employs the verb. It is not possible to decide with certainty whether the metaphor in the present passage is that of soldiers standing firm in battle, or whether the figure is taken from the amphitheatre. Lightfoot accepts the latter alternative. 'Here,' he says, 'the metaphor seems to be drawn rather from the combats of the Roman amphitheatre. Like criminals or captives, the believers are condemned to fight for their lives: against them are arrayed the ranks of worldliness and sin: only unflinching courage and

64

steady combination can win the victory against such odds.'
The language of ver. 30 would seem to support this view.

The phrase **in a common spirit**—literally, ' in one spirit '—
has been variously interpreted. By some, **spirit** is interpreted
as the Holy Spirit ; by others as the human spirit ; and by
others still as a disposition or temper. The last of these is
the interpretation adopted in our translation. Each of the
three meanings of **spirit** may be said, however, to contribute
to the conception which the Apostle intends to convey by
the phrase. In 1 Cor. 12 : 13 and Eph. 2 : 18 we have precisely
the same expression, and in both cases the reference is obviously
to the Holy Spirit. The word ' spirit ' (*pneuma*) also denotes
the human spirit, ' the higher part of our immaterial nature,
that in which the agency of the Holy Spirit is especially seen
and felt ' (Ellicott). In the very next clause Paul speaks of
the ' soul ' (*psyche*), the seat of the sensations, affections,
desires, and passions. From the fact that he mentions both
spirit and soul it would appear that he is personifying the
Christian community at Philippi. The Church is to act as if
it possessed one *pneuma* and one *psyche*. Looked at from
this point of view, the **spirit** in our passage is the human spirit,
or, more strictly, the spirit of the personified community.
Paul, however, would not think of the spirit in this sense as
something altogether apart from the Holy Spirit of God.
' Indeed,' remarks Ellicott, ' in most cases in the New Testament it may be said that in the mention of the human *pneuma*
some reference to the eternal Spirit may always be recognized.'
So here, where the community is personified, we may assume
that the Holy Spirit is as definitely in the Apostle's mind as
in 1 Cor. 12 : 13 and Eph. 2 : 18. Now, this spirit of the
community, in which the Holy Spirit is working, may well be
thought of as the disposition of the community, so that they
who interpret **spirit** here as disposition or temper (as is done
in our translation) are fully justified. Thus the three meanings
of **spirit**—the Holy Spirit, the human spirit, and a disposition
or temper—all contribute to form the resultant conception
that was in the Apostle's mind when he wrote **standing firm
in one spirit.**

The Apostle continues his statement of what he would fain learn concerning them in the words : **fighting side by side like one man for the faith of the gospel.** The words **fighting side by side tr**anslate one word in the Greek, a participle which literally means ' contending together with.' The verb—a compound—occurs also in 4 : 3, and nowhere else in the New Testament. The simple verb occurs once—in 2 Tim. 2 : 5—in the sense of ' contending in the games.' It can, however, be used of the contest of war as well as of the games. Here, seemingly, it is the encounters of the arena that are in Paul's mind, as in the rest of the paragraph, but the more serious and bloody contests rather than the merely spectacular and competitive. The Philippian Christians are like a group standing in the arena, surrounded by wily, fierce antagonists.

' Contending together with '—together with whom ? Some say together with Paul ; but it is far more probable, as being more in harmony with the context, that the meaning is ' together with each other,' or, as our translation has it, **fighting side by side.** Paul expects to hear, not merely of their standing firm, but of their standing firm *fighting*. To fight is one of the conditions of **standing firm.** When we cease to fight we are bound to fall.

The words rendered **like one man** literally mean ' with one soul.' We have just seen that the soul (*psyche*) is the seat of the sensations, affections, desires, and passions. Paul is still personifying the Christian community at Philippi. The members are not only to have one spirit (*pneuma*) : they are to fight side by side with one soul (*psyche*). Chrysostom, Theodore of Mopsuestia, and some of the best of the ancient versions join the words ' with one soul,' not with **fighting side by side,** but with **standing firm.** It is, however, better in every way, with almost all modern scholars, to take them with **fighting side by side.** Compare Acts 4 : 32, where we are told that ' there was but one heart *and soul* among the multitude of the believers.'

It is not surprising that the unity of the early Christian communities should so persistently be threatened, or that the Apostle should deem it necessary to foster it by frequent

66

and emphatic exhortation. 'Consider the case of these early converts. What varieties of training had formed their characters, what prejudices of diverse races and religions continued to be active in their minds ! Consider also what a world of new truths had burst upon them. It was impossible they could at once take in all these in their just proportions. Various aspects of things would strike different minds, and difficulty must needs be felt about the reconciliation of them. In addition to theory, practice opened a field of easy divergence. Church life had to be developed, and Church work had to be done. Rules and precedents were lacking. Everything had to be planned and built from the foundation' (Rainy, *Expositor's Bible*, p. 82).

The rendering **for the faith of the gospel** agrees with the text of the R.V. as against the margin, which has ' *with* the faith of the gospel '; according to the latter rendering Paul is personifying the faith of the gospel, and urging the Philippians to assist the faith in its struggle against opposing forces. ' Striving in concert with the faith ' is the translation of Lightfoot, who adopts this interpretation. Analogous instances of personification in the New Testament are supposed to lend support to this way of taking the words, such as, for example, the personification of ' truth ' in 1 Cor. 13 : 6 and 3 John 8, and of the ' gospel ' in 2 Tim. 1 : 8. But no such personification of ' faith ' as Lightfoot finds here has been found elsewhere ; and his interpretation misses the emphasis which Paul is laying here, and throughout the paragraph, on the necessity of co-operation with each other on the part of the Philippians. The interpretation adopted in our translation is that of most modern scholars. It is *for* **the faith of the gospel** that the Apostle exhorts his readers to fight.

What are we to understand by **the faith of the gospel?** Here only does the phrase occur. It surely must mean more than ' the teaching of the gospel,' which is Lightfoot's interpretation. It means the faith that has resulted from **the** preaching of the good news concerning Christ. The most vital consequence of its proclamation was the trust produced thereby in the Christ proclaimed. This trust was the heart and centre of the experience and life engendered by the acceptance of the good news, and it was not unnatural that ' trust ' or ' faith ' should come to be used for the experience or life as a whole. ' The Faith ' later became a technical expression for the whole content of the Christian religion, and it is by no means impossible that we have here an early sign of the tendency to use the word in that way. The very existence of the new religion at Philippi was at stake, and the Philippians must fight to preserve it.

Moule and Hughes take the meaning here to be that the Philippians are to strive to win fresh adherents to the gospel. This is doubtless an essential element in all true fighting for the faith, but there is no reason for restricting the present reference to definite attempts to extend the bounds of the Christian community. There were other ways in which they could fight for the faith.

28 **Never be scared for a second by your opponents.** The verb here used for ' to scare ' is extremely rare, occurring nowhere else in the Greek Bible. It was employed in reference to startled, shying horses. Paul is anxious that the Philippians should not lose their self-control before the onslaught of their opponents. In the notes on chap. 2 : 12 ff. the suggestion is made that in that portion of our epistle the Apostle is comparing and contrasting himself with Moses when he was giving his final injunctions to the children of Israel as described in the closing chapters of the Book of Deuteronomy ; and it is not impossible that already in the present passage Deuteronomy may have been in his mind, for the choice of the unusual verb may well be due to the fact that the injunction of Moses in Deut. 31 : 6—' nor be affrighted at them ' —employs a verb which means ' to tremble ' or ' to quiver.' Was it the use by Paul of this particular verb that suggested to Trapp his reference to the horse in Job ? ' He that feareth God,' he comments, ' need fear none else, Psalm 3. But with the horse in Job 39 : 22, he mocketh at fear, and is not affrighted , neither turneth he back from the sword.'

The Philippians are not to be scared **for a second.** Whatever happens, whatever their opponents may do, they must not for an instant permit themselves to be scared out of their calm, steady self-control.

The word here used for ' opponent ' is found also in Luke 13 : 17, 21 : 15, 1 Cor. 16 : 9, 2 Thess. 2 : 4, 1 Tim. 5 : 14. Clearly the hostility with which Paul had had to contend at Philippi was still active against those who had believed through his ministry. See ver. 30. Just as the city of Philippi was a Roman colony surrounded by foes against whom it was ever on its guard, so the Christian community had to stand its ground against the enemies by whom it was encircled. These opponents were probably the heathen inhabitants of Philippi. The Jews were few ; and as Paul had himself been opposed by the pagan inhabitants, we infer, on the basis of ver. 30, that the present opponents of the Philippian Christians were also pagan. Referring to Paul's attitude to Jewish propaganda, Kennedy remarks that ' when warning his readers against Jewish malice, what he usually fears is not that they will be terrified into compliance, but that they will be seduced from the right path.' This consideration lends support to the view that in our present passage the Apostle has heathen opponents in mind. Kennedy also calls attention to the fact that the remains which have been discovered at Philippi would seem to show that the pagan inhabitants were 'an extraordinarily devout community.' Their very devoutness may have led them to persecute the Christians. Perhaps some of the latter were being forced into some sort of compromise by the threats of their antagonists. It is evident that the Apostle does not regard the peril as negligible.

Some writers identify the opponents here spoken of with the persons against whom Paul warns his readers in 3 : 2 ff., but the suggestion is most improbable. We do not think that the verses in chap. 3 formed part of the original letter to the Philippians ; and in any case the persons spoken of there are Jews, whereas the present opponents (as we have just seen) are the heathen inhabitants of the city.

From the courageous steadfastness which the Apostle urges his readers to exhibit there will emanate a twofold result.

Your fearlessness, he says, **is a clear omen of ruin for them and of your own salvation**—at the hands of God. In the Greek this is a relative clause : **your fearlessness** rightly interprets the relative pronoun.

Their fearlessness is, first, **a clear omen of ruin for them,** that is, for their opponents. **For them** goes, not with **ruin,** but with the whole phrase, **a clear omen of ruin. A clear omen** translates one word in the Greek, a word not found in the New Testament outside the Pauline epistles, and in them only in Rom. 3 : 25, 26, 2 Cor. 8 : 24, and the present passage. It signifies a proof based upon the evidence of facts. The fearless behaviour of the Philippian Christians would be a *fact* which their opponents would not be able to ignore, whose evidence they would not be able to gainsay.

An omen of ruin ! The word **ruin** is the common New Testament expression for eternal perdition—the antithesis of **salvation** ; and inasmuch as the two words are contrasted in the present passage, it seems best to take them in their full sense of eternal perdition and eternal life. But how would the fearlessness of the Philippian Christians be for their opponents an omen of eternal perdition ? The opponents would recognize in their behaviour something superhuman, something which could only come from God, and so would see that they themselves were pitted, not against a few helpless men and women, but against the very power of God. And what could be the issue of that but eternal perdition ? The persecutors could reverse Paul's great question in Rom. 8 : 31 and say : ' If God is against us, who can be for us ? ' Time and again in the story of the Christian Church the fearlessness of the persecuted has forced the persecutors into a recognition of the utter hopelessness of their own position. The candle lit by the martyrs has oftentimes revealed to their torturers that the path they were treading was one that led to eternal perdition.

Their fearless attitude would also be an omen **of your own salvation.** It has frequently been remarked that here we should have expected ' but to you of salvation,' to correspond with the preceding clause. That is what we actually find in the A.V. ; and it cannot be denied that the best-attested text seems at first sight to be lacking in symmetry. It is, however, as a matter of fact the more probable text. Paul is speaking of the influence exerted by the demeanour of the Philippian Christians upon their persecuting opponents, and after saying that it will be to them an omen of eternal ruin, he adds (possibly more or less as an afterthought) that it would also reveal to them that the persons whom they were persecuting were on the path that leads to eternal salvation. The persecutors would see that God was against themselves and at the same time recognize that He was on the side of the Christian believers. The spirit in which Stephen endured his martyrdom had been for Paul himself a token of his own perilous position, and of Stephen's salvation, while the spirit of One greater than Stephen had constrained the army-captain who stood by his cross to say: ' This man was certainly a son of God ' (Mark 15 : 39).

The words **at the hands of God,** as the punctuation of **our** translation makes clear, do not go closely with **your own salvation.** It is the omen supplied to the persecutors by the fearlessness of the Christians that is from God. The evidence furnished by their behaviour is a gift from God to those who are persecuting them.

For on behalf of Christ you have the favour of suffering no 29 **less than of believing in him.** This is an explanation of the statement just made, that the clear omen was God's gift to the persecutors. It was the fearlessness of the Christians that furnished the omen, and the omen was God's gift inasmuch as the suffering that occasioned the fearlessness was His gift to the Christians. When He gave to the Christians the gift of suffering on behalf of Christ, He was also at the same time giving to their opponents the double token—the token of their own perdition and of the Christians' salvation. The one gift involved the other.

To connect this verse closely with the immediately preceding words in this way is more natural than to connect it (as do some) with the words **never be scared,** as if Paul were saying, ' Do not be alarmed at the prospect of suffering, for suffering is a gift from God to you.'

Paul's statement literally rendered would run : 'the favour of suffering was granted to you.' Note the past tense : the gift was graciously bestowed upon them when first they believed. It is, of course, still in their possession, but it would have been nearer to the Apostle's actual words to render : 'you *have received* the favour of suffering.'

The favour of suffering was involved in the gift of faith. Some expositors appear to understand Paul to mean that God had meted out for the Philippian Christians a certain share of suffering which they were bound to endure ; but such a view is too mechanical. What Paul means is that when God bestowed on them the gift of the new life, He gave them something that was sure to come into collision with the evil world, and at the same time a spirit that would not flinch whatever consequences their defiance might entail. The gift is a gracious favour because it makes possible the fearlessness which is God's own omen for the persecutors. He provided the material, so to say, out of which the Christians themselves had to fashion His token. He furnished the gold which they were to mint into coins bearing His image and circulating for His glory.

They were called to suffer **on behalf of Christ,** that is, to help forward his cause and to enhance his glory in the eyes of men. The New Testament not infrequently speaks of suffering for his cause as an honour and a privilege. Compare Acts 5 : 41 : 'The apostles left the Sanhedrin, rejoicing that they had been considered worthy of suffering dishonour for the sake of the Name.' See also Rom. 5 : 3 and Col. 1 : 24. The same attitude to suffering has illumined the dark story of persecution ever since. In his letter to Magdalen Pica, Countess of Mirandola, on the subject of her purpose to enter the Order of St. Clare, Savonarola says of the saints and the 'religious' : 'So possessed are they by love of him that for his sake no toil is heavy, no adversity is bitter ; nay, they do count it honour and hold it in high esteem if they are able to suffer even in some small degree for his sake who for them deigned to die upon the Cross " (*Spiritual and Ascetic Letters*, p. 12). Trapp here quotes the saying of Careless, the martyr : ' Such an honour it is as the greatest angel in heaven is not permitted to have. God forgive me mine unthankfulness.'

There is some emphasis on the word **you**, as if Paul were contrasting the Christians with their opponents in the matter of privilege. His readers might be tempted to envy their persecutors, but the believers, harassed and oppressed as they were, were the truly favoured ones—the fortunate and privileged recipients of God's great gift of suffering.

In the Greek, the Apostle, before actually mentioning the suffering, stops abruptly in the middle of the sentence in order to introduce the words rendered **no less than of believing in him**, so eager is he to emphasize the inevitable connexion between their suffering and their faith ; the gift of suffering is not an isolated boon : it is involved in the gift of faith ; when God gave the latter gift, he of necessity gave also the former. Note the conception of faith as a gift of God's grace.

The Greek is here somewhat irregular, but our translation 30 is certainly right in taking the clause as a description of the way in which the Philippians suffer—**by waging the same conflict that, as once you saw and now you hear, I wage myself.** The word rendered **conflict** originally signified a contest in the arena, whether gladiatorial or athletic, and that sense of the word would seem to be in the Apostle's mind here. In 1 Thess. 2 : 2 Paul uses the very same word of his experience at Thessalonica. The Christians are pictured as standing in the arena, pitted against deadly foes. Theirs is ' the same sort of conflict ' as Paul himself is waging ! It is not necessary to infer from these words that the Philippian Christians were in custody, as Paul had been at Philippi and now was in Ephesus. It is the same sort of conflict, even though it may not be identical with his in form. How the thought would enhearten his readers ! They could magnify Christ by their sufferings as he was doing by his !

As once you saw—that is, at Philippi. The conflict to which these words refer is recorded with fullness in Acts 16. Moule observes that one of the probable recipients of our epistle, namely the jailer, had not only seen Paul's sufferings, but had also himself inflicted some of them.

And now you hear : this refers to his present conflict waged in Ephesus, news of which would reach the Philippians through the present letter (which would be read in their assembly), through Epaphroditus the bearer of the letter, and doubtless through others also. Paul regards his experiences at Philippi and at Ephesus as aspects of the same conflict. All the varied struggles of Christian history are items of the one great conflict.

CHAPTER II

AN EXHORTATION TO HARMONY AND SELF-ABNEGATION
(II. 1–4)

1 So by all the stimulus of Christ, by every incentive of love, by all your participation in the Spirit, by all your affec-
2 tionate tenderness, I pray you to give me the utter joy of knowing you are living in harmony, with the same
3 feelings of love, with one heart and soul, never acting for private ends or from vanity, but humbly considering
4 each other the better man, and each with an eye to the interests of others as well as to his own.

The utter absence of severity of censure in this exhortation shows that the dissensions and disputes at Philippi had not yet reached an acute stage. The frequency and the urgency of the Apostle's appeals, however, imply that the danger of serious disruption was real. Paul's concern reveals itself in the elaborate fourfold adjuration with which the present paragraph opens.

1 In the statement of the last of the four grounds of appeal (that is, in the last clause of ver. 1) the Greek text in the best authorities exhibits an almost incredible breach of concord. All the uncial manuscripts as well as many of the cursives have this palpable grammatical error! The R.V. renders the clause literally : ' if (there are) any tender mercies and

compassions.' The word rendered ' tender mercies ' is (in the Greek) a neuter plural noun, and the word ' compassions ' a masculine plural noun ; but the word ' any ' (which should agree in gender and number with the noun with which it goes) does not agree with either of these, being masculine or feminine singular ; it does not agree in any respect with the noun ' tender mercies ' to which it stands in immediate proximity ! This strange perpetuation of a manifest inaccuracy bears witness to the unthinking fidelity of the early scribes. A conjecture suggested independently by Haupt and Kennedy and endorsed by James Hope Moulton seems to restore the original text. In the text as restored by this conjecture Paul, with impressive repetition, says with regard to each of the four bases of his appeal : ' if it has any force, if it carries any weight, I pray you,' etc. Our translation is an excellent rendering of the restored text.

There exists among expositors a lack of agreement on the question whether the four grounds on which Paul bases his appeal represent four things which should create in the hearts of the Philippians a considerate attitude towards the Apostle and his entreaty, or four things which should make them kindly disposed towards each other. On a priori grounds we should have expected the Apostle to base his appeal upon the things calculated to foster kindly feelings among the Philippians themselves, rather than upon the things calculated to make them considerate in their attitude to him and his petition ; and yet he expresses his appeal in ver. 2 (' fulfil ye my joy,' R.V.) in a way that would seem to favour the latter view. On the whole we incline to the view, held by the Greek Fathers, that the four adjurations present four grounds of appeal for considerateness towards himself ; and we shall interpret the appeals from that point of view, without, however, ignoring the other possibility. It goes without saying that, though the Apostle puts the appeal in the form of a request for the fulfilment of his joy, it is not his joy that he is concerned about, but the harmony among the Philippians that would complete his joy in them. His real appeal is for unity and harmony.

75

The four clauses which express the four grounds of appeal are capable of being interpreted in an almost bewildering variety of ways ; it will not be possible for us to do much more than select and state in each case the interpretation which seems to us to conform with the mind of the Apostle.

(*a*) **By all the stimulus of Christ.** The word rendered **stimulus** may mean ' consolation ' (A.V.), ' comfort ' (R.V.), ' encouragement,' ' exhortation.' The last of these is, we think, the meaning intended here. Paul has in mind the exhortation which he is now addressing to the Philippians. It is an exhortation ' in Christ ' ; Christ is the sphere in which it is addressed ; it is prompted by his spirit. If, says the Apostle, such an exhortation has any force, if it carries any influence with you, let it lead you to fulfil my joy by being united among yourselves. The constant use in the Pauline epistles of the cognate verb in the sense of ' I exhort ' or ' I beseech ' (see, for example, Rom. 12 : 1, 15 : 30, 16 : 17 ; 1 Cor. 1 : 10, 4 : 16, 16 : 15 ; Eph. 4 : 1 ; and especially 4 : 2 of our epistle) supports the adoption of ' exhortation ' as the meaning of the noun in the present passage.

(*b*) **By every incentive of love.** The word translated **incentive** occurs here only in the New Testament, and is not very far removed in meaning from the word ' exhortation ' in the preceding clause. Persuasion, appeal, exhortation, consolation, incentive—these are its meanings. Paul is referring still, we think, to the appeal which he is addressing to his readers—an appeal that springs from his love to them. If such an appeal has any influence with them, let them do its bidding. Surely love's appeal cannot go unheeded !

(*c*) **By all your participation in the Spirit.** Literally, ' if fellowship of spirit (means) anything.' This our translation interprets to mean ' if the fact that you all participate in the same Holy Spirit means anything.' This may well be **Paul's** meaning, in which case he appeals to the Philippians on the ground of their common Christian life. A community whose members are all inspired by the same Spirit should surely be free from disputes and dissensions. If this is the meaning of the clause, the nature of Paul's appeal is now changed.

Hitherto, if our interpretation of the preceding clauses is correct, he has based his request on the nature of the appeal which he is able to address to his readers, whereas now he appeals on the ground of his readers' common experience. It is possible, however, that he still has in mind the mutual relation of himself and his readers, in which case his words mean ' by all *our* participation in the Spirit,' the appeal being based on the fact that he and they together share in the same life of the Spirit. Because of this common participation an appeal from him should have force with them.

(*d*) **By all your affectionate tenderness.** **Affectionate tenderness** represents two nouns in the Greek, which the A.V. renders by ' bowels and mercies,' and the R.V. by ' tender mercies and compassions.' The former of the two is the same word that is rendered ' affection ' in 1 : 8, where the A.V. has ' bowels ' as here. See the note there. The second of the two nouns conveys the idea of pity to a greater degree than does the first. Here, as in the preceding clauses, the precise reference of the words is in doubt. It may be that the Apostle is appealing to the affectionate tenderness that should be operative among the members of the Philippian Church, binding them together and making dissension and disruption impossible. Or he may mean the affectionate tenderness which they should manifest towards him, the disposition that would make it impossible for them to turn a deaf ear to his entreaty. It may be urged as an objection to this last interpretation that a man of Paul's temper would never appeal to the pity of his readers ; but we must not be too certain that he is not doing so here ; for the way in which he heaps up his grounds of appeal betokens an earnestness that would not hesitate to appeal even to their pity. It is possible, however, that Paul is thinking of his own affectionate tenderness towards them from which, as from his love, his appeal proceeds. Surely the thought of his affectionate pity could not fail to move them.

Whatever be the exact force of the four clauses in ver. 1, 2 there can be no question of the Apostle's intense earnestness. He entreats his readers to ' fulfil his joy by being of the same mind.' **I pray you**—so his words run in our translation—**to give me the utter joy of knowing you are living in harmony.** The Philippians are already a source of joy to him. He has told them in 1 : 4 that he always prays for them ' with a sense of joy'; and in 4 : 1 he addresses them as his ' joy and crown.' Still, his joy in them is not complete : an arc of the circle of his joy is wanting. He urges them to complete the circle—to fulfil the joy they are capable of affording him. This they can do by living in harmony among themselves. Their factiousness robs him of a portion of his due joy in them. It is not his own joy, as we have seen, that the Apostle is concerned about. As Calvin puts it, ' he felt small anxiety for himself, if but the Church of Christ might prosper' (quoted by Moule). The reason he frames his request in the way he does is that it thus furnishes for his readers an additional motive, reminding them that by living in harmony they would be perfecting his joy in them. There is something sublime in Paul's joy in his converts. To another Macedonian Church he writes : ' How can I render thanks enough to God for you, for all the joy you make me feel in the presence of our God ? ' (1 Thess. 3 : 9).

It is the utter joy of knowing that they are **living in harmony,** or, to render the words literally, ' thinking the same thing,' that the Apostle seeks. The very same expression is used in 4 : 2, where Paul entreats Euodia and Syntyche to ' agree' in the Lord. The phrase means more than to hold in common a particular opinion ; it refers rather to unity of sentiment and feeling ; so that our translation is justified when it renders **living in harmony.** The verb that is used in the phrase is found also in 1 : 7, in the Greek that underlies the words ' to be thinking of you all.' See the note there. It is interesting to find the very expression used in the present passage employed in a touching epitaph of a married couple (from Rhodes, 2nd century B.C.) which runs as follows : ' Saying the same things and thinking the same things, we have come the long way to Hades.'

Paul adds with the same feelings of love. Love, mutual and **equal, is to inhabit and actuate every heart in the Church.**

With one heart and soul. This phrase represents Greek words
which literally mean ' sharing the same soul (*psyche*), thinking
the one thing.' ' Sharing the same soul ' renders just one
word, an adjective which occurs here only in the New Testament. It takes us back to the words ' like one man ' in 1 : 27.
We there saw that the *psyche* is the seat of the sensations,
affections, desires, and passions ; and we suggested that Paul
was personifying the community. Here he seems to revert to
that personification. The Philippian Church is to share one
psyche. It is not to be divided up into groups, each having,
as it were, its own separate soul. And the members are to
' think the one thing.' We saw a moment ago that the words
living in harmony in the present verse mean literally ' thinking the same thing.' Paul now, in the earnestness of his soul,
repeats the phrase in a slightly stronger form—' thinking the
one thing.' His desire is not that they should hold in common
a particular opinion, but rather that one sentiment should
pervade the whole community. The Apostle is concerned to
produce among the Philippians not a uniformity in belief and
opinion, but rather a unity of spirit and sentiment.

In the words **never acting for private ends** the Apostle con- 3
tinues his statement of the life he desires them to live. The
R.V. has ' *doing* nothing through faction.' No participle is
expressed in the Greek : it is left to the reader to supply one.
Some scholars are of the opinion that the participle to be
supplied is not ' doing ' (as in the R.V., and as is implied in
our translation), but ' thinking ' or ' being mindful of,' as
the last clause of ver. 2 would seem to suggest. Some, indeed,
refuse to supply a participle at all, preferring to regard these
opening words of ver. 3 as an imperative : ' nothing for
private ends ! ' The context, however, shows that a participle
is to be supplied. In any case there is no ambiguity in the
meaning. Nothing is to be done for private ends ! Paul
employs here the very noun which he uses in the phrase ' for
their own ends ' in 1 : 17, where he is describing the motives
of the preachers whom he condemns. As was observed in the
note on 1 : 17, the context must in each occurrence determine
the exact significance of the noun. ' The word,' says Moule,

79

' may denote not merely the *combined self-seeking* of partisan-ship, but also a solitary ambition, working by intrigue.' It is the latter meaning that is adopted in our translation, but seeing that Paul is here deprecating factiousness and pleading for unity, the former would be the more suitable meaning. In other words, ' party ends ' would bring out the Apostle's meaning more exactly than **private ends**. The advantage of party is never to be a motive for action. The interests of a section of the community should never be allowed to override the interests of the community as a whole.

The preposition used with the noun in the present passage is not the same as that used with the same noun in 1 : 17 ; here the very preposition shows that what Paul is deprecating is the pursuit of party ends as a rule or principle of conduct : nothing is to be done ' according to ' or ' by way of ' party ends. The comprehensiveness of the injunction should be noticed : the Philippians are *never* to find their motive in party interest. How different would have been the story of the Christian Church if this precept had furnished for Christians a universal rule ! Paul could see before his very eyes, as 1 : 17 shows, the evil results of factiousness : small wonder that he charges the Philippians to renounce utterly the spirit of faction. Ignatius echoes the very words of Paul when he says to the Philadelphians : ' I beseech you to do nothing for party ends, but (to do all things) in accordance with the teaching of Christ ' (chap. 8).

Another motive for action is deprecated by the Apostle in the words **or from vanity**. Here only does the noun occur in the New Testament, but the corresponding adjective is used in Gal. 5 : 26. Both the A.V. and the R.V. render the noun by ' vainglory.' Like the English word ' vanity,' the Greek word etymologically suggests a conceit that is hollow, groundless, pretentious. Personal conceit, as well as partisanship, is condemned as a motive and principle of action. Factiousness and vanity—these were the evils that menaced the Christian community at Philippi. The former is often the bane of active, vigorous Churches.

The spirit which the Apostle would fain see flourishing

among the Philippians is set forth in the remaining words **of** this paragraph. After his warning against partisanship and vanity he proceeds : **but humbly considering each other the better man.** This is the opposite of vanity. Instead of **humbly,** both the A.V. and the R.V. have ' in lowliness of mind.' The noun which they thus render occurs seven times in the New Testament, the R.V. renderings varying between lowliness, lowliness of mind, and humility. There enters into the formation of the noun (just as ' low ' enters into the formation of ' lowliness ') an adjective which in classical Greek connotes abject self-abasement. In the New Testament, however, it is entirely free from any suggestion of meanness. The exaltation of the adjective and its derivatives and cognates in the New Testament answers to the exaltation of the virtue itself by Christianity. Paul is not here demanding on the part of the Philippians a state of mind that is abject and servile. Christian humility is a due sense of one's own unworthiness, a disposition that recognizes in oneself room for improvement, a readiness to see and to rejoice in the good in others. Paul asks them to consider **each other the better man.** ' This explains,' says Plummer, ' what is meant by humblemindedness. The Christian knows that he has many defects and failings which are unknown to his fellows, and which he has no right to suppose that they have. On the other hand, he sees in them virtues which he knows that he does not possess.' Wesley, in one of his many letters to Thomas Wride, the eccentric preacher, complains of his lack of the very spirit which Paul here urges his readers to cultivate. ' Alas ! alas ! ' writes Wesley, ' you have now confirmed beyond all contradiction what many of our preachers, as many as have had any intercourse with you, alleged concerning you ! I am persuaded, had I read your last letter (that of the 17th inst.) at the Conference, condemning, with such exquisite bitterness and self-sufficiency, men so many degrees better than yourself, the whole Conference, as one man, would have disclaimed all connexion with you. I know not what to do. You know not what spirit you are of. Therefore there is small hope of cure. I have no heart to send you anywhere. You

have neither lowliness nor love. What can I say or do more ! '
(*Letters*, p. 190).

4 Just as the last clause of ver. 3 refers to the grace that is
the opposite of vanity, so it is *possible* to regard ver. 4—**and each
with an eye to the interests of others as well as to his own**—
as pointing to the spirit that is the antithesis of partisanship,
for, according to what appears to be the true text, the Apostle
twice employs in this verse the word **each** in the plural ; and
this plural (of which there is no other instance in the New
Testament) is capable of being explained as a reference to
the various groups into which the Church at Philippi was
divided. This interpretation, however, is exposed to some
serious objections, of which one is that it makes Paul sanction,
not only the continued existence of these groups in the Church,
but even the right of each group to consider its own interests !
So we prefer to take the plural as the plural of emphasis,
giving the meaning ' each and all.' Every single member
is to have at heart the interests of the other members as well
as his own. The Apostle does not prohibit interest in one's
own affairs ; it is selfish preoccupation with one's own affairs
that he condemns. We must love our neighbour—*as ourselves*.

Some commentators interpret this verse in a way that
brings it into closer harmony with the last clause of ver. 3.
According to their interpretation Paul speaks, not of the
interests of others, but of the ' good qualities ' of others, urging
his readers to be on the outlook for the virtues of their fellow-
members. While this interpretation is possible, it does
not suit Paul's language as well as the one adopted in our
translation, for the Greek participle underlying the words
with an eye to connotes the idea of aim or object ; and the
Apostle is more likely to have spoken of the *interests* of their
fellow-members as an object for his readers to aim at than
of their *virtues*. Unselfishness is the one and only guarantee
of unity. Where selfishness exists, harmony is impossible.

THE EXAMPLE OF CHRIST (II. 5–11)

5 Treat one another with the same spirit as you experience in
6   Christ Jesus. Though he was divine by nature, he did

not snatch at equality with God but emptied himself 7
by taking the nature of a servant ; born in human guise 8
and appearing in human form, he humbly stooped in his
obedience even to die, and to die upon the cross. Therefore 9
God raised him high and conferred on him a Name above
all names, so that before the Name of Jesus *every knee* 10
should bend in heaven, on earth, and underneath the earth,
and every tongue confess that 'Jesus Christ is Lord,' to 11
the glory of God the Father.

In order to give greater force to the entreaty which he has
just addressed to his readers, the Apostle sets before them the
example of their Lord.   Compare Rom. 15 : 3 and 2 Cor. 8 : 9.
In our endeavour to arrive at the correct interpretation of the
present passage we must ever bear in mind that it is introduced for a practical purpose.   At the same time the passage
reveals an exact balance of clauses (see Moffatt, *Introduction
to the Literature of the N.T.*, p. 167), which seems to point to
careful construction.   It is not impossible that Paul is making
use of the words of some early poem or hymn.

The paragraph presents as many and as great difficulties
as perhaps any passage in the epistles of St. Paul.   'The
diversity of opinion prevailing among interpreters,' says
Bruce, 'is enough to fill the student with despair, and to
afflict him with intellectual paralysis' (*Humiliation of
Christ*, p. 8).

Before we consider the verses *seriatim* let us glance at the
question whether or not the passage speaks of the pre-existent
Christ.   Does the Apostle, or does he not, carry back the
example of Christ to his pre-incarnate state ?   In the opinion
of some interpreters the paragraph is concerned solely with
the example afforded by the life of the historical Christ, and
it must be admitted that this is a quite possible, and in some
ways attractive, interpretation.   If, however, with Westcott
and Hort, the R.V., and the majority of interpreters, we take
the clause **born in human guise** closely with the words that
precede it, and so make it a part of the description of the way
in which Christ Jesus emptied himself, this interpretation is

impossible, for in that case the self-emptying is clearly regarded as the outcome of a pre-incarnate volition.

Whether we take that particular clause with the words which precede or with those which follow, the probability is that the passage embraces the pre-incarnate as well as the incarnate life of Christ. This is the opinion of Lipsius, Dibelius, and almost all recent English writers. See Lightfoot's reasons for adopting this view (*Philippians*, pp. 131, 132). There are several passages in Paul's letters which point to his belief in the pre-existence of Christ. In Rom. 8 : 3 and Gal. 4 : 4 he speaks of God ' sending ' His Son ; and in 2 Cor. 8 : 9 he employs language which makes it clear that in his view the pre-existence was not merely ideal, but real and actual. The pre-existent Christ was possessed of the power of thought and will. ' The only pre-existence in which apostolic writers are interested is not ideal but real and personal. The love which entered history in Jesus could come only through a personal channel' (Mackintosh, *Doctrine of the Person of Christ*, p. 447).

This conception of a personal pre-existence teems with difficulties ; but into these it is evident that we cannot now attempt to enter. The inadequacy of the term ' person ' is obvious (see Mackintosh, *op. cit.*, p. 452), and the fact that we are compelled to think in terms of time affects all our thought. Nor is it part of our present task to inquire how the Apostle arrived at his conception of the pre-existent Christ. We may be sure that a vital factor in the formation of his thought was his own experience of the Risen Lord. He who had come to mean so much to him surely did not begin to exist when Jesus was born in Bethlehem. Nor need we hesitate to believe that Paul was influenced by Jewish and Alexandrian speculations.

5 **Treat one another with the same spirit as you experience in Christ Jesus.** The very novelty of this rendering may repel some readers, for it is so utterly different from the familiar renderings of the A.V. and the R.V. And yet it is almost certainly correct. This way of taking the verse is adopted by Deissmann, Lipsius, Dibelius, Kennedy, Jones, Hughes, and others. The words of the Apostle literally rendered, are :

' Think this in (or, among) yourselves which also in Christ Jesus.' No verb is actually expressed in the relative clause. Both the A.V. and the R.V. supply the verb ' was.' But the verb that most naturally suggests itself is that which is found in the first part of the verse. When we supply this verb we get : ' think among yourselves that which also you think in Christ Jesus.' The word ' think ' is the word we have already met in 1 : 7 and 2 : 2 and which occurs again several times in chaps. 3 and 4. It connotes more than mere thought. The action of the heart is embraced within its meaning as well as that of the head. It speaks of sympathetic interest and care. Paul's injunction, then, means : ' have among yourselves the disposition which is yours in Christ Jesus ' ; ' show among yourselves the spirit you experience in him ' ; or, as our translation has it, **treat one another with the same spirit as you experience in Christ Jesus**. He urges them to put into practice in the life of the Christian community the spirit engendered in their hearts by communion with Christ. One advantage which this interpretation has over the old is that it enables us to give to the phrase **in Christ Jesus** its customary Pauline significance, namely, ' in living union with the Risen Christ.'

Now comes the statement of the great example. **Though 6 he was divine by nature, he did not snatch at equality with God**—so it opens. It will help us if we place side by side with this rendering those of the A.V. and the R.V. The former has : ' who, being in the form of God, thought it not robbery to be equal with God ' ; and the latter : ' who, being in the form of God, counted it not a prize to be on an equality with God.' The participial clause which is literally rendered in both versions (' being in the form of God ') is rightly construed in our translation as having a concessive force (**though he was**), for the simple and natural implication of the words is, as Lipsius observes, that the lofty state here predicated of the Christ might well have allured him into that very path upon which, according to the next clause, he refused to enter.

The participle translated ' being ' in the A.V. and the R.V. is not from the ordinary Greek verb ' to be.' In classical

85

Greek the participle would mean ' being by nature,' or, as the R.V. margin renders, ' being originally.' In later Greek, however, the verb frequently means no more than simply ' to be,' and it is precarious to say (as does Plummer) that the participle itself ' points clearly to the pre-existence of Christ.' Nor does Gifford (*Incarnation*, pp. 11-21) succeed in showing that the participle implies that Christ continued ' in the form of God ' even after he had emptied himself.

The Greek word translated ' form ' in the A.V. and the R.V.—*morphē*—is found elsewhere in the New Testament only in Mark 16 : 12. In our translation the word ' form ' is used—in ver. 8—to render a different Greek word (*schēma*). Lightfoot (pp. 127-33) has a long detached note in which he discusses the meanings of these two Greek words. He traces the meaning of *morphē* in the earlier and later philosophers, but as the word undoubtedly came to be used in a loose, popular sense, it is now very generally felt that in the attempt to arrive at its precise significance in the present clause not much is gained by tracing its philosophical history. At the same time it seems certain that the word ' always signifies a form which truly and fully expresses the being which under-lies it ' (Kennedy). Moulton and Milligan (*Vocabulary*, p. 417) quote passages from the papyri which support this statement, and Lightfoot's examination of the use in the Pauline epistles of compounds in which the word we are discussing forms an element would seem to show that the Apostle recognized this significance of the word (pp. 130, 131). Though the word does not actually mean **nature,** yet a thing cannot be said to be in the *morphē* of another unless it possesses the essential qualities of that other. All this goes to show that the render-ing of our translation—**though he was divine by nature**—represents the meaning of the clause, especially as the participle may not be without some tinge of its classical meaning, ' being by nature.' ' He was in nature essentially Divine ' is Findlay's paraphrase of the clause (*Epistles of Paul the Apostle*, p. 199) ; and Mackintosh says regarding our para-graph : ' It is asserted—and on the assertion hinges the thrilling moral appeal of the passage—that before he came as man, Christ's life was Divine in quality; not merely *like* God, but participant in His essential attributes' (*op. cit.*, p. 67). With the description of Christ in this clause compare 2 Cor. 4 : 4, Col. 1 : 15, 16, Heb. 1 : 3.

Though the pre-existent Christ was thus divine by nature, he did not, says the Apostle, snatch at equality with God. We can best examine this statement by considering separately the following two questions : (*a*) What are we to understand by equality with God ? (*b*) What does the clause say regarding the attitude of Christ Jesus towards this equality with God ?

(*a*) What are we to understand by equality with God ? Is being equal with God synonymous with being divine by nature ? So some interpreters maintain. But, as Kennedy says, ' there is absolutely nothing in the text to justify the supposition.' Lipsius justly observes that the change of expression tells against the identification. The one expression is more naturally taken as referring to essential being, the other as referring to state or condition.

Many who do not hold that the two expressions mean the same thing, yet maintain that equality with God is something which Christ must have possessed in his pre-incarnate state in virtue of his being divine by nature. So Gifford, for example (*op. cit.*, p. 55). But equality with God and divinity of nature do not of necessity go together in Paul's thought of Christ, as is shown by the fact that he is able to foresee the time when the Son himself, his work completed, shall be subjected to the Father (1 Cor. 15 : 28) ; for we can scarcely believe that Paul would think of the Son as having at that time ceased to be divine by nature.

But if equality with God is not in Paul's mind an inevitable concomitant of Christ's divine nature, is it something which he thought of as being possessed by Christ in his pre-incarnate state ? Or did the Apostle think of it as something which Christ could achieve in the future ? Was it equality with God that he achieved at his exaltation ? It is this latter view that we regard as the more probable. But let us turn to the other question.

(*b*) What does the present clause say regarding the attitude

of Christ to **equality with God**? Paul here uses a noun—
harpagmos—which occurs nowhere else in the Greek Scriptures,
and is met with but rarely outside of the Scriptures. The verb
which he employs in this clause he has just used in ver. 3 when
he says **humbly** *considering* **each other the better man.**

Now, this noun *harpagmos* may be either active or passive
in meaning, that is to say, it may mean either ' a snatching '
or ' a thing snatched.' Is it active or is it passive in the
present clause ?

The form of the word suggests the active sense, and in
that sense it seems to be understood by the A.V., which has
' thought it not robbery to be equal with God,' that is, ' deemed
it no usurpation on his part to be equal with God.' Several
of the Latin Fathers interpret the clause in this way ; but in
recent times Webster and Wilkinson are almost alone in so
doing. In their view, the clause expresses Christ's ' consciousness of his essential deity in his pre-existent state,' and so
enhances ' the condescension of his humiliation.' There are,
however, several objections to this way of interpreting the
words. For one thing, if this were the meaning, we should
have expected the next clause to be introduced by ' nevertheless ' or ' and yet.' For another, the drift of the passage does
not lead us to expect just here a statement of Christ's consciousness of his right to equality with the Father.

The R.V. takes the noun in a passive sense—' counted it not
a prize to be on an equality with God.' It is true that it is a
different form of the word that naturally bears the passive
meaning ; but the distinction between the two forms had
become blurred at the time when the books of the New Testament were written. The form used here by Paul may well
bear the passive sense, and so in all probability it should be
understood. But when we have decided to take it in that
sense we have still to decide between the two possible meanings
of ' booty to be retained ' and ' booty to be snatched.'

The former of these meanings associates itself with the
view that equality with God is already possessed by Christ
in his pre-existent state. If it be adopted, the sense of
the clause will be that Christ did not look upon his equality

with God as a thing to be retained and held fast at all costs. The latter meaning, on the other hand, goes with the view that equality with God is not something already possessed by Christ. This second meaning suits the derivation of the word better than does the former. The cognate verb appears invariably to denote snatching something not yet possessed. So, in spite of Lightfoot's contention that a phrase practically identical with that here used by Paul had come to mean ' to prize highly,' ' to set store by ' (the idea of robbery or plunder having entirely passed out of it), we prefer to think that Lipsius correctly gives the meaning of Paul when he says : ' The sense is : Christ regarded this equality with God (which, though in divine form, he did not yet possess) not as a booty, that is to say, not as an object which he might violently and against the will of God snatch for himself . . . but rather as something attainable only through self-emptying and by the favour of God.' This is also the interpretation adopted by Kennedy, and it is the one that is assumed in our translation. It may perhaps be said in criticism of the rendering in our translation that it does not sufficiently bring out the thought of mental judgment or decision expressed in the Greek.

It has been suggested by various writers that there is in the mind of Paul a contrast between the spirit that animated Christ and the spirit manifested by some person or persons who *did* attempt to reach equality with God. The negative form of expression gives some countenance to the suggestion, as Kennedy and Dibelius have observed. The contrast, according to some, is with Adam (compare Gen. 3 : 5, 6). Dibelius thinks the humility and condescension of Christ are set over against the arrogant behaviour of Satan and certain other denizens of the spirit-world whose self-seeking spirit is depicted in the tenth chapter of the *Ascension of Isaiah.*

So far from snatching at equality with God the pre-existent 7 Christ emptied himself by taking the nature of a servant. The rendering emptied himself, in which our translation agrees with the R.V., is nearer the Greek and in every way more satisfactory than that of the A.V. ' made himself of no reputation.'

89

Of what did Christ empty himself? Paul does not specify. Several interpreters, influenced by the contrast between the divine nature of Christ referred to in ver. 6 and the nature of a servant which he assumes, maintain that it was of his divine nature that he divested himself. But the retention of the divine nature and the assumption of the nature of a servant are not incompatible; and it may be doubted whether the Apostle would regard as possible the surrender by Christ of his divine nature.

According to others, it was of his **equality with God** that he emptied himself; but if the interpretation of this phrase which we have adopted is the correct one (that is to say, if the phrase refers to something which he did not yet possess in his pre-incarnate state), it follows that this explanation must be set aside. We are not limited, however, to the divine nature and equality with God as possible objects of the self-emptying. Even if equality with God did not yet belong to the pre-existent Christ, there were conditions of glory and majesty that inevitably pertained to his divine nature; and if some specific secondary object must be found for the verb **emptied,** we may well think of these conditions as that object. So Lightfoot says: ' he divested himself, not of his divine nature, for this was impossible, but of the glories, the prerogatives, of Deity.' Compare John 17:5.

It is possible that the Apostle was not thinking of any definite object for the verb. His words may have been intended to express a general antithesis to snatching at equality with God. In the *Journal of Theological Studies*, vol. xii, pp. 461-3, W. Warren suggests that the verb here needs no secondary object, but means ' to pour out,' with ' himself ' as the direct object. He gives examples of the use of the verb in this sense. Liddell and Scott refer to a passage in which it means to pour (medicine) away. Taylor (*Sayings of the Jewish Fathers*) has compared Isa. 53:12 with vers. 7 and 8 of our passage (see Kennedy, p. 439*a*), and there the prophet says of the Servant that ' he poured out his soul unto death.' That this verse from Isaiah has some connexion with our passage would seem to be confirmed by the fact that in the

very next clause mention is made of a **servant,** and that in
ver. 8 Christ is said to have been obedient **unto death.**

Whatever may have been the exact meaning the Apostle
attached to the words **emptied himself,** he goes on to tell that
it was **by taking the nature of a servant** that Christ did empty
himself. **By taking** correctly expresses his meaning, for he
uses a participle whose action is contemporaneous with that
of the verb **emptied,** and by which the action of the verb is
explained. The word **nature** in this clause is the same as that
used in ver. 6, for which in both places the A.V. and the
R.V. have ' form.' It points to the reality of the state now
assumed by Christ. Not in appearance only did he become a
servant. Was it to God or to man that he became a servant ?
The obedience spoken of in ver. 8 is naturally understood as
obedience rendered to God, and that supports the view, probable on other grounds, that it was God's servant he became.
Vincent and Plummer combine the two ideas. The word
rendered **servant** is the common word for slave, and points to
the completeness of Christ's surrender to the will of God.
How great the contrast between the path he chose and the
path he rejected !

In this verse Paul is speaking of the Incarnation itself, not
of a pre-incarnate act of self-renunciation which prepared the
way, so to speak, for the Incarnation. He speaks of a real
kenosis. But it is evident that the present passage supplies
but little foundation for the elaborate theories that are called
' kenotic.' Nor do these theories afford us much help in our
endeavour to understand the person of our Lord. ' It is not,
I am sure,' says Bethune Baker, ' to any theory of depotentia-
tion of God that we can look to give us the conditions under
which we can explain Jesus as both human and divine—the
fact of the *Deus homo* ' (*Modern Churchman,* September 1921,
p. 292). The verb **emptied** is ' not used or intended here in a
metaphysical sense to define the limitations of Christ's incarnate state, but as a strong and graphic expression of the completeness of his self-renunciation ' (Vincent).

Christ's self-renunciation did not cease when he entered into 8
human life. In this verse Paul tells of the path of humiliation

which in his incarnate life he trod. Its opening clause (**born in human guise**) is commonly reckoned as a part of ver. 7, and construed closely with the words that precede. It may, however, quite naturally be taken, as in our translation, with the words that follow : **born in human guise . . . he humbly stooped.** The A.V. has ' and was made in the likeness of men ' ; and the R.V. ' being made,' etc. The same word ' likeness ' is used in Rom. 1 : 23, 5 : 14, 6 : 5, 8 : 3 ; as well as in Rev. 9 : 7. Rom. 8 : 3 speaks of God ' sending His own Son in the guise of sinful flesh.' The word suggests similarity and nothing more ; it does not imply, as the word *morphē* would have done, the reality of Christ's humanity. On the other hand, there is nothing in the clause to suggest that his humanity was not real—that he was man in appearance only. What the clause sets forth is his likeness to other men. The verb whose participle is rendered **born** in our translation does not here, as Ellicott points out, imply merely ' to be born.' Perhaps the meaning of the clause can best be expressed by a paraphrase, thus : ' Having come into human life, and being like men in general.'

To emphasize Christ's likeness to other men Paul adds another clause—**and appearing in human form.** The noun **form** applies only to outward appearance—to that which is apprehended by the senses. Elsewhere in the New Testament it is found only in 1 Cor. 7 : 31 (' for the present phase of things is passing away '). Seeing that the whole paragraph reveals a rhetorical structure, Dibelius opines that the word **form** and the word **guise** in the preceding clause are parallel synonyms. **Form,** however, implies external semblance even more clearly than does **guise.** The participle also speaks of outward impression, and is well rendered **appearing.**

As man, then, **he humbly stooped in his obedience even to die, and to die upon the cross.** The R.V. renders more literally : ' he humbled himself, becoming obedient even unto death, yea, the death of the cross.' Paul is here certainly speaking of our Lord's self-humiliation in the days of his flesh, and not repeating in other words (as some have held) the statement of the pre-incarnate renunciation. The tense of the verb

' sums up the holy course of submission either into one idea, or into one initial crisis of will ' (Moule).

It is to the will of the Father, whose servant he became (ver. 7), that his obedience is rendered. Compare Rom. 5 : 19 and Heb. 5 : 8. In the Greek the words **even to die** go closely with the reference to his obedience, and it would be slightly more in accord with the language of Paul to say : ' he humbly stooped in an obedience that was ready even to die.' He went in his obedience even as far as death itself. ' Usque ad mortem ' is the rendering of the Vulgate. The word **cross** is without the definite article in the Greek—' and to die upon a cross '—which serves to emphasize the nature of the death of shame and suffering to which he stooped. Such a death marks the utmost limit of self-renunciation. Gal. 3 : 13 (which quotes Deut. 21 : 23) reveals the horror with which the Jew regarded crucifixion ; and the feelings of the Romans find expression in the words of Cicero, who says : ' To bind a Roman citizen is an outrage ; to scourge him a crime ; it almost amounts to parricide to put him to death ; how shall I describe crucifixion ? No adequate word can be found to represent so execrable an enormity ' (*in Verrem*, 5 : 66). In his *pro Rabirio*, again, he says : ' Far be the very name of a cross not only from the body, but even from the thought, the eyes, the ears of Roman citizens ' (5 : 10). With the present clause Heb. 12 : 2 should be compared.

This verse is the first of three in which the Apostle sets 9 before his readers the other side of the great picture. After the humiliation comes the exaltation. **Therefore God raised him high.** The exaltation is not so much a reward (though Lipsius and others so speak of it) as a direct, natural, and inevitable consequence of the humiliation. It is the inversion, so to speak, of the self-emptying and of all the self-renunciation that followed upon it. The reference is to the Ascension and the subsequent state of glory and power at God's right hand. The divine law which decrees that exaltation shall follow self-humiliation had been enunciated by our Lord (Matt. 23 : 12 ; Luke 14 : 11, 18 : 14b), and now ' was gloriously fulfilled in his own case ' (Meyer, quoted by Vincent). The suggestion of the present passage is that the same law will operate in the case of the Christians at Philippi if they manifest the same spirit of self-abnegation.

And conferred on him, continues the Apostle, **a Name above all names.** As compared with the word 'give' of the A.V. and the R.V., the word 'confer' better suits the dignity of the Greek word used by Paul, which speaks of a gracious bestowal. The same verb is used in 1 : 29 in the clause 'you have the favour of suffering.' Our translation agrees with the A.V. in having '*a* Name,' but '*the* Name,' as in the R.V., is much better attested. The Name conferred on Christ is above *all* names, as Bengel observes, and not merely above all human names. Compare Eph. 1 : 20, 21, where we read of the Father seating the Son at His own right hand 'above all the angelic Rulers, Authorities, Powers, and Lords, above every Name that is to be named not only in this age but in the age to come.'

What is the Name which the Son receives from the Father ? Lightfoot suggests that 'we should probably look to a very common Hebrew sense of "name," not meaning a definite appellation, but denoting office, rank, dignity.' The suggestion, however, has not met with much favour. Alford, Ellicott, and some few other expositors take 'Jesus' to be the name. The new name, however, was conferred at the exaltation, whereas 'Jesus' was the Son's name in the days of his humiliation. Moule, who does not himself accept this view, observes that those who hold it might contend that the elevation of the name 'Jesus' 'for ever into the highest associations, in the love and worship of the saints, was as it were a new giving of it, a giving of it as new.' But the suggestion does not rob the objection of its force. Vincent regards 'Jesus Christ' as the name, but this view is exposed to the same objection. Theodoret suggests 'God' or 'Son of God.'

Recent exposition has been tending strongly towards the view that the Name is 'Lord'—the title that actually occurs in the confession in ver. 11. Lightfoot admits that if the Apostle has in his mind some one definite term, 'Lord' is probably the one intended. 'Lord' is the rendering of the

94

Hebrew Yahweh in the LXX, and the title was common in Gentile religion. ' To St. Paul and his age,' says Maurice Jones, ' the Christ, Incarnate, Crucified, and Risen, has become equated with the Most High God of the Jews, and for him is claimed exclusively the honour associated in paganism with the supreme deity.'

This verse and the next state the purpose of the Father in **10** exalting the Son and conferring on him the Name above all names—so that before the Name of Jesus *every knee should bend* in heaven, on earth, and underneath the earth, *and every tongue confess* that ' Jesus Christ is Lord,' to the glory of God the Father.

The words in italics are quoted from Isa. 45 : 23, where Yahweh foretells the universal worship that would one day be paid to him : ' As I am God and God alone, I swear by myself, I swear a true word, never to be recalled, that every knee shall bow to me, and every tongue swear loyalty.' This verse is quoted also in Rom. 14 : 11, where the reference is to the worship of God. In our passage, as will be shown below, the words are probably used of the adoration to be paid to the Son, which points to the lofty place that he occupied in the thought of Paul and the early Christians. There may also be some connexion between our passage and 1 Enoch 48 : 5, where we read : 'All who dwell on earth shall fall down and worship before him, and will praise and bless and celebrate with song the Lord of Spirits.' It is significant that in the immediate context in Enoch (vers. 2 and 3) reference is made to the naming of the Son of Man.

Answering to the words in heaven, on earth, and underneath the earth the A.V. has : ' of things in heaven, and things in earth, and things under the earth ' ; and the R.V. is virtually the same. In the Greek three adjectives are used which may be either masculine or neuter. If the writer intended them as neuter—and Lightfoot thinks he did—the words are a general expression for the whole universe ; such an interpretation reminds us of Rom. 8 : 22, where the Apostle speaks of the ' entire creation ' being affected by the redemption wrought by Christ. If, on the other hand, the adjectives

95

are masculine, the reference seemingly is to the angels, the living, and the dead. The view which identifies those **underneath the earth** with the dead is more probable than that which sees in the words a reference to demons. Fanciful explanations such as that which finds here a reference to Christians, Jews, and pagans, are not worthy of serious attention. Combinations of the three adjectives here used, or of similar adjectives, are to be found in the papyri (see Moulton and Milligan, *Vocabulary*, p. 236). Compare Rev. 5 : 13.

The **Name of Jesus** means, not the Name Jesus, but the Name belonging to Jesus. **Before** translates the common Greek preposition whose ordinary meaning is ' in.' ' In ' is the rendering of the R.V., whereas the A.V. has ' at.' Is the Name of Jesus here thought of as the *object* or as the *medium* of worship and homage ? Is the worship paid directly *to* his Name, or to the Father *in* his Name ? Each view has its advocates. It is highly probable that the words speak of the direct ascription of worship to the Son. That is what the general drift of the passage would lead us to expect ; and it is the confession of *his* lordship that is described in the parallel clause. Lightfoot cites several instances of the construction employed here, in each of which direct adoration is obviously intended. **Before** is thus seen to be an excellent rendering of the preposition. The **Name of Jesus** stands for ' Jesus as bearing the new Name of Lord conferred on him by the Father.'

11   Universal confession of the lordship of Jesus Christ—that aspect of the purpose of the exaltation—is the subject of this verse. The verb rendered **confess** may mean ' to confess with thanksgiving,' ' to proclaim joyfully.' That is its most prominent meaning in the LXX, and the meaning adopted by Lightfoot in our present passage. But elsewhere in the New Testament its commonest meaning is ' to confess ' simply, and no imperative reason suggests itself for departing from that meaning in the present verse.

Jesus Christ is Lord—that is what every tongue will confess. Here we have the earliest creed of the Christian Church (see Rom. 10 : 9 and 1 Cor. 12 : 3 ; there may also be a reference to this early creed in Eph. 5 : 26, where see Moffatt's translation). **Lord** was the title most commonly applied to Jesus by the early Christians ; it is used of him about two hundred and fifty times in the epistles of Paul. As we have already seen, it is the word employed in the LXX to translate the Hebrew name Yahweh. According to the early chapters of the Acts of the Apostles, the title was applied to Jesus Christ in the first days of Jewish Christianity (compare also 1 Cor. 16 : 22) ; and its ready adoption by those who entered the Church from paganism is not difficult to understand, for it was a common term in the mystery cults (see Kennedy, *Vital Forces of the Early Church*, chap. 8, on ' The Lordship of Christ '). **Lord** was one of the most vital terms in the pagan world of that age, as it also was within the pale of the Christian fellowship. Kennedy observes that in our day it ' has become one of the most lifeless words in the Christian vocabulary,' and adds that ' to enter into its meaning and give it practical effect would be to recreate, in great measure, the atmosphere of the Apostolic age.'

The verse closes with the words **to the glory of God the Father.** This is the ultimate purpose of all that is spoken of in vers. 9–11. The words are not to be taken in immediate connexion with **Jesus Christ is Lord,** as though they formed part of the confession. They remind us of the great saying of 1 Cor. 15 : 28 : ' When everything is put under him, then the Son himself will be put under Him who put everything under him, so that God may be everything to everyone.' Here is struck ' the final chord of the Pauline theology ' (Kennedy, in Peake's *Commentary*, p. 813*b*). Compare John 13 : 31 and 17 : 1 ; and the Odes of Solomon 10 : 5. Even the exaltation finds its climax and completion in a self-surrender to the Father on the part of the Son.

AN APPEAL TO THE CHURCH TO WORK OUT ITS OWN
SALVATION (II. 12–18)

**Therefore, my beloved, as you have been obedient always and 12
not simply when I was present, so, now that I am absent,
work all the more strenuously at your salvation with**

13   reverence and trembling, for it is God who in his goodwill
14   enables you to will this and to achieve it. In all that you
15   do, avoid grumbling and disputing, so as to be blameless
      and innocent, *faultless children of God* in *a crooked and*
      perverse generation where you shine like stars in a dark
16   world; hold fast the word of life, so that I can be proud of
      you on the Day of Christ, because I have not run or *worked*
17   *for nothing.* Even if my life-blood has to be poured as a
      libation on the sacred sacrifice of faith you are offering to
18   God, I rejoice, I congratulate you all—and you in turn must
      rejoice and congratulate me.

The counsel which the Apostle now addresses to his readers is the natural sequel to the great paragraph that precedes it. The word therefore in ver. 12 shows that the connexion of thought is close. The great statements made regarding Christ Jesus were introduced for a practical purpose. The Apostle's enunciation of truths concerning his Saviour is never merely theoretical. The object is ever to save and nourish souls, and build up the communities of the saints.

What kind of counsel should we expect the Apostle to base upon the example set by Christ Jesus ? Surely not the counsel that each individual addressed should be concerned about his or her own personal salvation. An appeal to work out one's own individual salvation—however appropriate it might be under different circumstances—would be singularly inappropriate coming immediately after the great passage in which is described the self-sacrifice of our Lord. For this and other reasons we believe that the meaning commonly given to the injunction addressed to the Philippians in ver. 12 charging them to work at their salvation is erroneous. Paul is not urging them as individuals to work at their personal salvation : he is urging the whole body of Christians at Philippi to work out their salvation *as a community*.

We have already seen (see p. 62) that the whole section of our epistle extending from 1 : 27 to 2 : 18 is a closely-woven unit in which the Apostle impresses upon his readers the duty of their forming a harmonious body free from disputes and dissensions. From the beginning to the end of this section Paul is instructing and exhorting the Philippians with regard to their common life ; and it would be strangely incongruous to introduce into the heart of the passage an injunction bearing upon the personal salvation of the individual members of the Church. And this is precisely what the Apostle does if the common interpretation of ver. 12 is correct. In the notes that follow we shall endeavour to show that the social interpretation is the natural one to give to the Apostle's words. There is nothing in the phraseology of the paragraph that tells against this interpretation ; on the contrary, everything would seem to support it. See the article on ' Work out your own Salvation ' in the *Expositor* for December 1924, pp. 439-50, where this interpretation is set forth more fully.

Before we proceed to examine the paragraph in detail another preliminary remark may be added. The verses seem to us to furnish clear evidence that Paul is here comparing and contrasting himself with Moses when he was giving to the children of Israel his parting injunctions as described in the closing chapters of Deuteronomy. This thesis has some bearing upon our contention that the Apostle is addressing the Philippian Church as a whole and not as individuals ; for Moses addresses his words to Israel as a community, and if it is established that Paul has in mind the analogy between the lawgiver and himself, some support is given to the view that he is concerned about the welfare of the Philippians as a body, and not primarily about the personal salvation of the individual members of the Church. In any case, the suggestion sheds some light on the thought of Paul in the present passage. In ver. 15 there is an obvious reference to the ' Song of Moses ' in Deut. 32 ; but that is not the only point of contact between this paragraph and Deuteronomy. Indeed, we have already noticed in 1 : 28 a possible allusion to the words of Moses in Deut. 31 : 6. It has also been suggested that in 1 : 19 ff. the Apostle has in mind certain resemblances between his own lot and the circumstances of Job. If these suggestions regarding Moses and Job are well founded—as we believe them to be—

they reveal to us one source of strength and solace of which Paul availed himself in his prison.

12   The language of ver. 12 leaves us in some doubt whether the two clauses in which Paul speaks of his presence and of his absence should be taken with **you have been obedient** or with **work at your salvation.** The R.V. reproduces the ambiguity of the Greek. Literally the clauses mean 'not as in my presence only, but now much more in my absence.' Our translation deftly separates them, and perhaps by so doing succeeds in expressing Paul's exact meaning. Both clauses should be taken, we think, with **work at your salvation,** the meaning being : 'In consonance with your invariable obedience in the past, work all the more strenuously at your salvation now in my absence, and not in the spirit that will do its best only when I am present.' The Apostle's language is somewhat involved, but this, we think, expresses his meaning with fair exactness.

He addresses his readers as **my beloved.** The epithet is of frequent occurrence in his epistles, and is found in a similar use in the papyri, both in Christian and in non-Christian letters. Its frequency in Paul betrays the warmth of his love for his converts ; and to no group would he apply it more wholeheartedly than to the Philippians. In 4 : 1 we find it twice in one verse.

In the clause **as you have been obedient always** the Apostle, with the tact so characteristic of him in all his dealings with his converts, indicates that the past behaviour of the Philippians gives him confidence as he addresses to them the present injunction. A contrast between the attitude of the children of Israel to Moses and the attitude of the Philippians to himself would seem to be in his mind. In Deut. 31 : 27 Moses charges the children of Israel with having been rebellious against the Lord while he was yet alive with them. Unlike the Israelites in their rebellious mood, the Philippians have always been obedient. Obedient to whom ? There has been much discussion as to whether obedience to God or to the Apostle is meant. It is with rebellion against Yahweh that Moses charges the Israelites, and that may suggest that Paul is thinking of obedience to God. In either case the meaning is the same, for the Philippians' obedience to God would take the form of compliance with the injunctions and precepts of the Apostle.

What precisely does Paul mean by his ' presence ' and his ' absence ' ? Does he, as is commonly supposed, mean just his presence at, or absence from, Philippi ? We are confident that he means something other than that. Moses, after charging the Israelites (in Deut. 31 : 27) with rebellion against Yahweh while he was yet alive with them, adds : ' And how much more after my death ? ' We think that when Paul says ' now much more in my absence ' he is alluding to the words of Moses. And does not the use of the word **now** imply that the change from presence to absence either had just taken place or else was just about to take place at the time when Paul was writing ? Some years, however, had passed by since he was at Philippi. Paul is referring to his presence in this life, and to his impending departure from this life. Note how in ver. 17 he speaks as though the surrender of his life were imminent. Moses in Deut. 31 : 29 predicts with sorrow what will happen after his death : ' For I know that after my death ye will utterly corrupt yourselves, and turn aside from the way which I have commanded you.' Paul, on the contrary, with a confidence springing from his experience of the unbroken obedience of the Philippians in the past, urges them all the more strenuously after his death to work out their own salvation. We say ' their *own* salvation,' for there is more emphasis on the pronominal adjective than the rendering of our translation would lead us to suppose. The point of the emphasis is that the Philippians must now act for themselves. Hitherto, though separated from them, the Apostle has been able to guide and encourage them by letter or by spoken message entrusted to some travelling friend. Soon he will be gone beyond their reach. The great heart that has sheltered them will soon have ceased to beat !

As we have seen, the words **work at your own salvation** have reference not to the personal salvation of the individual members of the Church at Philippi, but to the well-being of the community as a whole. Some would render : ' work at the salvation of one another,' or ' promote the welfare of each other.' But although the Greek can bear this rendering, we do not think it represents exactly what Paul means. The Apostle is addressing the Philippians as a group, charging them to be concerned about the well-being of their community, threatened as it is with disruption. Thus interpreted, his injunction comes naturally after vers. 5–11. It is to the performance of an act of self-renunciation resembling that of Christ that he urges his readers.

Our translation says **work at**, whereas the R.V. has ' work out ' ; and there is something to be said for the latter rendering. The verb is a favourite one with Paul, occurring twenty times in his epistles, and elsewhere in the New Testament only twice or thrice. It suggests the idea of working *out*, of bringing to completion. *Usque ad metam*, says Bengel, in his comment on the present passage. The Church at Philippi is urged to work at its salvation until its salvation is complete, until its health is fully established. Every trace of dissension should go. Paul might have addressed to the Philippians the words ' Clean out the old dough that you may be a fresh lump ' (1 Cor. 5 : 7).

They are to work out their salvation **with reverence and trembling**. The A.V. and the R.V. render more literally and baldly ' with fear and trembling.' The phrase does not occur in the New Testament outside the Pauline epistles. It seems to have acquired an idiomatic meaning—a meaning less forcible than one would expect from the words of which it is composed. Neither in 2 Cor. 7 : 5 nor in Eph. 6 : 5, where the phrase is found, is the meaning ' with fear and trembling ' suitable. It should also be noticed that in both of these passages the words are used to describe an attitude towards *men*. The phrase doubtless bears some such meaning as is given to it by three old interpreters quoted by J. H. Burn in a note in the *Expository Times* for September 1923 (p. 562), whose renderings are as follows : ' with respect and reverence ' (Thomas Belsham) ; ' with the most submissive deference and solicitude ' (Edward Harwood) ; ' with humility and concern ' (J. Pierce). As we interpret the passage, the phrase describes, not the attitude towards God in which the individual Philippian should seek to work out his own personal salvation, but rather the spirit that should characterize the behaviour of each member in his relation to the rest of the community. This brings the use of the phrase in our passage into line with the other Pauline occurrences.

Ver. 13 supplies a ground for the injunction of ver. 12. Even **13** after the Apostle's death they should strive to make the Church perfect, for the work of salvation that is going on in the community is God's own working ! Unless they worked at their salvation they would be impeding His work ! **It is God,** says Paul, **who enables you to will this and to achieve it.** In this rendering the verbs **enable** and **achieve** represent the same Greek verb—a verb which connotes *effective* working. An effective divine energy is at work in the community, and if the Philippians only avail themselves of its presence, co-operate with it, and permit it to express itself in their working, the inevitable result will be not only the willing, but also the achieving, by them of the salvation of the community. We should perhaps have expected that, to describe the Philippians' part, Paul would have used the same verb that he uses in ver. 12, and have said : ' It is God who enables you to will this and to work it out ' ; but instead of this he repeats the very verb which he employs of God's own effective working. Surely there is significance in this double use of the same verb. It is implied that their actual working cannot fail to be effective. If God is allowed to work in their working, the end will be achieved. He works both the willing and the achieving. The hidden working of their minds and hearts in the direction of harmony, no less than its actual achievement, is His work.

Our translation says that God does all this **in his goodwill.** Literally rendered, Paul's words are ' on behalf of (the) good-will.' The noun is the same as that used in 1 : 15 to express the motive of the preachers who receive the Apostle's com mendation. It is usual to interpret the goodwill in our present passage as the goodwill of God, the phrase thus meaning : ' **in** fulfilment of His benevolent purpose ' (Lightfoot). The rendering **in his goodwill** is another way of saying this. **It is** possible, however, to understand the phrase in a way that is nearer to the natural meaning of the Greek, and at the same time in accord with our interpretation of the passage as a whole. With some of the ancient versions, as well as with some modern interpreters, we prefer to regard the goodwill spoken of here as the goodwill that should characterize the Christian community at Philippi. The phrase means ' to promote the (virtue of) goodwill,' the whole verse stating that ' it is God who is working among them both the willing and the working to promote goodwill.'

Once more there seems to be a point of contact with Deuteronomy. Time and again Moses tells the children of Israel that whereas he is not permitted to remain with them, Yahweh will be with them. In Deut. 31 : 8, for example, we read : ' And the Lord, he it is that doth go before thee ; he will be with thee, he will not fail thee, neither forsake thee.' Is there no connexion between such promises made by Moses and the declaration of Paul that God is working among the Philippians ? Even if Paul is taken away, God will continue to work among them !

14   The abrupt way in which this fresh command is introduced— **In all that you do, avoid grumbling and disputing**—without the least hint of any change in the course of the writer's thought, clearly suggests that he is now expanding the previous injunction. By avoiding grumbling and disputing in all that they did the Philippians would be working out their salvation. What are we to understand by **grumbling** and **disputing** ? The Greek has two nouns, each in the plural. ' Do all things without murmurings and disputings ' is the rendering of the R.V. Most expositors interpret the former word as describing an attitude towards God ; but the probability is that in this verse both nouns refer to attitudes towards men. This is the only occurrence of the former of the two in the Pauline epistles, but it occurs thrice elsewhere in the New Testament (in John 7 : 12, Acts 6 : 1, 1 Pet. 4 : 9), and if its meaning in these passages is anything to go by, it stands for murmuring or grumbling against men in our passage also. The other of the two nouns—' disputings '—naturally refers to disputes in the

community. In the papyri it sometimes denotes a legal ' inquiry ' or ' session ' for the hearing of cases (see Milligan, *Selections*, p. 34), and here the reference probably is to outward disputes and wranglings. Clearly grumbling and disputing were the evils that constituted the malady of the Philippian Church.

The comprehensiveness of the prohibition should be noted. Just as in ver. 3 of this chapter the Philippians are urged *never* to act for private ends or from vanity, so here they are charged to avoid grumbling and disputing *in all they do*. Paul is eager to rid the Church of every particle of the unholy leaven of strife and contention. Compare the unrestricted injunctions of 1 Cor. 10 : 31 and Col. 3 : 17.

Paul proceeds to state what his readers would become by 15 avoiding grumbling and disputing in all that they did. The somewhat elaborate statement may haply be intended as another gentle reminder that improvement was possible. See on 1 : 3-5.

First of all, they would be **blameless**; no one would be able to point to anything worthy of censure in them. Moulton and Milligan (*Vocabulary*, p. 26) observe that the adjective here used is common in sepulchral epitaphs in conjunction with another adjective which means ' kind.' Then they would be **innocent.** This adjective occurs twice elsewhere in the New Testament—in Matt. 10 : 16 (' *guileless* like doves ') and Rom. 16 : 19 (' *innocents* in evil '). The English word ' innocent ' may mean either ' harmless ' or ' guiltless.' Although both the A.V. and the R.V. have ' harmless ' here, it is the other meaning that should be given to the word **innocent** in our translation, for the rendering ' harmless ' is due to a mistaken etymology. The word used by Paul does not properly mean ' harmless ' at all. The fundamental notion of the adjective is freedom from foreign admixture ; it is used of wine that is unmixed with water, and of metal that contains no alloy. It describes anything that is in its true and natural condition (see Trench, *Synonyms*, pp. 205, 206). ' Blameless ' signifies that no one would be able to point to any flaw in the Church : ' innocent ' means that actually no impure ingredient would be present. The former relates to the verdict of outsiders who pass judgment, the latter describes intrinsic character.

The rest of the description—*faultless children of God* in a *crooked and perverse generation*—is an adaptation of words that occur in the ' Song of Moses ' (see Deut. 32 : 5). As translated in the R.V., this verse in Deuteronomy thus speaks of fickle Israel : ' They are not his children, it is their blemish ; they are a perverse and crooked generation.' From the first half of this Deuteronomic verse the Apostle fashions a description of the Philippians—' unblemished (or faultless) children of God.' The second half of the verse Paul deftly applies to the opponents of the Philippians—the **crooked and perverse** generation by whom they are surrounded. Note that in our text the word **in** is not printed in italics, as it does not form part of the verse that is quoted.

The word rendered **faultless** originally and properly means ' blameless,' but through the influence of the Hebrew word for ' blemish ' it came to mean ' free from blemish,' the meaning which it almost invariably bears in the LXX, and probably its one and only meaning in its eight occurrences in the New Testament. They would be God's children—sharing His nature—without a blemish ! Grumbling and disputing obscure and destroy the august relationship !

In a crooked and perverse generation : our translation agrees with the A.V. and the R.V. in these two epithets. The generation among whom the Philippians live is crooked and twisted ; it is not in line with the truth, but curved and distorted from the straight. **Where you shine,** adds the Apostle, **like stars in a dark world.** Shine is an improvement on the ' are seen ' of the R.V., and **stars** is a far better rendering than the ' lights ' of the R.V. text. The margin of the R.V. more correctly has ' luminaries.' **Like stars** is perhaps reminiscent of the LXX of Daniel 12 : 3 : ' and they that be wise shall shine as the stars of heaven.' Only in Rev. 21 : 11 does the word here rendered ' star ' occur again in the New Testament.

Is Paul thinking of the influence of the Philippian Church

upon the evil world around it, or only of the contrast between the Church and the world ? The question is usually discussed in connexion with the interpretation of the opening clause of ver. 16.

The opening words of this verse form in the Greek a parti- 16 cipial clause which in the A.V. and the R.V. is rendered ' holding forth the word of life.' It is possible, however, to render ' holding fast the word of life.' Indeed the latter is perhaps the more natural meaning of the verb, and there is evidence for it in the papyri. If the idea of influence is present in the last clause of ver. 15, then ' holding forth ' would be a suitable rendering in the present context. If, on the contrary, Paul is thinking of contrast only in ver. 15, ' holding fast ' would be the more appropriate rendering. On the whole, the idea of contrast is more probable than that of influence, and it has the advantage of associating with itself the more natural meaning of the participle in ver. 16. ' The connexion of thought is this : the world is dark, but you are points of light ; don't let yourselves be extinguished, as you will be if you give way to bad temper and strife. Adherence to the gospel implies that stedfast obedience to God, that humble, unselfish spirit, which is equivalent to real " life " ' (Moffatt, in *Expositor*, November 1916, p. 344).

It goes without saying that contrast involves influence. Even if Paul has nothing other than contrast in his mind in the last clause of ver. 15, that contrast would of necessity involve some influence. They could not shine like stars without thereby exerting an influence. We are reminded of the words of Jesus : ' So your light is to shine before men, that they may see the good you do and glorify your Father in heaven ' (Matt. 5 : 16).

Our translation rightly renders the participle by means of an imperative : **hold fast the word of life.** There is, we think, a slight break in the thought between ver. 15 and ver. 16, and we are at liberty to discuss the force of the closing words of ver. 15 independently of the meaning of the opening words of ver. 16. In ver. 16 Paul sums up, so to say, all his injunctions in the preceding verses. ' Hold fast,' he says, ' the word of life :

maintain your hold upon the principles enunciated in the message that brought life to you ; do not relax your grip upon the truths which I declared unto you.' Nowhere else in Paul does the phrase **the word of life** occur.

To the injunction Paul subjoins an inducement to obedience. **Hold fast the word of life,** he says, **so that I can be proud of you on the Day of Christ.** The Day of Christ is the day already alluded to in 1 : 6 and 1 : 10—the day of his Parousia (see the note on 1 : 6). ' *With a view to* the Day of Christ ' is what Paul actually says in the present passage ; the pride in the Philippians which he desires is something that is to be reserved, as it were, for the great day. It is then that he will require it. What he desires is of course something very different from the vanity which he condemns in 2 : 3. In 1 : 26, using the very noun that he uses here, Paul speaks of himself as the ground of exultant joy to his readers ; so here it is a ground of noble exultation that he requests his readers to provide for him. Compare 2 Cor. 1 : 14 and 1 Thess. 2 : 19, 20.

The basis of the pride which he prays may be his on the great day is expressed in the words **because I have not run or** *worked for nothing.* He pictures himself looking back upon his life from the standpoint of the Day of Christ, and finding that his toil has not been in vain. He asks the Philippians to make it possible for him to enjoy such a retrospect. The phrase **for nothing,** which in the New Testament is used only by Paul, is found in the papyri of water running to waste (see Moulton and Milligan, *Vocabulary*, p. 340). Paul does not want to discover when he comes to the Day of Christ that all his efforts have run to waste.

The words **worked for nothing** are in our text printed in italics as being reminiscent of Isa. 49 : 4 and 65 : 23. A very similar phrase is used in Gal. 4 : 11, where Paul says : ' Why, you make me afraid I may have spent my labour on you for nothing ! ' Compare also 1 Thess. 3 : 5, where the Apostle speaks of the possibility that his ' labour had been thrown away.' Lightfoot thinks the metaphor is taken from fruitless training for the games on the part of unsuccessful athletes. Deissmann suggests another source for the metaphor. ' In fact,' he writes, 'with regard to all that Paul the weaver of tent-cloth has to say about *labour*, we ought to place ourselves as it were within St. Paul's own class, the artisan class of the Imperial age, and then feel the force of his words. They all become much more lifelike when restored to their original historical *milieu*. " I laboured more abundantly than they all "—these words, applied by St. Paul to missionary work, came originally from the joyful pride of the skilled weaver, who, working by the piece, was able to hand in the largest amount of stuff on pay-day. The frequent references to " labour in vain." are a trembling echo of the discouragement resulting from a width of cloth being rejected as badly woven and therefore not paid for' (*Light from the Ancient East*, p. 317).

Paul's appeal to the Philippians so to live that his toil will not have been in vain reminds us of the appeal of Savonarola addressed to the Brethren of his Convent at Florence on the fifth of August, 1497 : ' Remember, I pray you, the sufferings of our holy father Dominic, whose feast we keep to-day, and strive to live so godly as that his sufferings and labours on our behalf may not have been in vain ' (*Spiritual and Ascetic Letters*, p. 59).

In the A.V. and the R.V. ver. 17 opens with ' yea,' a word 17 18 which is not definitely represented in our translation. Inasmuch as the word used by Paul commonly means ' but,' it is customary to discuss the nature of the contrast that was in his mind as he wrote. As, however, the word is frequently used to give emphasis to the words which it introduces, or even just to introduce an accessory idea, there is no need to assume that a definite contrast was present in the Apostle's mind. The mention of his labours for his readers leads the Apostle to say that there is no limit to the sacrifice that he would joyfully make on their behalf ; and the order, in the Greek, of the two little words rendered **even if** shows that he fully anticipates that he will soon be called upon to surrender his life His use of the present indicative, too, in the opening clause of ver. 17 shows not only that he is anxious to bring the hypothesis vividly before the minds of his readers, but also that the possibility of his execution is vividly present to his own mind. He speaks of his life-blood being poured out as a libation on their sacrifice, using the verb that he also uses in 2 Tim. 4 : 6 where he says, ' The last drops of my own sacrifice are falling.'

There has been much debate regarding the exact meaning of the words in which Paul speaks of the sacrifice of the Philippians. Literally rendered, his words run, ' upon the sacrifice and service of your faith.' What precisely does that mean ? Is their faith the victim, so to speak, that is offered in sacrifice ? If so, by whom is it offered ? Is Paul the priest ? Or are the Philippians themselves the priests ? Each of these views has its advocates. Our translation—**on the sacred sacrifice of faith you are offering to God**—regards their faith as the thing offered, and interprets the word ' service ' of the act of offering that sacrifice of faith to God. This may well be Paul's meaning, though we must own to the feeling that it would suit his words better to take faith as that which offers the sacrifice and renders the service. Their adherence to the new faith entails the offering of a sacrifice to God which is at the same time the rendering of a service to Him. The two nouns ' sacrifice ' and ' service ' have in the Greek but one article, which shows that together they form one conception. What the Philippian Christians sacrifice is their comfort, their ease, their worldly prosperity, and possibly in some cases their very lives. Their sacrifice is akin to Paul's own sacrifice, for, as he has reminded them in 1 : 30, where he employs a different metaphor, they are waging the same conflict that he himself is waging.

If we bear in mind the analogous nature of the two sacrifices —that of Paul and that of his readers—it will help us to understand his words about rejoicing in the remainder of ver. 17 and in ver. 18. **Congratulate** is scarcely adequate to express the meaning of the verb so rendered in our translation. ' To rejoice with ' is its simple and proper meaning. Paul has in mind, we believe, when he uses that verb, not felicitation merely, but rather a participation in the joy of another. He declares that he himself rejoices in his own sacrifice even if it should mean the outpouring of his very life-blood. He also takes for granted that they too rejoice in their sacrifice, and tells them that he participates in their joy. Then in ver. 18 he asks them in turn, or in the same way (compare Matt. 27 : 44), to adopt a similar attitude towards the double sacrifice. Let them rejoice in their own sacrifice—as he has assumed in ver. 17 that they are doing—but let them participate also in his joy in his own sacrifice. Let there be a mutual sharing of joy. There is a correspondence in sacrifice : let there be also a correspondence in joy ! Notice the word **all** ; once more the Apostle hints that he does not countenance their divisions. What a mighty encouragement it would be to the Philippians amid their trials and difficulties to know that he and they are thus bound together in mutual suffering and in mutual joy ! Paul's declaration of his joy in his sufferings would help them to rejoice in theirs. A great verse in Colossians gives us another glimpse of Paul's joy in his sufferings : ' I am suffering now on your behalf,' he says, ' but I rejoice in that ; I would make up the full sum of all that Christ has to suffer in my person on behalf of the church, his Body ' (Col. 1 : 24).

PAUL'S PURPOSE TO SEND TIMOTHEUS (II. 19-24)

I hope in the Lord Jesus to send you Timotheus before long, 19 that I may be heartened by news of you. I have no one 20 like him, for genuine interest in your welfare. Everybody 21 is selfish, instead of caring for Jesus Christ. But you 22 know how he has stood the test, how he has served with me in the gospel, like a son helping his father. I hope 23 to send him then, as soon as ever I see how it will go with me—though I am confident in the Lord that I shall be 24 coming myself before long.

The section of the epistle in which the Philippians are urged to cast out the leaven of dissension and discord has now come to an end. A fresh subject is introduced. The Apostle hopes to send them Timotheus, and even sooner to send back their own envoy Epaphroditus. Timotheus is the subject of vers. 19–24, Epaphroditus of vers. 25–30.

Simple as the paragraph that speaks of Timotheus seems, it has been, and probably will always remain, the subject of some perplexing questions. Timotheus was to carry to Philippi the news of the issue of the Apostle's imprisonment (see on ver. 23), and Paul evidently expects that the issue would soon be determined. Seeing that the Apostle is so loath to part with Timotheus, and as the delay would not have been long, why does not Epaphroditus postpone his departure until the issue is known? This is but one of many questions raised by the paragraph. It is possible that, if we had full knowledge of all the circumstances, the difficulties would disappear; but it would be idle to pretend that they do not exist. It is not easy to abstain from wondering whether we have in vers. 19–24 a brief Pauline note, similar to the notes which have been incorporated in the Pastoral Epistles, written to correspondents whose identity can no longer be determined, at a time when the Apostle chanced to be surrounded by persons who had not drunk deeply of the spirit of Christ. If that be so, the crisis anticipated in ver. 23 would be some less momentous event than the issue of the Ephesian imprisonment, and Paul's confidence that he would soon see his correspondents would be more firmly based than the hope he entertained of seeing the Philippians when he wrote our epistle. Such a note might well have been sent to the Philippians themselves, and it may have found its way into our epistle attracted by the presence of the twin passage concerning Epaphroditus. Our misgivings do not perhaps furnish an adequate reason for detaching the paragraph from its traditional context; and so we leave it— but with some hesitation—in that context, and expound it as a part of our epistle.

19 **I hope in the Lord Jesus to send you Timotheus before long.** The Lord Jesus was the sphere in which the hope had its being. Paul's confidence that he would soon be coming himself was also 'in the Lord' (ver. 24). It has become almost an instinct with him to refer all things to his union with his Lord.

The object of the mission of Timotheus is stated in the words **that I may be heartened by news of you**. Does the Apostle, then, send Timotheus just for his own satisfaction ? By no means ! Our translation ignores a slight nuance that is unmistakably present in Paul's words. His statement, exactly rendered, would run : ' that I *also* may be heartened by news of you.' The implication is clear that the Philippians will be heartened by the coming of Timotheus. The enheartening of his readers is so obviously a purpose of the mission that the Apostle is content to allude to it in this indirect way. Indeed, the Greek words which are rendered **to send you Timotheus** would suggest to the Philippians that he was being sent for their good.

The verb rendered **I may be heartened** is one of great interest. Here only does it occur in the New Testament. Into its composition there enters the noun *psyche* (soul)—see the notes on **I : 27**—and its meaning is ' to be stout of soul,' hence, ' to be of good courage.' It is touching to see this verb used in a second-century letter of consolation in place of the customary greeting which would scarcely accord with the character of the letter (see Milligan, *Selections*, p. 96). The imperative is common in sepulchral inscriptions meaning ' Farewell ! ' or ' Be it well with thy soul ! '

We gather from the Apostle's words that he fully expects to get news of the Philippians. But he does not yet know (as ver. 23 shows) whether Timotheus is to bear to Philippi news of his acquittal or of his condemnation. If Timotheus bears tidings of condemnation, would Paul in that event expect to get news from Philippi before his execution ? Or is he for the moment assuming that his imprisonment will issue in his release ?

How close is the bond that binds the Apostle and his readers in the communion of saints ! With the possibility of execution staring him in the face, he would be heartened by news of them. For that refreshment his soul craves. He assumes that the news when it comes will be of such a nature as to hearten him. The assumption is a delicate hint of his confidence in his readers. And what news does he expect to receive ? Surely the news that peace and harmony are now firmly established among them.

20   In vers. 20-22 the Apostle sets forth Timotheus's qualifications for the task he is about to undertake. Vers. 20, 21 set him in contrast with others who lack fitness, while ver. 22 speaks of the readers' knowledge of his character and past services.

I have no one like him, runs ver. 20, **for genuine interest in your welfare.** This rendering expresses Paul's meaning exactly. Literally rendered, the opening words of the verse would run : ' I have no one like-minded,' and the question arises, ' Like-minded with whom ? ' Our translation assumes that the Apostle means ' like-minded with Timotheus ' ; and this interpretation is much more probable than that assumed in some of the ancient versions and held by several writers on our epistle, according to which Paul says, ' I have no one like-minded with myself.' The second half of the sentence —**for genuine interest in your welfare**—is in the Greek a relative clause, and suits the interpretation adopted in our translation better than it suits the other interpretation. Moreover, as Lightfoot has pointed out, if Paul had meant like-minded with himself, he must certainly have written, ' I have no one *else* like myself.'

It is a Greek adverb that underlies the word **genuine.** The whole verse may be literally rendered thus : ' I have no one like him, of the kind that will genuinely care for your welfare.' The cognate adjective is found in 4 : 3 of our epistle (' my *true* comrade '), and in 2 Cor. 8 : 8, 1 Tim. 1 : 2, Tit. 1 : 4, but in the present passage alone does the adverb occur. The primary meaning of the adjective is ' belonging to the race ' or ' born in wedlock.' It sometimes bears this primary meaning in the papyri. In the earliest dated Greek papyrus that we possess (a marriage contract of 311–310 B.C.) it is used in the phrase ' lawful wedded wife.' ' Legal,' ' suitable,' ' genuine,' are other meanings it bears in the papyri. See Moulton and Milligan, *Vocabulary*, pp. 128, 129. Lightfoot in our present passage paraphrases the adverb thus : ' as a birthright, as an instinct derived from his spiritual parentage.' The adjective, as we have just noted, is used in

1 Tim. 1 : 2, where Paul is represented as speaking of Timotheus as his 'lawful son in the faith,' and Lightfoot thinks that here in Philippians Paul, by the use of the adverb, means to imply that Timotheus, who 'recognised this filial relationship' (as ver. 22 shows), had 'inherited all the interests and affections of his spiritual father.' On this interpretation what Paul says is : 'I have no one like him who will take in your welfare such an interest as I, his spiritual father, take.' No one could take Paul's place among the Philippians as Timotheus could. Moulton and Milligan, however, give it as their opinion that Lightfoot 'rather overdoes the consciousness of the word's ultimate origin.' It is quite possible that the Apostle did not mean more than he is represented as saying in our translation.

The verb in this clause—' to care for '—is the verb used in the prohibition ' never be anxious ' in 4 : 6. But there is no real contradiction. Timotheus's care for the Philippians is a legitimate concern for the welfare of others, whereas the temper deprecated in 4 : 6 is that which refuses to cast its burden on the Lord. Paul employs the cognate noun in 2 Cor. 11 : 28, where he speaks of his own ' care of all the churches.'

Everybody is selfish, instead of caring for Jesus Christ. 21 This short verse has occasioned much discussion. With most expositors we feel constrained to think that the context calls for some restriction of the sweeping and severe indictment. It was surely not meant to apply to all the Christians in Ephesus, but only to such as could have been regarded by the Apostle as available for the mission to Philippi. Note that in ver. 20 Paul says, ' I have no one like him '; he does not say, ' I know of no one like him ' or ' There is no one like him.' Besides, we must not attach to the words too literal and strict a meaning. Paul does not quite mean all that his words seem to mean, any more than he does when he condemns the preachers in 1 : 15 ff. (see p. 45). Temporary annoyance has led to an exaggeration of statement (see Moffatt, *Introduction to the Literature of the N.T.*, p. 175). The suggestion has been made—and it is by no means improbable

—that Paul, in his eagerness to keep Timotheus by him, had proposed to his other coadjutors that one of them should undertake the journey to Philippi, and that, when they one and all refused, his distress at the prospect of parting with his trusty lieutenant led him to give utterance to this unduly severe impeachment. He could attribute their reluctance only to the fact that they were more concerned about their own interests than about the interests of their Lord.

22   But, continues the Apostle, **you know how he has stood the test.** The R.V. follows the A.V. in the less perspicuous, because over-literal, rendering, ' But ye know the proof of him.' The word rendered ' proof ' means either the process of proving or the result of the proving. Here it bears the latter meaning. We might render ' You are acquainted with his tested character,' but the true force of the sentence is best given in English by the use of some such idiom as is employed in our translation. The test which Timotheus had stood was furnished, as the rest of the verse implies, by his co-operation with Paul in the work of the gospel. The Philippians had had ample opportunity for observing Timotheus as he was undergoing the test ; he was present when Paul first proclaimed to them the good news (Acts 16), and had seemingly paid Philippi at least one visit since that time. We know from 1 Thess. 3 : 1, 2 that Paul sent him back to Thessalonica from Athens, and he may well have visited the Philippians on that occasion.

It is because the Philippians know how Timotheus has co-operated with Paul that they know how he has stood the test. **You know . . . how he has served with me in the gospel, like a son helping his father.** The original meaning of the word rendered **served** is ' to serve as a slave.' It reminds us of the description of Paul and Timotheus in the opening salutation as ' slaves of Christ Jesus.' The Greek suggests that the Apostle was on the point of writing the present sentence in a form slightly different from the form which it actually assumed ; and the sudden change sheds a beam of light on his nature. Our translation does not show this ; indeed only by means of an excessively literal rendering can it be shown. What Paul actually says is : ' You know . . . how, as a son [serveth] a father, he served with me.' But it is made quite clear by the form of the sentence in the Greek that when he began to write it he intended to say : ' You know . . . how, as a son [serveth] a father, he served me.' He is checked, however, by the innate delicacy of his nature ; he will not permit the form of the sentence to hint that he thinks of Timotheus as his slave. The mere suggestion was intolerable ; for were they not both slaves of the same Master ? It is worthy of note that this casual and undesigned token of Paul's inherent delicacy of feeling comes in the verse that follows immediately after the one in which he appears to be guilty of ungracious petulance ! Had the cloud disappeared so soon ?

I hope to send him then, continues the Apostle, **as soon as** 23 **ever I see how it will go with me.** The word him is not without some emphasis, as if Paul were saying, ' This, then, is the man whom I hope to send—one so well qualified for the task.' He hopes to send him as soon as ever he knows what the issue of his imprisonment is going to be. And it would not be long before his fate would be decided, for he tells his readers in ver. 19 that Timotheus would be sent ' before long.'

Though, he adds, **I am confident in the Lord that I shall be** 24 **coming myself before long.** This confidence, like the hope in ver. 19, is **in the Lord.** Plummer calls attention to the remarkable fact that Paul uses more decided language about his own coming than about the sending of Timotheus ; he hopes to send Timotheus (vers. 19 and 23) ; he is confident of coming himself (ver. 24). This may be regarded as supplying an additional reason for wondering whether the present passage is in its true context. The very same adverb **before long** is used in this verse as in ver. 19. One cannot but wonder why, if the Apostle could so ill afford to part with Timotheus, he should be in so great a hurry to send him to Philippi when he is so confident that he himself will be going soon. I Cor. 4 : 17 and 19 offers a striking parallel to vers. 23 and 24, for there also Paul speaks of sending Timotheus and of coming himself.

PAUL'S DECISION TO SEND EPAPHRODITUS AT ONCE
(II. 25-30)

25 As for Epaphroditus, however, my brother, my fellow-worker, my fellow-soldier, and your messenger to meet my wants,

26 I think it necessary to send you him at once, for he has been yearning for you all. He has been greatly concerned

27 because you heard he was ill. And he was ill, nearly dead with illness. But God had mercy on him, and not only on him but on me, to save me from having one

28 sorrow upon another. So I am specially eager to send him, that you may be glad when you see him again, and thus

29 my own anxiety may be lightened. Give him a welcome in the Lord, then, with your hearts full of joy. Value

30 men like that, for he nearly died in the service of Christ by risking his life to make up for the services you were not here to render me.

In the last paragraph we met certain Christians who, as it seems, refused to undertake the journey to Philippi even at Paul's urgent entreaty. Now we are introduced to one who is pining to go to Philippi! The passing glimpse of him afforded by the present paragraph reveals one of the most attractive and heroic characters to be found in the annals of early Christianity. All we know of him is what we can gather from this passage and from the mention of his name in 4 : 18. Incidentally the paragraph exhibits Paul himself as a man of marvellous tenderness, forgetful of his own needs where the happiness and well-being of others are concerned.

Some features of the little drama that comes before us only reveal themselves when we read between the lines. The course of events would seem to have been on this wise. The Philippians had sent one of their number, Epaphroditus by name, to the Apostle on a twofold mission. He was, first, the bearer of a gift, presumably a gift of money (see 4 : 18). But his task was not accomplished when the gift had been delivered. It was the intention of the Philippians (who may have furnished him with the means of his maintenance) that Epaphroditus should remain with the Apostle so long as he had need of him. The messenger himself was a gift, so to speak, from the Philippians. And right worthily had he played his part, displaying a devotion which brought on a sickness that was all but mortal. The Philippians heard of his illness and were troubled. Epaphroditus in turn heard of their dismay. He yearned to be back amongst them, knowing that nothing but the sight of him restored to health would put an end to their anxiety. Paul observed the yearning, and made up his mind to send him to his friends. Epaphroditus was doubtless taken aback when Paul suggested that he should return. What would his friends at Philippi think? How would they look upon his desertion of the Apostle—for so they would regard his return? Paul tells him that he will assume the responsibility. He dictates our epistle, of which Epaphroditus himself doubtless was the bearer, and inserts this gracious passage, telling of Epaphroditus' devotion, and bespeaking for him a cordial welcome. With such a testimonial in his hand, Epaphroditus consents to go. How could his friends possibly chide him?

As for Epaphroditus, however, writes the Apostle, **my 25 brother, my fellow-worker, my fellow-soldier, and your messenger to meet my wants, I think it necessary to send you him at once.**

However marks the difference between the case of Epaphroditus and the case of Timotheus, who cannot be sent till Paul sees how things will go with him. Epaphroditus can and will be sent without any delay. The name 'Epaphroditus' arrests us; high-sounding as it is, it was by no means uncommon, for it meets us often in the papyri and in inscriptions. It means 'charming,' and Epaphroditus was worthy of his name. The word embodies the name of the goddess Aphrodite, but 'no scruple appears to have been felt among the primitive Christians about the retention of such pre-baptismal names' (Moule).

In Col. 1:7, 4:12 and Philem. 23 we meet with the name 'Epaphras,' which also is common in inscriptions. Of the person who bears the name, Paul speaks in terms of high commendation. Now as 'Epaphras' is a shortened form of Epaphroditus, and as the three letters in which the two names occur may have been written during the same imprisonment, the question whether Epaphras and Epaphroditus are the names of one and the same person could not fail to arise. Those scholars who find one person only behind the two forms of the name argue that it would be strange if two persons bearing this name were with Paul during his imprisonment. Notice, too, that what is said of Epaphras in Colossians would suit Epaphroditus admirably. Most scholars, however, rightly reject the identification. The name, in both its forms, is common ; and in Col. 4 : 12 Paul speaks definitely of Epaphras as one of the Colossians, whereas every clause of the Philippian passage implies that Epaphroditus was a member of the Church at Philippi.

My brother, my fellow-worker, my fellow-soldier—so does the Apostle describe Epaphroditus. The same three terms are found in Philem. 1 and 2, but of three different persons. Reference has already been made (in the note on 1 : 12) to the use of **brother** as a term applied to members of the same religious community. Here it describes Epaphroditus as a fellow-believer, though more than that must surely be involved in the use of the phrase **my brother.** There would be no necessity to speak of him as a Christian in a letter to the Philippians. **My brother** depicts him as one with whom Paul is associated in Christian fellowship. The two men are united in the bonds of a mutual Christian affection. **Fellow-worker,** a term applied in 4 : 3 to other members of the Philippian Church perhaps now dead, is not seldom used by the Apostle of those who shared with him in the work of the Lord, as, for example, of Prisca and Aquila in Rom. 16 : 3. **Fellow-soldier** reminds us that Christian toil is also a conflict. Elsewhere in the New Testament the exact term is used only of Archippus in Philem. 2. Some have thought that when he speaks of Epaphroditus as his **fellow-soldier** Paul is thinking of their conflicts at Philippi ; but there is no apparent reason for thus restricting the reference. The Apostle may be thinking chiefly if not wholly of the conflicts at Ephesus.

Brother, fellow-worker, fellow-soldier ! How intense must have been the devotion of Epaphroditus to the Apostle himself and to the cause of their common Master to evoke so noble a commendation ! Lightfoot calls attention to the ascending scale—common sympathy, common work, common danger and toil and suffering ; and Kennedy quotes the words of Anselm : ' Frater in fide, cooperator in praedicatione, commilito in adversis.'

But the description of Epaphroditus is not yet completed. Paul adds **and your messenger to meet my wants.** A quite literal rendering of his words would be ' and your apostle and minister of my need ' ; but our translation rightly binds the two terms together, as Lightfoot also does, to form one idea— **your messenger to meet my wants.** The second of the two nouns—' minister '—is a word of high and holy associations. It is the usual word for priest in the LXX ; and is common in inscriptions and elsewhere of one who has performed some distinguished public service. A cognate noun is used in vers. 17 and 30 of this chapter of the service rendered by the Philippians. There is a deliberate choice of sacred and noble words to describe Epaphroditus as the envoy of the Philippians, for Paul would lift to a lofty plane the service they rendered to him. Compare 4 : 18, where he speaks of their gift as a sacrifice to God. The former of the two nouns employed in the present passage—' apostle '—is in our translation, as in the R.V., fitly rendered **messenger.** It does not here bear the full meaning it acquired in the Christian vocabulary, any more than it does in 2 Cor. 8 : 23. Theodoret speaks of Epaphroditus as the ' bishop ' of Philippi, but the title has no sort of justification in our passage. Nor is it necessary, with Moule, to see in the use of the word ' apostle ' a mark of gentle pleasantry, as if Paul thought of Epaphroditus as a missionary bearing to him a gospel.

I think it necessary, says Paul, **to send you him at once.** There is nothing in the Greek answering to **at once.** Would not some such expression have been introduced into the present sentence if the paragraph about Timotheus had immediately preceded ? May we not see in its absence **another**

indication that the earlier paragraph is not original ? The word **necessary** occupies an emphatic position in the Greek as the first word of the whole paragraph, showing that Paul is anxious to impress upon the Philippians the fact that the immediate return of Epaphroditus was in his eyes a matter of necessity. It was not a matter of choice. They must not blame their envoy for returning now : Paul adjudged it to be necessary. The verb in the present clause, though in the past tense in the Greek, is rightly rendered by the present **I think,** for it is an example of the common epistolary use of the past, the writer placing himself at the point of view of the readers as they read the letter. The past tense is surely not to be interpreted, as it is interpreted by Adeney in Peake's Commentary, to mean that Epaphroditus has already been sent. The manner in which Paul bespeaks for him a cordial welcome (vers. 29, 30) almost amounts to a proof that he was the bearer of the letter.

Trapp has his own characteristic explanation of the necessity for the immediate return of Epaphroditus. He had been long enough away from his pastoral duties at Philippi ! ' It is not meet,' runs his comment, ' that a pastor be long absent from his people. Moses was away but forty days, and before he came again Israel had made them a golden calf. A godly minister when he is abroad is like a fish in the air ; whereinto if it leap for recreation or necessity, yet it soon returns to his own element.'

That Paul should have it in his power to decide that Epaphroditus is to return shows that the Philippians had placed their messenger at the disposal of the Apostle ; and, further, the fact that Paul says **to send him,** and not ' to send him *back,*' indicates, as Bengel saw, that Epaphroditus had not been sent by the Philippians on a brief and hurried mission, but rather with the intention that he should remain with the Apostle. A smaller man than Paul would have retained him.

26 Paul now gives the reason for his decision to send Epaphroditus at once : **for he has been yearning for you all.** The rendering **he has been yearning** reproduces the thought suggested by the Greek that the yearning had been going on

for some time. The same verb is used in 1 : 8, where Paul says, ' God is my witness that I yearn for you all ' (see the note there). Some authorities read in our present passage : ' he has been yearning *to see* you all.' So the margin of the R.V. The evidence for the two readings is fairly evenly balanced, and the difference of meaning is slight. Lightfoot says with truth that the language seems to gain in force by the omission of the words ' to see.' In Rom. 1 : 11, 1 Thess. 3 : 6, and 2 Tim. 1 : 4 the verb here used for **yearning** is followed by ' to see,' and it is possible that reminiscence of these passages is responsible for the insertion of the infinitive in those authorities that have it here.

The yearning of Epaphroditus is impartial ; he yearns for them *all*. Paul makes it clear that their messenger does not look with favour upon their divisions. It may be that the news of the dissensions had intensified Epaphroditus' yearning to be back. ' His heart,' says Trapp, ' was where his calling was.' Far from attempting to stifle this natural yearning, Paul countenances and encourages it.

He has been greatly concerned, continues the Apostle, **because you heard he was ill.** Not only had news of the illness of Epaphroditus reached the Philippians : news of their consequent distress had reached him. **He has been greatly concerned** is scarcely strong enough as a rendering of the verb used by Paul. Elsewhere in the New Testament the verb is found only in Mark 14 : 33, and the parallel passage Matt. 26 : 37, where it is used to describe the agitation of our Lord in Gethsemane. In the present passage ' distressed ' or ' agitated ' would have expressed the meaning more exactly.

Epaphroditus was distressed because his friends had learnt of his illness ! Even though the sickness had been contracted in the execution of their commission, he is grieved because they have come to know about it. Their grief distressed him more than did his own sickness. They might be disappointed because of his premature return, but their hearts could not fail to be softened to tenderness when they read Paul's statement of his unselfish desire to spare them grief on his account.

In the *Journal of Theological Studies* for July 1917 (pp. 311,

312) Moffatt calls attention to an analogous case of unselfish concern disclosed in a second-century papyrus letter. It is one of the Oxyrhynchus papyri—a letter sent by a soldier to his mother. She had heard that her son was ill, and he is annoyed that she should have been troubled by a report that was exaggerated. True, he had not written to her for some time ; but the reason for that was to be found not in his sickness, but in the pressure of his military duties. ' So,' he writes, ' do not grieve about me. I was much grieved to hear that you had heard about me, for I was not seriously ill.' The two cases are not quite parallel, for the report that had reached the Philippians was no exaggeration. ' Still,' says Moffatt, ' both Epaphroditus and this soldier were unselfishly concerned about those who cared for them.'

27 No, the report which had reached Philippi was not in the least degree exaggerated. **And he was ill,** says Paul, **nearly dead with illness.** The all but fatal nature of the illness is emphasized again in ver. 30. It may be that Paul lays all this stress on the seriousness of the illness partly because he suspected that when Epaphroditus reached Philippi he would do his utmost to minimize its gravity, and thereby weaken in the eyes of the Philippians the Apostle's reason for sending him back.

But God had mercy on him. Epaphroditus recovered. Paul regards recovery and escape from death as a mercy. Nor has he the least doubt that the recovery came from God. So Wesley, writing in July 1775 to James Dempster, an American preacher, says : ' Last month I was at the gates of death. But it pleased God just then to rebuke the fever, so that my pulse began to beat again, after it had totally ceased. Since that time I have gradually been recovering strength, and am now nearly as well as ever. Let us use the short residue of life to the glory of Him that gave it ! ' (*Letters*, p. 252). The closing sentence of Wesley's letter reminds us of Chrysostom's comment on the present passage (quoted by Moule) : ' Those who are departed this life can no longer win souls.'

The Apostle regards himself as coming within the range of the Divine mercy that had brought Epaphroditus back from the region of death, for he adds : **and not only on him but on me, to save me from having one sorrow upon another.** Commentators for the most part assume that Paul has here in mind two definite sorrows. His words, however, do not of necessity demand so precise an interpretation. He may only mean—and so our translation seems to understand his words—that the recovery of Epaphroditus saved him from the superaddition of one more sorrow to the many that pressed upon him already. Still, it is not impossible that he is thinking of two definite sorrows. One, of course, is the sorrow that would have resulted from the death of Epaphroditus, and the other probably the bitterness of his captivity, rather than the anxiety caused by the illness of his devoted helper.

In the *Expositor* for November 1916 Moffatt cites the interesting passage in the *Confessions* of Augustine (ix. 3) in which use is made of some of the words of this verse. ' When,' writes Moffatt, ' the Milanese scholar, Verecundus, lent his villa at Cassiciacum to Augustine, for the purpose of a religious retreat, he remained at Rome, unwilling to join the party. Shortly afterwards he died, but not before he had become a Christian. This sad news reached the party, yet they comforted themselves with the thought that he had not died outside the pale of the Church. '' Thus Thou hadst mercy not on him only, but on us also, lest we should be tortured with unbearable grief as we recalled the kindness of our friend to us and yet were unable to count him as one of Thy flock.'' '

So, continues Paul, **I am specially eager to send him.** Here 28 again the epistolary past is used which the R.V. renders ' I have sent.' See on ver. 25. The present sentence also contains an adverb, in the comparative degree, which may mean either ' with greater eagerness,' referring to the spirit in which Paul is sending Epaphroditus, or else ' with more haste,' referring to the outward manner of his dispatch. It may be that both meanings should be found in the word ; but, if choice has to be made, the context would seem to point to the meaning ' with more haste ' as the more fitting in the present case, the reference being to the fact that

THE EPISTLE OF PAUL TO THE PHILIPPIANS

THE EPISTLE OF PAUL TO THE PHILIPPIANS

Epaphroditus was being sent with a greater dispatch than the Philippians expected or were likely to appreciate.

The reason for this special hurry is stated in the words **that you may be glad when you see him again.** Our translation is at one with the A.V. and the R.V. in taking again with see. On the whole, however, the better course is to take it with **may be glad.** ' That you " may recover your cheerfulness " ' is Lightfoot's rendering. Their recovered cheerfulness would be reflected upon the spirit of the Apostle, for he proceeds to expand the reason for his action in the words **and thus my own anxiety may be lightened.** He employs in saying this an adjective, occurring nowhere else in the New Testament, into the composition of which there enters the Greek word for ' grief.' ' Grief ' or ' sorrow ' would, then, we think, serve to express his meaning better than ' anxiety.' Paul does not say, as the preceding clause might perhaps have led us to expect him to say, ' and thus I too may be glad,' for, even when he should feel the cheering influence of their recovered gladness, his own spirit would not be altogether free from sorrow. His sorrow would be lightened ; it would not wholly vanish. Some drops of joy from their overflowing cup would find their way to him, helping to compensate for the departure of his devoted minister.

29 The Apostle now in plain entreaty bespeaks for Epaphroditus a cordial Christian welcome. **Give him a welcome in the Lord, then**—that is, ' seeing that he is returning at my instance, and that I am sending him for your joy, and for the alleviation of my own grief.' The phrase **in the Lord** suggests some amount of apprehension on Paul's part that the Philippians, chagrined at Epaphroditus' premature relinquishment of his charge, might fail to welcome him in a spirit worthy of their common faith. In Rom. 16 : 2 Paul himself explains the very phrase he uses here ; for he there says with respect to Phoebe : ' Receive her in the Lord as saints should receive one another.'

With your hearts full of joy : the welcome is to be wholehearted and abundant. No particle of chagrin or resentment is to have a place in their hearts. Joy is to occupy the whole space. Literally the words may be rendered ' with all joy,' as in the R.V. The sense is not, as some explain, ' with every kind of joy '—it is not easy to attach an intelligible meaning to such a phrase here—but, ' with joy unmixed and unreserved,' or, in the words of our translation, **with hearts full of joy.**

Value men like that, adds the Apostle. Such characters, whenever found, are too precious to be set at naught. The idea of honouring, as well as of valuing, is present in the Apostle's words. The Philippians must not only appraise such men at their true worth : they must also give them the honour which is due to the nobility of their character. It is often easy for a Church to value and honour the wrong persons. Quiet, unobtrusive workers, even though they be the salt of the earth, are apt to be overlooked and lightly valued. Words addressed by the Apostle to another Macedonian Church may be placed by the side of this injunction. ' Brothers,' he says to the Thessalonians, ' we beg you to respect those who are working among you, presiding over you in the Lord and maintaining discipline ; hold them in special esteem and affection, for the sake of their work ' (1 Thess. 5 : 12, 13). Compare also Heb. 13 : 7.

After soliciting due esteem and honour for the class of which 30 Epaphroditus is an example, Paul reverts to the case of Epaphroditus to find additional justification for his plea. **For,** he says, **he nearly died in the service of Christ,** or, more literally, ' for the work of Christ.' The authorities are evenly balanced between ' the work *of Christ* ' and ' the work *of the Lord.*' One good authority, however, has ' for the work ' simply ; and it is tempting, with Lightfoot and others, to regard this as the original reading, in which case the various additions will be attempts at explanation or elucidation. In Acts 15 : 38—a passage which may well reproduce Paul's own words—' the work ' is used in this absolute way for the work of Christ.

Epaphroditus came near to death. For ' to death ' Paul uses the very phrase he uses in ver. 8 of this chapter when he speaks of our Lord being obedient even ' to death.' Is there a hint that the spirit of Epaphroditus was akin to the spirit of his Master? Whether or no Paul meant that suggestion to be conveyed by his words, the spirit of the Cross was in the service of the devoted Philippian who came near to death **by risking his life.** In this latter phrase Paul employs a participle that comes nowhere else in the New Testament. Some scholars have thought that the word may have been coined by him. It is another word, differing only by the addition of a single letter, that is rendered 'not regarding' in the A.V. However, the verb actually used by Paul, and in the identical participial form here employed, has been discovered in an inscription found at Olbia, on the Black Sea. (See Deissmann, *Light from the Ancient East,* pp. 84, 85.) Epaphroditus had gambled with his life. In Eph. 4 : 14 Paul employs another gaming term which means 'playing with dice.' The word 'Parabolani,' the name of an order of laymen in the early Church who risked their lives in nursing cases of fever and plague, is closely related to the word used by Paul for **risking** in our present passage. It is possible that the metaphor of gambling was suggested to Paul by the name of Epaphroditus (see the *Expository Times* for October 1925, p. 46).

In what way did Epaphroditus hazard his life? All **the** Greek commentators say that it was by exposing himself to the risk of persecution. But the present verse seems clearly to suggest that the reference is rather to the risk of ill-health involved in his fervent devotion to the Apostle. Whether Paul has in mind any hazard other than that due to his labouring beyond his strength can only be a matter of conjecture. What Paul says here of Epaphroditus reminds us of what he says elsewhere of Prisca and Aquila : 'Salute Prisca and Aquila, my fellow-workers in Christ Jesus, who have risked their lives for me ' (Rom. 16 : 3, 4).

Epaphroditus' motive in hazarding his life is stated in the words **to make up for the services you were not here to render me.** This is a most happy rendering of Paul's words, far superior to the more literal rendering of the R.V.—' to supply that which was lacking in your service toward me.' This rendering of the R.V. may give to the English reader the impression that the Apostle is cavilling at some lack or defect in the service of the Philippians. The very opposite is the truth. Paul refers to a lack that was unavoidable, the lack, that is, of their personal presence ; and in the very words by which he pays high tribute to the devotion of Epaphroditus he deftly tells the Philippians that by sending him they had done much to offset the lack which they could not help. There is no suggestion of remissness on their part. Paul indeed employs a word (cognate with the word ' minister ' applied to Epaphroditus in ver. 25) that speaks of the service of the Philippians as a sacred ministration. Epaphroditus had done his best to represent them all ; and the effort had proved too much for his strength. What is here said of Epaphroditus implies most clearly that he was one of the Philippians ; the Apostle would hardly have spoken to the Philippians of Epaphras the Colossian as he speaks here of Epaphroditus.

CHAPTER III

A WARNING AND A NEW STANDARD OF VALUES
(III. 1*b*-7)

I am repeating this word ' rejoice ' in my letter, but that does 1*b* not tire me and it is the safe course for you.—Beware 2 of these dogs, these wicked workmen, the incision-party ! We are the true Circumcision, we who worship God in 3 spirit, we who pride ourselves on Christ Jesus, we who rely upon no outward privilege. Though I could rely 4 on outward privilege, if I chose. Whoever thinks he can rely on that, I can outdo him. I was circumcised on the 5 eighth day after birth ; I belonged to the race of Israel, to the tribe of Benjamin ; I was the Hebrew son of Hebrew parents, a Pharisee as regards the Law, in point of ardour 6 a persecutor of the church, immaculate by the standard of legal righteousness. But for Christ's sake I have 7 learned to count my former gains a loss.

We have already in the Introduction (see pp. **xi, xii**) given reasons for believing that vers. 1*b*–19 of chap. 3 did not originally form part of the present epistle to the Philippians. They may have formed part of an earlier letter sent to Philippi, or of a letter addressed to some other Church. There can be no manner of doubt regarding their authorship ; and if we are right in thinking that they form no part of the present letter, that does not detract from their worth in the slightest degree. We shall take ver. 1*a* after vers. 1*b*–19, along with 3 : 20, 21 and 4 : 1.

1*b* Ver. 1*b* has been the subject of much discussion. It will help us if we approach the study of it from the quite literal rendering of the R.V., which runs thus : ' To write the same things to you, to me indeed is not irksome, but for you it is safe.' Paul does not say what the things are which he is repeating. Our translation—**I am repeating this word ' rejoice ' in my letter**—adopts one of several possible interpretations. Whether that is the most probable interpretation or not we shall have to inquire. Before we do that, let us glance at the words in which Paul makes his half-apologetic reference to the reiteration. He says it is not irksome to him to repeat, but that it is the safe course for his readers. Clearly he is solicitous lest the readers should be annoyed by the repetition. It is possible that he is using a line from some poem, for the words form the metrical line known as the iambic trimeter. Moule, with a view to the rhythm, renders thus : ' To me not irksome, it is safe for you.' The word translated ' irksome ' usually means ' hesitating, shrinking, dilatory, sluggish.' Some such meaning it bears in its other New Testament occurrences in Matt. 25 : 26 and Rom. 12 : 11. Here, however, it must mean ' causing hesitation or weariness.' **That, says Paul, does not tire me.**

Paul was alive to the need of repeating his admonitions. ' It is not sufficiently considered,' writes Dr. Johnson in the *Rambler*, ' that men more frequently require to be reminded than informed ' (quoted by Moffatt in the *Expositor*, November 1916, p. 347). ' Men,' comments Trapp on this verse, ' are dull to conceive, hard to believe, apt to forget, and slow to practise heavenly truths, and had therefore great need to have them much pressed and often inculcated.'

Let us now ask ourselves what it is that Paul is reiterating. What are the ' same things ' of which he speaks ? Let us suppose for the moment that the letter as we have it is just as it came from his hand. Evidently it is possible to regard the words which we are now examining as referring either to what Paul has just said in ver. 1*a*, or else to what he is about to say in vers. 2 ff. Some scholars adopt the former of these alternatives, in which case the ' same things ' which Paul is reiterating will refer to the injunction to rejoice. That he uses the plural, ' the same things,' is no objection to this view. This is the interpretation adopted in our translation, and it is the view of Baur, Alford, Ellicott, and many others. But while it is true that the note of joy is sounded throughout the epistle, not until we come to 3 : 1*a* do we find a direct injunction to rejoice. It is possible, of course, that in previous letters Paul may have urged upon the Philippians the duty of rejoicing, and that with so much persistence that he thinks it necessary to apologize for repeating the injunction in the present letter. But while this is possible, it is surely in the highest degree improbable. One brief reference would not lead him to apologize. Lightfoot observes that ' such an injunction has no very direct bearing on the *safety* of the Philippians,' and that ' its repetition could hardly be suspected of being *irksome* to the Apostle. But over against the former of these statements there are certain considerations that may be adduced. ' It is surely conceivable,' writes Moffatt, ' that Paul would regard any failure to '' rejoice in the Lord '' as a dangerous symptom. . . . It is never safe to grow dispirited. Christians need to be warned against the temper of melancholy and dulness as much as against false doctrines. Any failure to '' rejoice in the Lord '' means an imperfect sense of what he is to us, and it is always a safe thing to be warned of this inward danger ' (*Expositor*, November 1916, p. 347).

The other alternative is to regard ver. 1*b* as an introduction to the warning given in vers. 2 ff. That warning may have been given repeatedly in previous letters, and it has an evident bearing upon the safety of those to whom it is addressed. Moffatt (*loc. cit.*) concedes that this may be the true interpretation.

Lightfoot rejects both of these alternatives and suggests another explanation. In his view, the reference is to the warnings against the dissensions that existed among the Philippians. 'This topic,' he says, 'either directly or indirectly has occupied a very considerable portion of the letter hitherto ; and it appears again more than once before the close.' If it be retorted that there is no warning against dissension in the immediate vicinity of 3 : 1, Lightfoot's answer to the objection is that the Apostle was just about to reintroduce the subject when he was interrupted. This suggestion of interruption, however, is but a theory, admitting neither of proof nor of refutation.

So far we have been assuming that vers. 1*b*–19 form part of the original letter. As a matter of fact we think they should be detached from their present context. They form a fragment of a Pauline letter sent to some correspondents whom we cannot identify. If in that letter the words of ver. 1*b* served as an introduction to the warning that follows them, then we know that in the earlier portions of that letter, or in previous letters to the same correspondents, the Apostle had repeatedly issued warnings against the 'dogs' to whom he refers in vers. 2 ff. If, on the other hand, the words of 1*b* refer to warnings which had preceded them in the original letter, then we have no means of knowing what the 'same things' are. Whether vers. 1*b*–19 be an interpolation or not, we incline to the view that ver. 1*b* should be connected with the warning that follows in vers. 2 ff. Otherwise ver. 2 is introduced somewhat abruptly and awkwardly. If the passage is an interpolation, the mere fact that ver. 1*b* has survived as a part of it would point to an original close connexion with the words that follow.

2   Now comes the warning : **Beware of these dogs, these wicked workmen, the incision-party !** Before we examine these words in detail, it may be well to clear the ground by considering in a general way who these persons are against whom Paul is warning his readers. We may summarily dismiss the view which identifies them with the preachers condemned in 1 : 15 ff. ' They have nothing to do with the evangelists mentioned in 1 : 15 f. ; the latter preach Christ truly ; it is their motives, not the content of their gospel, to which Paul takes exception (Moffatt, *Introduction to the Literature of the N.T.*, p. 166). Everything points to their being Jews. But were they Jews unaffected by the Christian faith, void of all sympathy with it, and intolerant in their attitude to those who professed it ? Or were they Judaizers, that is, Jews who had adopted the new faith but were seeking to impose upon all converts, Gentile as well as Jewish, the burden of Jewish ritual, teaching that apart from circumcision there could be no access to God ? The context permits us to hold either of these views. Adeney (in Peake's *Commentary*) declares categorically that they were not Judaizing Christians, but ' simply Jews antagonistic to Christianity.' It may be that the Christians to whom Paul is writing were suffering grievously at the hands of persecuting Jews and sorely tempted to slide back into Judaism. The fact that the Apostle in his list of the outward privileges in which he could outmatch his antagonists includes his quondam persecution of the Church (ver. 6) lends some countenance to this view. The great majority of commentators, however, assume with little or no discussion of the question, that the persons against whom the warning is uttered are Judaizers. On the whole, this is the more likely view. The things which the Judaizers would seek to impose upon Christians were the very things which the non-Christian Jews valued most highly. The mere fact that Paul with deliberation sets forth the superiority of the new way of righteousness in Christ would suggest that he is warning his readers against opponents whose weapon is persuasion rather than persecution. Contrast the manner in which persecuting Jews are denounced in 1 Thess. 2 : 15, 16. His method of dealing with his opponents in our present passage is more closely akin to his method in Galatians and 2 Corinthians, where beyond question the Judaizers are the objects of his attack. The machinations of the Judaizers,

who so persistently harassed Paul and his converts, constituted the chief peril to which the earliest Christians were
exposed.

The word rendered **beware** in this verse literally means ' to
observe, look at.' The readers are to observe in order to be
on their guard against the peril. The Judaizing propaganda
had not, seemingly, made much headway among them. And
yet the repetition of the verb in each of the three clauses of
this verse shows that to the Apostle's mind the danger was
very real. It would have been an advantage if in our translation the impressive triple repetition of the imperative had
been reproduced : ' Beware of these dogs ! Beware of
these wicked workmen ! Beware of this incision-party ! '

By more than one expositor the three clauses of this verse
have been supposed to refer to three distinct and separate
classes of antagonists. B. Weiss, for example, understands
Paul to be speaking of the unconverted heathen, the self-
seeking teachers of 1 : 15 ff., and the unbelieving Jews. The
vast majority of interpreters, however, rightly assume that
the three clauses refer to the same persons.

These dogs ! Why does Paul use this discourteous term ?
Nowhere else in his extant letters is the word to be found.
Indeed in the whole of the New Testament the ordinary
word for ' dog ' occurs only five times. Whenever the dog
is mentioned in the Bible, it is with contempt. Each of the
odious and repulsive characteristics of the eastern dog has
been supposed to be the one uppermost in Paul's mind in
the present comparison—impurity, insolence, cunning, shame-
lessness, greediness, and so on. It may be, however, that
the Apostle employs the word as a general term of reproach,
as Jews and Greeks alike were wont to use it. In ver. 8 of this
chapter Paul speaks of the things held in veneration by these
persons as ' refuse,' and it may be that the same idea underlies his use of the term ' dogs.' The things on which they live
are but refuse and sweepings ! They devour, as Lightfoot
puts it, ' the garbage of carnal ordinances.' The Christians
who would not submit to their ordinances were placed by
the Judaizers outside the pale of God's family. They them-

selves were the children, all else were no better than dogs.
' And now Paul takes up the figure, and reverses the application. "Nay, nay!" cried the Apostle, "you are living
in the outside of things. You are magnifying ceremonies
and ordinances and institutions. You are dwelling in the
external. Yes, *you* are in the streets. *You* are the dogs "'
(Jowett, *Apostolic Optimism*, p. 38).

These wicked workmen. ' False workmen ' he calls them
in 2 Cor. 11 : 13. Kennedy finds in this description of them
clear evidence that they were within the Christian Church ;
that is, they were Judaizers and not Jews merely. Christian
workers in a sense they were, but they were not worthy of
the title. Trench says of the epithet applied to them in
this clause that it ' affirms of that which it characterizes that
qualities and conditions are wanting there which would
constitute it worthy of the name which it bears ' (*Synonyms*,
p. 315).

The incision-party. Both the A.V. and the R.V. have ' the
concision.' Paul uses here a noun found nowhere else in the
New Testament. It means a cutting, a mutilation, an incision.
The abstract term is used for the concrete, and is well rendered
by the phrase **the incision-party.** There is an evident play
upon words, such as is found in other places in the epistles of
Paul. The Apostle would not and could not apply to the
Judaizers the term ' circumcision ' (*peritomē*), seeing that it
' though now abrogated in Christ had still its spiritual aspects '
(Ellicott) ; so he calls them the **incision** (*katatomē*). The
cognate verb is used in the LXX of the mutilations that
were forbidden by the Law, as in Lev. 21 : 5 ; and it is employed
in 1 Kings 18 : 28 of the self-inflicted mutilations of the
prophets of Baal. The noun is used of ordinary, literal cutting
in the papyri and elsewhere. The Judaizers' carnal, unspirit-
ual view of circumcision, the rite in which they gloried and
which they were eager to foist on all Christian converts,
turned it into a mere incision, a mere laceration with no more
spiritual meaning and value than the wounds of the prophets
of Baal.

Paul now explains why he cannot speak of the Judaizers as **3** the circumcision-party. The rite, it is true, was cardinal in their view ; and yet he deliberately refuses to apply the term to them, using instead this other term of bitter sarcasm— the **incision-party**! Why does he deny to them the name which they would have chosen for themselves ? Because in his view they had forfeited their right to that name. The right had passed to others. ' I can only call them,' he seems to say, ' the incision-party ; I cannot call them the circumcision-party for *we*—you and I and all true Christians—are the true Circumcision.' There is emphasis on the word **we**— *we* (not they) **are the true Circumcision.**

Circumcision was the symbolic rite of the covenant existing between Yahweh and His people Israel. It had value and significance only as a symbol of the covenant-relation. There was, however, a persistent tendency to make it a thing of value in itself, something other than the mere sign that it actually was. The Judaizers were Jewish Christians who had brought this unwholesome tendency with them from Judaism even into the Christian Church. Their attitude to circumcision was proof that they were blind to its real character. To exalt a rite to a place of pre-eminence is to destroy that rite. The Judaizers were strangers to the true secret of the new life of freedom in Christ. Such men had no place in the new covenant. Paul and those of like mind were the ones who appreciated and enjoyed the blessings symbolized by circumcision. The rite as a rite had been abrogated in Christ, but the things for which it stood remained, having found in him their consummation and their glory. So they who were ' in Christ ' were the true Circumcision. The Judaizers had no right to the name.

The great spiritual teachers of Israel were ever insisting on the truth that it was the spirit behind the symbol that mattered, and not the symbol itself. This is the lesson taught by some of the sublimest utterances of the Old Testament. See Deut. 10 : 16, 30 : 6 ; Jer. 4 : 4. The inutility of the mere outward rite finds frequent expression in the letters of Paul. ' He is no Jew,' he writes to the Romans, ' who is merely a Jew outwardly, nor is circumcision something

136

outward in the flesh ; he is a Jew who is one inwardly, and circumcision is a matter of the heart, spiritual not literal—praised by God, not by man ' (Rom. 2 : 28, 29). He tells the Colossians that they ' have been circumcised with no material circumcision that cuts flesh from the body, but with Christ's own circumcision ' (Col. 2 : 11).

The remainder of this verse consists of three clauses which explain who the we are, and set forth the characteristics of those who are worthy to be called the true Circumcision. In the Greek the clauses are participial, and there is only one article with the three participles, showing that the three clauses are to be taken closely together as component parts of the description. Who are the true Circumcision ? **We who worship God in spirit, we who pride ourselves on Christ Jesus, we who rely upon no outward privilege.**

We who worship God in spirit. The word here used for worship originally meant ' to serve for hire.' It spoke of a service rendered not of compulsion, but spontaneously and willingly. For that reason it came to be used of the service rendered to the gods. In Biblical Greek it refers without exception to the service of the true God or of heathen deities. In our present passage the R.V. has ' who worship by the Spirit of God,' following a slightly different text for which the authority is decidedly stronger than for the text followed in our translation. This same verb ' to worship ' is used absolutely, that is, without an expressed object, in Luke 2 : 37, Acts 26 : 7, Heb. 9 : 9, 10 : 2, a fact which may be regarded as giving support to the text followed by the R.V. Still, it is possible that the other text, the one underlying our translation, is the true and original text. The analogous construction in Rom. 1 : 9 perhaps favours it, for there Paul speaks of God as the God ' whom I serve in my spirit.' The Apostle's meaning in our clause may well be that the worship of the true Christian is offered in the domain of the spirit, not in the realm of external rite and ceremony as is that of the Judaizers. If this be his meaning, he would at the same time think of this worship as made possible by the impulse of the Divine Spirit, so that both our translation and that of the R.V. may accord with the thought that was in the Apostle's mind. The worship of the Judaizers had its being in the realm of things external, lacking the inspiration of the Divine Spirit, that ' gracious power of God which evoked faith in Jesus as the crucified and risen Christ and then mediated to the receptive, obedient life all that the Lord was and did for his own people ' (Moffatt, *Paul and Paulinism*, pp. 36, 37). Compare John 4 : 24.

We who pride ourselves on Christ Jesus. The verb used in this clause is one of Paul's favourite and characteristic words. Though this is its solitary occurrence in our epistle, it is found over thirty times in his letters, and twice only in the remaining books of the New Testament. A cognate noun is used in 1 : 26 and 2 : 16 of our epistle. In the present passage the A.V. has ' rejoice,' and the R.V. ' glory.' If the rendering of our translation is to be adequate, we must give to the word ' pride ' its noblest meaning. Perhaps ' exult ' brings out the sense as well as any single English word can bring it out. The word speaks of the triumphant, exulting mood of those who in Christ have discovered the secret of life and joy. It is the word used in Rom. 5 : 11, where Paul says, ' We triumph in God through our Lord Jesus Christ ' ; and also in Gal. 6 : 13, 14, where there is the same kind of contrast with the Judaizers that we have in our present passage. ' Why,' says the Apostle to the Galatians, ' even the circumcision-party do not observe the Law themselves ! They merely want you to get circumcised, so as to boast over your flesh ! But no boasting for me, none except in the cross of our Lord Jesus Christ, by which the world has been crucified to me and I crucified to the world.'

We who rely upon no outward privilege. This is the very opposite of what the Judaizers are doing ; they rely upon a rite—an outward privilege—for justification with God. That is the broken reed on which they lean. **Outward privilege** in this clause translates the ordinary Greek word for ' flesh,' and the rendering is fully justified. ' Flesh ' in Paul stands for the lower side of human nature, the seat and vehicle of evil, hostile to God and His will. By a natural extension or transference of its meaning the word came to stand for any and all of the things in which that evil nature seeks to find satisfaction. Vers. 4 ff. bring before us the kind of things Paul has specially in mind in the present clause. It may be that he is thinking chiefly of circumcision, but the word covers such things as descent, nationality, and even legal righteousness. As Calvin puts it, ' Carnem appellat quidquid est extra Christum.' Compare 2 Cor. 11 : 18.

The closing part of the description which he has just given **4** of the true Circumcision reminds the Apostle that all the outward privileges on which the Judaizers rely were present, or had been present, in his own case in a pre-eminent degree. It is sometimes said that he singles out his own case because the Philippians, being Gentiles, would not possess these grounds of confidence, whereas he himself did possess them. If, however, these verses were not originally part of our epistle, they may for aught we know have been addressed to some Jewish Christians. It is more probable that Paul specifies his own case to prevent his readers from thinking that he disparages these outward privileges just because he does not possess them. The Judaizers may have hinted that envy lay at the root of his attitude.

Though, he says, **I could rely on outward privilege, if I chose.** According to the strict, literal meaning of his words, he seems to say that he is actually so relying ; but the whole context makes it clear that that cannot be the sense intended. We are bound to give to his words some such meaning as is given to them in our translation. ' The Apostle,' observes Lightfoot, ' for the moment places himself on the same standing-ground with the Judaizers and, adopting their language, speaks of himself as having that which in fact he had renounced.' With the present passage we should compare 2 Cor. 11 : 18 ff.

Without a trace of misgiving the Apostle goes on to say that none of the Judaizers had as much right to rely on outward privilege as he himself had. **Whoever thinks he can rely on that, I can outdo him.** Then follows a catalogue of the things in which he might have boasted had he been so disposed (vers. 5 and 6). As we read the list we are reminded by contrast of the way in which Bunyan disclaims for himself all such possible grounds for boasting : ' For my Descent then, it was, as is well known by many, of a low and inconsiderable Genera- tion ; my Father's House being of that Rank that is meanest and most despised of all the Families in the Land. Wherefore I have not here, as others, to boast of noble Blood or of a high- born State according to the Flesh ; though, all things con- sidered, I magnify the heavenly Majesty, for that by this door he brought me into this world, to partake of the Grace and Life that is in Christ by the Gospel ' (*Grace Abounding*, § 2).

5　The various items of outward privilege are now enumerated, and in so terse a manner that (as Bengel observes) Paul might have been counting them on his fingers.

I was circumcised on the eighth day after birth. He begins with the rite that was central in the scheme of the Judaizers. Circumcision was the outward privilege on which above all others they relied. And Paul had been circumcised ! Yes, on the eighth day after birth—the day named in the Law for the circumcision of native-born Jews (see Gen. 17 : 12, Lev. 12 : 3). No Ishmaelite he, for the Ishmaelites were not circumcised before they had reached their thirteenth year (compare Gen. 17 : 25). Nor was Paul a proselyte born of heathen parents. He was born within the pale of Judaism, of parents punctilious in their observance of the letter of the Law.

I belonged to the race of Israel. In these words the Apostle claims direct Israelitic descent. ' His parents were not grafted into the covenant people, but descended from the original stock ' (Lightfoot). The preceding clause declared that his parents were not heathen ; the present clause tells that they were not proselytes. Israel was the covenant-name of the people of Yahweh. We are reminded of 2 Cor. 11 : 22 : ' Are they Hebrews ? so am I. Israelites ? so am I.' Com- pare, too, Rom. 11 : 1 : ' Then, I ask, has God repudiated his People ? Never ! Why, I am an Israelite myself, a descendant of Abraham, a member of the tribe of Benjamin ! '

As in this verse from Romans, so in our present passage the Apostle specifies the tribe to which he belonged. Not every Jew at that time knew to what tribe he belonged. Paul belonged to the tribe of Benjamin. The tribe of Judah itself was scarce more honourable than the tribe of Benjamin. Benjamin was the child of Rachel, the beloved wife of Jacob (see Gen. 35 : 16-18). He alone of the sons of Jacob was born in the Land of Promise. The tribe of Benjamin alone remained faithful to Judah and the house of David at the time of the disruption (1 Kings 12 : 21) ; and it alone with Judah formed the nucleus of the new settlement in Palestine after the return from the Exile (Ezra 4 : 1). Ehud, the left-handed hero whose story is told in Judges 3 : 12-30, was a Benjamite ; so also was Mordecai, the deliverer of the Jews in the Book of Esther. Greater than either of these was Saul, the nation's first king, who also belonged to the tribe of Benjamin (compare Acts 13 : 21). The Holy City stood within the borders of the tribe of Benjamin. To this tribe was assigned the post of honour in the armies of the nation : ' Blow ye the cornet in Gibeah, and the trumpet in Ramah : sound an alarm at Beth-aven ; behind thee, O Benjamin ' (Hosea 5 : 8). Compare Judges 5 : 14. The words of Jacob's prophetic blessing of Benjamin recorded in Gen. 49 : 27— ' Benjamin is a wolf that raineth : In the morning he shall devour the prey, and at even he shall divide the spoil '— came to be applied to Paul. Tertullian, for example, in his *Adversus Marcionem* (v. 1). states that Jacob ' foresaw that Paul would spring from Benjamin, " a ravening wolf, devouring his prey in the morning " : that is, in early life he would lay waste the flocks of God as a persecutor of the Churches ; then towards evening he would provide food : that is, in his declining years he would train the sheep of Christ as a teacher of the nations ' (Moffatt, *Paul and Paulinism*, pp. 1, 2).

I was the Hebrew son of Hebrew parents. This rendering is much to be preferred to that of the R.V., ' a Hebrew of Hebrews,' for this latter phrase is liable to be understood in the sense of ' a Hebrew of superior eminence,' whereas the preposition ' of ' means ' descended from.' Paul may be referring not merely to his immediate parents, but to his ancestry as a whole, for the phrase may mean ' a Hebrew of Hebrew ancestry.' Already in the words I belonged to the

race of Israel the Apostle has claimed direct Israelitic descent. What more does he claim for himself in the present clause? Whenever the word ' Hebrew ' is used in the Old Testament of the chosen race, the idea of contrast to or distinction from other nations is present. In the New Testament the term bears a narrower meaning. Both ' Hellenists ' and ' Hebrews ' are Jews, the difference between them being that the former are Jews who speak Greek, whereas the latter are Jews who, whether dwelling in Palestine or not, continue to use Hebrew (or Aramaic). Later, it is true, we find the term ' Hebrew ' applied to Greek-speaking Jews, but Paul employs it here in the narrower sense. He belonged to a family that held fast to the old tongue. How long the family had lived in Tarsus we do not know; but even there it had maintained its devotion to the Aramaic language; we know that Paul himself spoke it (see Acts 21 : 40, 22 : 2, 26 : 14). Along with the language many old customs and habits would doubtless be retained. Proudly does Paul declare himself to be **the Hebrew son of Hebrew parents.**

Of the four items thus far enumerated not one depended upon Paul's own choice. Now come three other distinctions, each of which is the product of his own volition.

A Pharisee as regards the Law. The word ' law ' is without the article in the Greek, but our translation is right in referring it to the Mosaic Law, which is always with Paul the great embodiment of the conception of law. It was upon their fidelity to the Law that the Judaizers prided themselves; its authority was the one thing on which they insisted. How did Paul fare in this regard? What attitude had he assumed to the Law? As regards the Law he was a Pharisee! What more perfect proof could he adduce of his devotion to the Law? The complete and exact fulfilment of its demands was the *raison d'être* of the Pharisaic party; and this was the party to which Paul had attached himself! We remember how he shouted to the members of the Sanhedrin, ' I am a Pharisee, brothers, the son of Pharisees! ' (Acts 23 : 6), and how a short time before in his address to the people he had declared that he was ' educated at the feet of Gamaliel in all the strictness of our ancestral Law ' (Acts 22 : 3). As he stood before king Agrippa, he said of the Jews : ' They know, if they chose to admit it, that as a Pharisee I lived by the principles of the strictest party in our religion ' (Acts 26 : 5). No Judaizer could lay claim to completer devotion to the Law than was involved in being a Pharisee.

But had he manifested any fervour in his devotion to the 6 faith of his fathers ? Here again the Apostle challenges comparison with his traducers. **In point of ardour,** he says, **a persecutor of the church.** We can imagine with what sad irony these words were written. As Lightfoot puts it, he is condemning while he seems to exalt his former self. Had any of the Judaizers done more to prove their ardour than he had done ? The word ' ecclesia ' which he here uses embodies the conception of the Church as the true heir and successor of the chosen race. In his blindness he had persecuted the ' ecclesia ' ! (See Acts 9 : 1, 2.) Paul never ceased to be mortified by the recollection of his persecution of the Church. The note of bitter remorse can be heard in his words to the Corinthians : ' For I am the very least of the apostles, unfit to bear the name of apostle, since I persecuted the church of God ' (1 Cor. 15 : 9). Compare also Acts 22 : 4, 5 ; 26 : 9-11, Gal. 1 : 13, 14 ; 1 Tim. 1 : 13.

Pharisee though he was, vehement as had been his ardour, had he in actual practice met all the demands of the Law in his search for righteousness before God ? Even by this microscopic test he stands approved, for he can say of himself that he was **immaculate by the standard of legal righteousness.** Like the young ruler in the Gospel story, he could claim to have observed all the commands of the Law (Mark 10 : 20 = Matt. 19 : 20 = Luke 18 : 21). There was no flaw in his observance. He had left nothing undone.

All this the Apostle could claim for himself. But, he adds 7 with dramatic abruptness, **for Christ's sake I have learned to count my former gains a loss.** Notice the contrast between gains in the plural and loss in the singular. Each of the outward privileges in his catalogue had at one time been in his view a distinct and separate gain ; now he ties them all up, so to speak, in one bundle and labels them a loss! Once they were separate items of profit : now they form one item of loss. Loss, be it noticed ; for they are worse than useless. They are actually a hindrance, standing in the way of him who seeks the only true and satisfying righteousness, the righteousness that is in Christ. They bar the way by fostering a spirit of self-righteousness.

I have learned—the form of expression points to some moment at which the old standard of values passed away and the new took its place. And what moment can that have been but the moment of enlightenment on the way to Damascus ? The form of expression also speaks of the continued supremacy of the new standard : from that moment on the Damascus road he has never wavered in his fidelity to the decision then made. There is no suggestion of regret at the surrender of things once valued so highly. That surrender had been made for Christ's sake, or as the Apostle puts it in the next verse, ' in order to gain Christ.' He had gained much more than he had lost.

LOSS AND GAIN (III. 8–11)

8 Indeed I count anything a loss, compared to the supreme value of knowing Christ Jesus my Lord. For his sake I have lost everything (I count it all the veriest refuse) in order
9   to gain Christ and be found at death in him, possessing no legal righteousness of my own but the righteousness of faith in Christ, the divine righteousness that rests on faith.
10   I would know him in the power of his resurrection and the fellowship of his sufferings, with my nature transformed to
11   die as he died, to see if I too can attain the resurrection from the dead.

In the last paragraph Paul has enumerated various items of outward privilege on which he once relied, and could still rely if he were so disposed (vers. 5, 6). Then comes the great declaration that for Christ's sake he has learned to count these former gains a loss. This declaration he now proceeds to amplify.

Indeed, he says, **I count anything a loss, compared to the** **8** **supreme value of knowing Christ Jesus my Lord.** The word **indeed** denotes that in the Apostle's view the statement of ver. 7 is inadequate : he is constrained to supplement and reinforce it. In the opening clause of ver. 8 he employs the present tense (**I count**), and not the perfect as in ver. 7. Also, he now speaks of counting **anything** a loss. Some think that in *both* these respects he is deliberately varying or expanding the statement of ver. 7. Others think that the only variation intended by Paul just here is that represented by the change in the tense of the verb. This is the view of Ellicott, who takes **anything** in ver. 8 to mean simply any one of the things mentioned in vers. 5 and 6. Still another view is that the only advance in the first clause of ver. 8 as compared with ver. 7 is that now Paul makes it clear that the things which he counts a loss are not confined to the items already given. This last is, we think, the right view. Paul is not emphasizing the fact that he *still* regards things in a certain way. What he does is to enlarge the bounds of his statement so as to include, not merely the things which at one time had been his ground of confidence, but all things whatsoever. Nothing can compete with Christ for his allegiance ; nothing can alter the judgment which he formed when he found him.

He counts anything a loss, he says, **compared to the supreme value of knowing Christ Jesus my Lord.** Both the A.V. and the R.V. have ' for the excellency of the knowledge of Christ Jesus my Lord.' It is difficult to see how in this clause the preposition ' for ' can bear the meaning ' for the sake of ' which some scholars would give to it, seeing that Paul does not say ' for the knowledge,' but ' for the excellency of the knowledge.' Our translation is undoubtedly right in rendering **compared to the supreme value of knowing Christ Jesus my Lord.** The supreme value of knowing him renders everything else worthless in comparison. It goes without saying that the knowledge of which Paul speaks is more than an intellectual apprehension of truth concerning Christ Jesus. ' It reaches,' as Jones puts it, ' far beyond mere intellectual knowledge, includes faith, service, and sacrifice, and is analogous to the

familiar Pauline phrase " to be in Christ." ' Most impressive
is the use by the Apostle of the full name and title **Christ Jesus
my Lord.** He speaks of knowing him in the fullness of all that
he is and all that he does for men. Impressive also is the use
of the pronominal adjective **my**, which speaks at the same
time of personal surrender and of personal appropriation.

This is with Paul no empty vaunt, nor do his words speak of
a merely abstract or academic comparison of values. Not only
does he *count* everything a loss for Christ's sake : for his sake
he has actually suffered the loss of everything. **For his sake
I have lost everything.** Everything ! The expression is not
quite the same as that rendered **anything** in the preceding
sentence. It pictures the things of which Paul has suffered
loss, not as separate items, but as one collective whole. It is
permissible to draw from the tense of the verb in the present
sentence the inference that the Apostle has in mind some
definite moment at which he suffered the loss of everything ;
and that can only be the moment of his conversion. Further,
the verb is in the passive voice, and it is sometimes maintained
that by the use of the passive the Apostle is drawing attention
to the overwhelming power of the new forces that came into
play at his conversion, when he was mulcted of everything,
having, as it were, no choice but to surrender. This thought
must not, however, be pressed too far, for, seeing that Paul
proceeds to dilate upon the motive by which he was actuated,
it is evident that the voluntary character of the surrender is
not absent from his mind.

Does the Apostle in any way regret the surrender ? Does
his heart conceal any secret misgiving as to the wisdom of the
course he has taken, any secret longing after the things he has
lost ? By no manner of means ! Lest any such thought
should arise in the minds of his readers he hastens to add
I count it all the veriest refuse. Our translation takes these
words as a parenthesis in order to bring the statement of purpose that follows into dependence upon the words **for his sake
I have lost everything** which precede. The run of the Greek,
however, would seem to be against this ; and would it not be
slightly tautological to say in the same sentence ' *for his sake*

I have lost everything *in order to gain Christ* ' ? The statement of purpose, commencing with the words **in order to gain Christ,** is dependent, we think, on all that precedes it in ver. 8. The decision which Paul made at his conversion as well as his attitude of mind ever since that momentous occurrence—all was and is in order that he might gain Christ.

The Greek word that underlies the expression **the veriest refuse** is found nowhere else in the New Testament. The A.V. and the text of the R.V. both have ' dung ' ; the margin of the R.V. has ' refuse.' These two renderings correspond with two suggested derivations of the word. Whichever be the true derivation, the word means ' food that is rejected,' in one case food rejected by the body as lacking nutriment, in the other food rejected as unfit for the table and thrown to the dogs. The latter meaning would seem to suit the present context better than the former, especially if Paul still has in mind the thought of a feast, which thought, as we inferred from his use of the word ' dogs,' he seems to have had in mind when writing ver. 2 (see the notes there). As compared with Christ, everything is as the refuse of a feast, even the things on which the Judaizers, who think of themselves as God's favoured children sitting at His table, rely for their acceptance with Him.

From the last clause of ver. 8 to the end of ver. 11 there extends a statement of Paul's motive or purpose in making the surrender of all things—of the gain that explains and compensates for the loss. As the exact interpretation of the passage has been the subject of much controversy, it will clear the ground if, before examining its clauses in detail, we state our view of the structure of the passage as a whole. The last clause of ver. 8—**in order to gain Christ**—is a general statement of the Apostle's motive and purpose. Ver. 9 contains a statement of the gain which he expected after death. We may regard this gain spoken of in ver. 9 as in a sense a corollary of the more general gain of the last clause of ver. 8. Vers. 10 and 11 do not, in our view, break fresh ground ; they contain a further statement of Paul's motive, bringing out more fully what is involved in the purpose already stated in the last clause of ver. 8 and in ver. 9. Ver. 10 answers to and expands the last clause of ver. 8, while ver. 11 answers to and re-states the corollary set forth in ver. 9.

The last clause of ver. 8, then, is a general statement of the Apostle's motive : **in order to gain Christ.** To gain Christ is to make Christ one's own, to appropriate in its fullness and richness the redeeming and saving grace that abides in him. Moule lays stress upon the fact that it is Christ himself that Paul would fain possess, ' not merely subsidiary and derived benefits, but the Source and Secret of all benefits.'

The verbs used by Paul in this context for losing and gaining are found also in the great saying of Jesus reported in Mark 8 : 36 (=Matt. 16 : 26, Luke 9 : 25), ' What profit is it for a man to gain the whole world and to forfeit his soul ? ' Kennedy suggests that the Apostle may have had the Master's saying in his mind. So far from gaining the world and forfeiting his soul, Paul forfeits everything and gains his soul by gaining Christ.

9   Ver. 9, as has already been stated, speaks of an experience that is a natural sequence of gaining Christ and accordingly forms part of the Apostle's motive and purpose. **And be found at death in him**—so runs our translation. The words **at death** are not actually represented in the Greek, but are inserted to make clear the true meaning of the expression ' to be found in him.' In the *Expository Times* for October 1912 (p. 46) Moffatt cites from Epictetus an analogous use of the same verb. 'It occurs,' he writes, ' in the fifth chapter of the third book of the Dissertations. " Don't you know," says Epictetus, " that disease and death are bound to overtake (or, surprise) us doing something ? . . . Now, what would you like to be doing when you are overtaken ? For my part, may I be overtaken when I am attending to nothing else than my own will, seeking to be imperturbable, unhindered, uncompelled, free ! I want to be found practising this." ' These words help us to appreciate Paul's meaning. When death overtakes him, he would fain be found in Christ. At the same time the rest of ver. 9 shows that he is thinking not merely of the moment when he would be surprised by death, but

also of the time when he would be standing before the judgment-seat of God. The state in which he would be found
at death would determine his standing at the Judgment. He
desires to be found **in Christ** at the Judgment as well as at
the moment of death. The righteousness he desires to
possess means a right standing before God's tribunal, a standing that would serve as a passport into the Kingdom. The
thought of ver. 9 is eschatological.

If at death and at the Judgment Paul is **found in Christ,**
that involves that his standing before God will not be dependent upon his own efforts to satisfy the demands of the Law.
So he expands the opening clause of ver. 9 by adding **possessing
no legal righteousness of my own.** The standing Paul desires
for himself when he appears before God's tribunal is not a
' legal ' one, that is to say, one emanating from the Law, or
resulting from his efforts to obey its commands. That would
be a righteousness ' of his own,' having no ground outside his
own efforts. He had, as a matter of fact, at one time assidu-
ously put forth such efforts in the hope of achieving righteousness. See ver. 6. But all his endeavours, sincere and wholehearted as they were, had not availed to effect his reconciliation
with God and to create the peace of mind for which he craved.
How could they, then, supply a basis for a right standing
before the throne of the holy God ? Compare Rom. 10 : 3.

If, however, the Apostle deprecates one righteousness it is
that he may possess another—**possessing no legal righteousness of my own but the righteousness of faith in Christ.** This
righteousness which he desires to possess at death and as
he stands before God's judgment-seat is a righteousness that
comes through faith in Christ. ' Through faith ' would have
been a more exact rendering than **of faith** in the present clause,
for the preposition used by Paul lays stress on the fact that
faith is the medium of obtaining this righteousness. Faith
is the attitude towards Christ which brings about man's reconciliation with God and secures for him a right standing
before God's tribunal. ' Faith,' says Peake, ' is a very rich
idea with Paul ; it is that act of personal trust and self-
surrender, the movement of man's whole soul in confidence

towards Christ, which makes him one spirit with Him ' (*Quintessence of Paulinism*, p. 30).

The desired righteousness is further described as **the divine righteousness that rests on faith.** These few words bring before us the ultimate source of righteousness as well as the human condition of its obtainment, which has already been mentioned in the foregoing clause. The true righteousness is **divine,** or ' from God,' as the Greek may be literally rendered. There may be intended in this description of the true righteousness as ' from God ' a contrast both with Paul's description of the deprecated righteousness as **legal** or ' from law,' and also **with** his description of it as ' his own.' The condemned righteousness has its source in the Law and in man's own attempt to obey its behests. The exalted source of the true righteousness is God Himself. Apart from His favour there can be no righteousness. He is the author of atonement, ever seeking man's reconciliation to Himself. The Scriptures abound with declarations of His longing desire to reconcile man to Himself. Moreover, the means of reconciliation is the provision of His love. In this sense, too, the true righteousness is divine. In Rom. 5 : 17 Paul speaks of ' those who receive the overflowing grace and free gift of righteousness.' At the same time this divine righteousness **rests on faith.** There are conditions to be satisfied on man's part : he must accept and appropriate the free gift. Apart from that personal trust and self-surrender called faith there can be no reconciliation and no right standing before God.

10   We have already expressed our view that in vers. 10 and 11 the Apostle is not breaking fresh ground, but re-stating what is involved in the motive or purpose stated in the last clause of ver. 8 and in ver. 9. This interpretation is in complete accord with Paul's language (see Moulton, *Prolegomena*, pp. 217, 218). Ver. 10 expounds what is involved in the purpose stated in the words ' in order to gain Christ ' (ver. 8). **I would know him,** says the Apostle, **in the power of his resurrection and the fellowship of his sufferings.** This rendering represents Paul's meaning exactly. The knowledge of the power of Christ's resurrection and of the fellowship of his sufferings is **not** dis-

tinct from and additional to the knowledge of Christ himself, as the rendering of the A.V. and the R.V. might lead the reader to suppose. Paul desires to know him by knowing the power of his resurrection and the fellowship of his sufferings, or (as our translation puts it) to **know him in the power of his resurrection and the fellowship of his sufferings.** All the knowledge for which he yearns is knowledge of Christ himself.

Paul would know him, first, **in the power of his resurrection.** It is curious to find Bengel maintaining that the word here rendered **resurrection** should be taken, not in its usual sense of resurrection from the dead, but as referring to the first advent of Christ. The reference is to the resurrection of Christ from the dead, and the power of his resurrection is the power with which as Risen Lord he is endowed. The Apostle desires to know Christ by experiencing the power which he wields in virtue of his resurrection, to know him, that is, as the redeeming, saving Lord he now has become. Thus to share in his Lord's resurrection-life and resurrection-power he sometimes describes as being 'raised with Christ' (see Eph. 2 : 5, 6, Col. 3 : 1).

But he would fain know Christ also in **the fellowship of his sufferings.** It is significant that the Greek does not repeat the definite article with the word **fellowship,** thus showing that to know Christ in the power of his resurrection and to know him in the fellowship of his sufferings are not two distinct and separable experiences, but rather two aspects of the same experience. This in itself is strong evidence that by knowing Christ in the fellowship of his sufferings Paul does not mean enduring outward sufferings similar to those which he endured in the days of his flesh. The very language intimates that the knowledge of Christ in the power of his resurrection and the knowledge of him in the fellowship of his sufferings are too closely related as aspects of the one experience to permit us to interpret the former of an inward experience and the latter of an outward endurance. The thought here is utterly different from that of Col. 1 : 24. Moreover, however willing the Apostle might have been to face and even to welcome hardship and persecution on the principle enunciated in Rom. 8 : 28, we can hardly suppose that the endurance of such sufferings would form part of his motive and purpose. Just as to know Christ in the power of his resurrection is an inward experience capable of being described as being raised with Christ, so to know him in the fellowship of his sufferings is to pass through an experience possessing some analogy with his passion. To rise with him into new life and power presupposes a dying to the old life. One is the counterpart of the other. Compare Rom. 6 : 4–8 and Gal. 2 : 19, 20.

This interpretation of **the fellowship of his sufferings is con-**firmed by the clause that immediately follows : **with my nature transformed to die as he died.** The R.V. renders more literally ' becoming conformed unto his death.' Our translation is certainly justified in interpreting the clause of an inward transformation of nature. The verb whose participle Paul here uses is found nowhere else in the New Testament, but a cognate adjective is used in the twenty-first verse of this chapter as well as in Rom. 8 : 29. It is by no means improbable that in the present clause Paul is making use of the language of the Mystery Cults. If the fact of such usage could be established, it would reinforce the view that the clause speaks of an inward transmutation rather than of a following in the footsteps of the Master even as far as the endurance of physical death. In the vicinity of the present clause, terms are used which beyond all doubt had their place in the vocabulary of the Mysteries, such as ' knowledge ' (ver. 8) and ' mature ' (ver. 15). To say that he employs the language of the Mysteries is not to say that his ideas were derived from the Cults, or even that the terms have for him the same meaning that they had in the Cults ; though, on the other hand, there is no valid reason for confining Paul's connexion with the Mysteries to a bare use of similar or identical terms. See Moulton, *Religions and Religion*, pp. 40, 41. In the Mysteries the initiates by the performance of certain rites shared in the experiences of the dying and rising redeemer-god, seeking thus to obtain a transformation of their nature and an assurance of a blessed immortality. It may be that it was the thought of this assurance of immortality vouchsafed to the members of the pagan Cults that led Paul to think of his own hope of immortality (see ver. 11). Be that as it may, in the last clause of ver. 10, which we are now considering, he expresses the desire that in his being there should take place something that was analogous to the death of Christ. Perhaps he thought that the use of terms familiar in the Mystery Religions would make it easier for his readers to grasp his meaning, though the transformation of which he speaks is free from any admixture of the magical element so prominent in the pagan Cults.

The concluding clause of ver. 10, then, as we interpret it, speaks of an inward transformation. It is true that many interpreters, taking the preceding clause of outward suffering, see in the present clause a reference to physical death. Some of them, including Meyer and Beet, hold that the Apostle is thinking definitely of martyrdom ; others, while interpreting the clause of ' a conformity with the sufferings of Christ's earthly life, even unto death ' (Vincent), do not find in it a distinct contemplation of martyrdom. The only satisfactory explanation of the words, however, is that adopted in our translation—the interpretation that discovers in them a reference to an inward transformation of nature. With this agrees Wesley's succinct comment : ' So as to be dead to all things here below.'

The question has often been asked why in this verse the clause that speaks of the power of Christ's resurrection should precede the clause that speaks of the fellowship of his sufferings ; and many are the answers that have been given. But if the interpretation of the passage adopted in these notes is correct, the order of these two clauses has no real significance, for they do not speak of two distinct experiences of which one precedes the other in time. They speak rather of two aspects of the same experience, and the order in which these are mentioned is not a matter of any real moment. Paul mentions the positive aspect first, which seems a natural thing to do.

Ver. 11 answers to ver. 9. It does not (as some scholars 11 maintain) depend just on the last clause of ver. 10, but on ver. 10 as a whole, expressing a result which Paul hopes may follow out of the experience described in that verse : **to see, he says, if I too can attain the resurrection from the dead.** The word **too,** which draws attention to the correspondence between the resurrection which Paul desires to attain and the resurrection of Christ himself, is not actually represented in the Greek. The manner in which Paul introduces this verse seems unmistakably to imply some sort of doubt or uncertainty on his part, though some scholars deny that this is so. The uncertainty of which he is conscious is not a doubt regarding survival after death. The resurrection from the dead here stands for all that Paul conceives the life after death to be for those who are truly in Christ, the glorious and triumphant continuance of the life lived in him here below. It may be that the desire to express the full meaning of the resurrection accounts for the use by Paul here of the rare double compound *exanastasis*, a form found nowhere else in the New Testament. The common word for ' resurrection ' is the simple *anastasis*, which is used in ver. 10. No satisfactory explanation has ever been offered of the use of the uncommon form in ver. 11. Numerous suggestions have been made. Ellicott does not think any special significance attaches to the variation. But as the two forms occur in such close propinquity it is probable that there is some significance in the change of word. Can it be that *exanastasis* is another of the terms that were employed in the Mystery Cults ?

Surprise is often expressed that Paul should be affected by any such doubt or uncertainty, however slight and transient, as this verse would seem to reveal. How, it is asked, could the writer of so confident a passage as Rom. 8 : 31–39 experience any doubt ? His words in 1 Cor. 9 : 27, however, remind us that he did not without intermission live in the sunshine of assured certainty. There is in our passage no distrust of God and the power of His grace, but rather a humble distrust of himself. Doubts and misgivings often visit even the children of God. So it was with Bishop Butler, as the following extract from Alexander Whyte's *Appreciation* (pp. 87, 88) will show : ' When Butler lay on his death-bed, he called for his chaplain and said to him, " Though I have endeavoured

to avoid sin, and to please God to the utmost of my power
yet, from the consciousness of perpetual infirmities, I am
still afraid to die." "My lord," said the chaplain, "you
have forgotten that Jesus Christ is a Saviour." "True,"
said Butler, "but how shall I know that He is a Saviour
for me?" "My lord, it is written, 'Him that cometh unto
Me, I will in no wise cast out.'" "True," said Butler, "and
I am surprised that though I have read that Scripture a
thousand times over, I never felt its virtue till this moment.
And now I die happy."'

CHRISTIAN PROGRESS AND ITS CONDITIONS (III. 12–16)

Not that I have already attained this or am already perfect, 12
but I press forward to appropriate it, because I have been
appropriated myself by Christ Jesus. Brothers, I for one 13
do not consider myself to have appropriated this; my
one thought is, by forgetting what lies behind me and
straining to what lies before me, to press on to the goal 14
for the prize of God's high call in Christ Jesus. For all 15
those of our number who are mature, this must be the point
of view; God will reveal that to any of you who look at
things differently. Only, we must let our steps be guided 16
by such truth as we have attained.

In the last paragraph the Apostle has set before his readers
the guiding purpose of his Christian life, the commanding
motive that explains his renunciation of all things. Now
with striking abruptness comes the declaration that the mark
at which he aims has not been reached, the purpose not yet
achieved. On the contrary, he is still engaged in a strenuous
endeavour to reach and to achieve. His words reveal an
obvious desire to prevent a misinterpretation of what he has
just said. It is equally obvious that in this repudiation of the
idea that he has reached perfection he has in mind some
persons, presumably among his readers, who maintained that
they themselves had arrived at perfection. It is possible
that along with this self-complacency there went (as Lightfoot

suggests) an Antinomian spirit, confounding liberty with licence, and regarding the Christian ' as already in such a sense arrived at his goal as to be lifted beyond responsibility, duty, and progress ' (Moule). It is possible also that it is of these same self-complacent persons that Paul speaks in vers. 18 and 19 of this chapter.

In his noble sermon on ' Christian Progress by Oblivion of the Past,' Frederick W. Robertson describes the present passage as ' one of the most encouraging in all the writings of St. Paul,' inasmuch as in it the Apostle ' places himself on a level with the persons whom he addresses,' giving them ' in himself a specimen of what frailty and weakness can achieve in the strength of Christ.' On the other hand, few passages in Paul's writings are more stringent and challenging, for if in the Apostle's case strenuousness so unremitting was necessary, who is there who can afford to abate one whit of his utmost endeavour ?

12   Not that I have already attained this. It is clear that he is anticipating a possible misunderstanding of what he has said about himself. In the Greek no object is actually expressed after the verb, that is, there is no Greek word to which the word this in our translation corresponds. The word this assumes that the object of the verb is the experience described in the verses that precede. Is this assumption justified? Does the Apostle's thought in this opening clause of ver. 12 definitely go back to what he has already written ? Chrysostom, followed by a long array of later interpreters, holds that already in the present clause Paul is thinking of the ' prize ' of which he speaks in ver. 14. But surely when no object is actually expressed it is more natural to seek for it, as our translation does, in what has already been said. But what precisely are we to include in the word this ? What exactly is it that Paul has not yet attained ? The closing words of the preceding paragraph spoke of the resurrection from the dead. Does the resurrection form part of the content of the word this? The A.V., by employing the same English word ' attain ' to represent two different Greek words in ver. 11 and in the opening clause of ver. 12, makes it appear as if the resurrection more

156

than aught else was in the Apostle's mind in the present clause. But, it may be asked, would it not be absurd to attribute to Paul so self-evident a statement as that he had not already attained the resurrection from the dead ? What necessity could there be for calling attention to so obvious a fact ? Absurd, however, as it may seem at first sight, it is just possible that that is what Paul is doing. In 2 Tim. 2 : 17, 18 we read of two men, Hymenaeus and Philetus, who ' have failed in the Truth by arguing that the resurrection has taken place already,' and it has been maintained that in our present passage Paul is combating some such heresy. Our knowledge of the heresy referred to in 2 Timotheus is scanty, but it seems to have involved the belief that all that God can do for man in Christ is attainable in this life, and that there is no higher experience to look forward to after death. If in our passage Paul is combating this belief, his meaning will be that he is not satisfied to think that already in this life he has received the best that God has to bestow. So the passage is interpreted by the writer on our epistle in Dummelow's One-volume Commentary, who finds here a challenge to certain ' perfectionists who imagined that Christ in their present state had reached the goal of his work of redemption.' This interpretation, however, fails to carry conviction. For one thing, we cannot be at all sure that the doctrine of a past resurrection was held as early as Paul's time (see the article ' Hymenaeus ' in the *Encyclopaedia Biblica*). The passage in 2 Timotheus is not at all likely to have come from his pen. Moreover, if Paul were refuting the doctrine, we might reasonably suppose that he would have made his purpose more apparent.

For these reasons a simpler and more straightforward interpretation is to be preferred. Paul means that he has not yet attained *even so far as it is attainable in this life* all that is involved in the experience he has described. Ver. 11, it will be remembered, is grammatically dependent on ver. 10, and speaks of an experience which is a corollary of the experience described in ver. 10, so that the latter experience more naturally suggests itself as the object of the verb in the opening clause of ver. 12 than does the former.

Paul adds **or am already perfect.** In a few authorities we find inserted before these words a clause meaning ' or have already been justified,' which Kennedy describes as ' the gloss, probably, of some pious copyist who imagined that the divine side of sanctification was left too much out of sight.' The authentic clause (**or am already perfect**) is in the R.V. more literally rendered ' or am already made perfect.' Paul uses a verb which he employs nowhere else, but which is common in the Epistle to the Hebrews. It is a cognate adjective that is rendered ' mature ' in ver. 15. The Apostle's disclaimer reminds us of Ignatius's disavowal of perfection in his letter to the Ephesians (3 : 1)—in which, however, a different verb is used—' I do not give you commands as if I were some one great, for though I am a prisoner for the Name, I am not yet perfect in Jesus Christ ; for now I do but begin to be a disciple, and I speak to you as to my fellow learners ' (Kirsopp Lake's translation).

Still, though he has not yet attained the experience for which he yearns, he is striving to achieve it. **But,** he says, **I press forward to appropriate it.** This rendering, perhaps, does not quite do justice to the note of contingency in Paul's words, which can be more literally rendered : ' I press forward to see if I am indeed to appropriate it.' The same two verbs that are used here are used also in Rom. 9 : 30, where Paul speaks of Gentiles, who have never ' aimed at ' righteousness, yet ' attaining ' righteousness. It is often said that the metaphor of a race is already in the Apostle's mind as he writes the present clause ; but that is doubtful. As Vincent points out, the verb rendered **appropriate** does not suit the metaphor, while the verb rendered **press forward** is elsewhere used by Paul without any such reference. The latter verb is the very word used in ver. 6 of this chapter for ' persecuting.' It pictures the Apostle pursuing the object of his quest with dogged perseverance. Of the other verb, **appropriate** is an excellent rendering. It is found in an early papyrus of colonists appropriating land. It suggests the idea of grasping, seizing tight hold of. Here again the object of the verb is in the Greek left unexpressed, but it is the same as the **object of**

I **have already attained** in the opening clause of the verse, and is succinctly stated by Wesley to be ' perfect holiness, preparatory to glory.' Even though Paul has not yet attained it, he is determined that it will one day be his. ' He is not paralysed by the distance which yawns between him and the ideal ' (Jowett).

And he gives a reason for thus pressing on to appropriate— **because I have been appropriated myself by Christ Jesus.** This rendering of the clause, which is substantially that of the margin of the R.V., is, we think, the correct rendering. It is significant that this is the meaning given to the clause by the Greek commentators. Ellicott objects to it on the ground that it ' introduces a reason where a reason seems hardly appropriate.' But why should the introduction of a reason at this point be deemed inappropriate ?

There are two other ways of taking the clause. We may render : ' whereunto, or for which purpose, I have been appropriated myself by Christ Jesus.' If this be the right way to take the words, the Apostle states, not that the reason he is pressing forward to appropriate is that he himself has been appropriated by Christ Jesus, but rather that the reason he was appropriated by Christ Jesus was that he might press forward to appropriate. Or again we may, as does the text of the R.V., connect the present clause closely with the (unexpressed) object of the verb **appropriate** in the preceding clause, thus : ' I press forward to appropriate that for which I have been,' etc. Neither of these renderings, however, is as satisfactory as the one adopted in our translation. Because at his conversion Christ had appropriated, had laid hold upon, him, Paul was pressing forward to appropriate that knowledge, that experience, of Christ of which he has spoken. Nothing less would accord with Christ's appropriation of him. His language shows that he thinks of Christ Jesus as having, as it were, laid violent hands upon him, constraining him into his salvation and impressing him for his service. He did not, however, look upon his conversion as an end, but as a means, a beginning, a summons to high and unremitting endeavour.

So eager is the Apostle to bring home to his readers the 13

fact that he does not regard himself as having reached perfection that he proceeds to repeat and to expand what he has just said in ver. 12. Brothers, he begins, I for one do not consider myself to have appropriated this. This rendering agrees with the margin, as against the text, of the R.V. in omitting the word ' yet.' Its inclusion would make very little difference to the meaning, and the authorities are fairly evenly balanced. Paul's language makes it almost impossible to avoid the inference that he is thinking of some among his readers who *did* regard themselves as perfect. Whatever they may think of themselves, he does not regard himself as perfect. It is because he has them in mind, seemingly, and because his words are in effect a censure on their self-complacency, that he introduces the word brothers. It is not so much ' with a view of arresting attention ' (Lightfoot) that the appellation is introduced, but rather with a view of mitigating any seeming severity in his words. The verb here well rendered consider is of frequent occurrence in the letters of Paul, particularly in Romans and 2 Corinthians. It connotes a careful weighing of the point under consideration. The Apostle's statement is no careless or casual remark, but represents his deliberate view of himself and his attainments.

So far is he from being satisfied with his attainments that he adds : my one thought is, by forgetting what lies behind me and straining to what lies before me, to press on to the goal. My one thought is—the Greek literally rendered would mean simply ' one thing ! ' and many views are held as to the exact force of this elliptical expression. Does Paul mean ' one thing I do ' (as the R.V. has it), or ' one thing I am concerned about,' or something else ? In any case the general meaning is clear, and our translation felicitously combines the two ideas of concern and action. The phrase bespeaks both singleness of purpose and concentration of effort. The figure of a race is now in the Apostle's mind, and in a race distractions are fatal. All Paul's activities are subordinated to one supreme end. In the sermon already referred to Robertson says : ' He who has not found out how directly or indirectly to make everything converge towards his soul's sanctification, has as yet missed the meaning of this life.'

Paul's one thought is to press on ; and he describes his manner of pressing on in the words : **by forgetting what lies behind me and straining to what** lies before me. First, then, he seeks to advance by forgetting what lies behind him. The word used for **forgetting** is, so far as the Pauline letters go, peculiar to this passage. It is another of the words from the vocabulary of the Mystery Cults employed in this chapter. What does the Apostle include in the phrase **what lies behind me ?** Some maintain that he means his old Jewish life, in particular the prerogatives enumerated in vers. 5 and 6 of this chapter ; others hold that the reference is to his new life in Christ, the part of his Christian course already covered ; while others still would include in the phrase the whole of the Apostle's past life both before and after his conversion. We have no hesitation in concluding that Paul is referring specifically to the part of his Christian course already traversed, and especially to the achievements and successes of his Christian career. A phrase identical with or similar to the one here rendered **what lies behind** is found in Jer. 7 : 24 (LXX), Luke 9 : 62, John 6 : 66, and the meaning of the phrase in these passages is sometimes said to favour the view that in the present Philippian passage the reference is to the Apostle's old, pre-Christian life. The reference of the phrase in these other passages, however, has no bearing whatsoever on its meaning in our passage. Paul is now clearly using the metaphor of a race, and it obscures and complicates the metaphor to see here a reference to the life he lived before he entered upon the Christian race. Moreover, in this whole passage he is combating self-satisfaction on the part of some Christians who imagined that they had reached perfection, and it is not easy to see how the forgetting on his part of anything other than his Christian achievements could have any bearing on his present purpose. It is the present participle of the verb ' to forget ' that Paul employs, thus signifying that his forgetting is continuous and ceaseless. **He forgets**

M

as he runs. Each success is allowed to slip into oblivion the moment it is achieved.

Lightfoot mentions the possibility (without, however, endorsing the suggestion) that Paul derives his metaphor in the present context not from the foot-race, but rather from the chariot-race. But there is not much that can be said in favour of the suggestion. Every word would suit a foot-race, and it is the foot-race that usually furnishes Paul's metaphors. Moreover, in this passage, where the need for effort is the theme, a race that demands the personal exertion of the participant is more likely to have suggested itself to the Apostle.

Not only does the Apostle describe himself as forgetting what lies behind him : he speaks of himself also as **straining to what lies before him.** It is obvious that the figure of a race is in his mind. He employs a graphic participle found nowhere else in his writings. It is a word that speaks of direction and posture, picturing the racer straining and stretching towards the object he is so eager to reach, as if trying to touch it from his present position. Bengel's comment is often quoted : ' The eye outstrips and draws on the hand, the hand outstrips and draws on the foot.' How intense must have been the Apostle's desire to advance in knowledge and experience of his Lord ! And how vital it is that we should be more intent on what we may become than on what we have already attained ! ' The runner,' says Chrysostom, ' does not count the laps that are passed, but those that remain.'

14 And what does the Apostle hope to reach by all this strenuous concentration ? His one thought is **to press on to the goal for the prize of God's high call in Christ Jesus.** It is the vision of the end of the race that ever directs and speeds his hastening feet. He will neither slacken nor stray so long as he keeps his eye on the goal. It is by contemplating the end that he hopes to attain the best that this present life can bestow. He employs again the expressive verb that is used in ver. 12 for ' pressing forward ' ; it represents him as pursuing the goal, resolute in his determination to bring it to bay.

The word translated **goal** is not a technical term for the end of a race. It means a mark to look at, or aim at. Here only is it found in the New Testament. The word **prize** occurs in one other place only in the New Testament, namely in 1 Cor. 9 : 24, but kindred words are used in Col. 2 : 18 and 3 : 15.

Some would make the goal and the prize in our passage two separate things ; but it is better to regard them as the same thing viewed in two different ways. Paul is thinking of the final, ultimate bliss to which God summons men. He regards it as the mark or goal the vision of which enables him to keep to the right course, to ' run without swerving ' (as he himself puts it in 1 Cor. 9 : 26). He thinks of it also as the prize which he hopes to attain, the contemplation of which keeps him from becoming satisfied with anything he achieves in this life.

He speaks of it as **the prize of God's high call.** This does not mean, as some maintain, that the prize is identical with, or consists of, God's high call, as though some noble summons at the end of the course constituted the prize. The phrase means rather ' the prize to which God calls.' It is the reward of obedience to His call. The call of God is **a high** or upward call because He summons men up to Himself. The author of the Epistle to the Hebrews speaks of it as a ' heavenly ' call (Heb. 3 : 1), and Paul writes to the Thessalonians of ' the God who called you to His own realm and glory' (1 Thess. 2 : 12). Paul heard God's call at his conversion, and through the intervening years it had not ceased to summon him upward.

The concluding words of this verse—**in Christ Jesus**—are by some expositors taken closely with **to press on,** but it seems more natural to take them with **God's high call.** The call is in Christ Jesus. How easily this phrase comes to Paul, for all that concerns his salvation lives and moves and has its being in Christ. Through him does God's call come, and in him it has its potency.

The Apostle finds stimulus in the thought of reward. So he does in 2 Tim. 4 : 8 (a verse which may well have come from his pen), where he says, ' Now the crown of a good life awaits me, with which the Lord, that just Judge, will reward me on the great Day.' Compare also Heb. 11 : 26, where it is said of Moses that ' he had an eye to the Reward.' To some it may seem unworthy to find incentive in the expectation of reward ; but when we consider the nature of the prize sought by Paul, we are not conscious of any unworthiness in his attitude. ' There is no unworthiness,' says Rainy, ' in devoting life to win this prize ; for it is a state of victorious well-being and well-doing ' (*Expositor's Bible*, p. 267).

15   The attitude which the Apostle has set forth as his own is in his eyes so obviously the right one that he cannot conceive of any other attitude approving itself to those who are competent to judge.   No other view should be possible for those who have arrived at maturity in Christian experience.   **For all those of our number who are mature,** he writes, **this must be the point of view.**   He includes himself in the same class with his readers, while at the same time hinting that they have not all reached maturity.

The word rendered **mature** is translated ' perfect ' both in the A.V. and in the R.V.   It is cognate, as we saw, with the verb used in the clause of ver. 12 in which Paul says that he has not yet reached perfection.   In ver. 12 the Apostle disclaims perfection, whereas here in ver. 15 he places himself among those who are perfect.   This seeming inconsistency has occasioned much discussion.   Some maintain that inasmuch as the two cognate words come so close together they must be used in the same sense, in which case the Apostle's words in ver. 15 must be ironical.   His meaning then would be : ' Those of our number who pride themselves on their imagined perfection should learn to look at things as I do.'   This is the interpretation adopted by Lightfoot, Jones, and others ; but it does not commend itself to us as the right interpretation.   There is no imperative reason why the adjective in ver. 15 should bear a meaning strictly analogous to that of the verb in ver. 12. Though the two words are kindred, the possibility of misunderstanding is obviated by the fact that those who are spoken of in ver. 15 as ' perfect ' are urged to seek the perfection which Paul disclaims for himself in ver. 12.   **Mature,** as in our translation, is a far more suitable rendering in ver. 15 than ' perfect.'   See Moffatt's note in the *Expositor* for November 1916, pp. 347, 348, and especially the apposite quotation from Epictetus. The word was used in the Mystery Cults, and Lightfoot (on Col. 1 : 28) speaks of it as ' probably borrowed from the ancient mysteries, where it seems to have been applied to the fully instructed, as opposed to the novices.' In early Christian literature it is used of baptized Christians as distinguished from catechumens. Perhaps it was tending to acquire some such meaning even in Paul's day. In any case, we do not think the term is used ironically in the present verse. We fail to detect a tone of irony in the passage. Paul is solemnly declaring what should be the point of view of those who are sufficiently advanced to understand and appreciate the genius of the new faith. The same adjective is used in 1 Cor. 14 : 20 (' In evil be mere infants, but be mature in your intelligence ') and in Heb. 5 : 14 (' Whereas solid food is for the mature, for those who have their faculties trained by exercise to distinguish good and evil ') and often elsewhere in the New Testament.

For such persons there must be no other point of view. They should have a point of view that is consistent with their maturity. The only true maturity is to strive after fuller maturity. Why should the laps that are past make one blind to the fact that there are more laps ahead ?

The verb which Paul uses in the phrase rendered **this must be the point of view** is the verb we have already met in 1 : 7, 2 : 2 (twice), 2 : 5, and it will meet us again three or four times in our epistle. (See the note on 1 : 7.) Moffatt, in the *Expositor* note to which reference has just been made, speaks of this verb's ' striking range of application ' in our epistle, and adds that ' here at any rate it denotes thought determining motives, and through motives conduct ' (p. 348). Paul demands of those who are mature more than mere right thinking : he demands that the whole disposition of their life be similar to that which he has described as his own.

The remainder of ver. 15 contains a word of encouragement to any of the readers who might be feeling ill at ease because of the discovery that their attitude did not tally with the Apostle's own. **God,** says Paul, **will reveal that to any of you**

who look at things differently. He still has in mind the mature, but he now speaks in the second person because his words are addressed to those of their number whose view he differentiates from his own.

Two slightly differing views are held regarding the exact meaning of these words. Frequently they are interpreted to mean : ' If, while your general attitude is unimpeachable, your view of the application of the general principle is in any particular case at fault, God will reveal to you the right view to adopt on that particular point.' So Rainy, for example, expounds the words on pp. 273 ff. of the *Expositor's Bible*. The other possible paraphrase would run on this wise : ' If your attitude comes short in any degree of the view I have set before you, God will enable you to acquire the correct point of view.' This latter explanation—which is the one represented in our translation—is the more natural interpretation of the Greek. Moreover, the run of the passage as a whole suggests that the Apostle is more concerned about the general attitude of those whom he addresses than about slight aberrations in detail that might accompany a correct general attitude. Paul means that if they do not see eye to eye with him in what he has said, divine guidance is at their disposal to enable them to gain the right point of view. Nothing is said regarding the manner in which the divine revelation would come to them ; but the Apostle is fully assured that his own view is in accord with the mind of God.

16 If this divine enlightenment is to come to them, a condition has to be satisfied ; it is of this condition that Paul speaks in the present verse. **Only, we must let our steps be guided by such truth as we have attained.** The Apostle now returns to the first person—possibly because the principle here laid down is of universal application. A literal rendering of the best-attested text of this verse would run : ' Only, whereunto we have attained, by the same let us guide our steps.' The less trustworthy text which underlies the A.V. inserts the word ' rule ' after ' the same,' and also appends a clause ' let us mind the same thing.' The R.V., while it does not read the word ' rule ' in the Greek text which it translates, nevertheless interprets ' by the same ' to mean ' by the same rule,' for it introduces the word ' rule ' in italics into its rendering.

What is the precise significance of this imperative condition which the Apostle lays down ? Does he mean (as some interpret his words) that those who would obtain the divine revelation must continue to walk in the same path, in the same straight line, in which they have hitherto been walking ? This can scarcely be his meaning, for the divine revelation of which he speaks is concerned with the necessity and duty of pressing forward and not becoming content with attainments already reached. He would not speak of advancing in a certain manner as a condition of receiving enlightenment on the necessity of advancing. It is much simpler to take the words to mean that fidelity to truth already attained is a condition of receiving fuller revelation. Those addressed are ' mature,' and some measure of divine revelation must have been vouchsafed to them. Let them be true to that. Let them ' guide their steps ' by such truth as they have already attained. Each single step should be determined by fidelity to truth already reached. Absolute fidelity in detail is ever the condition of further enlightenment. ' I still see the good in the inch,' wrote young Robert Louis Stevenson to his father, ' and cling to it. It is not much perhaps, but it is always something.' In every department of knowledge this principle applies. Of Romanes his biographer, Paget, says : ' The love of precision and completeness never dulled his care for the things that he could neither define, nor label, nor arrange ; in their fragmentariness he treasured them, in their reserve he trusted them, waiting faithfully to see what they might have to show him. And they did not fail him.'

An Exhortation to Imitate the Apostle (III. 17-19)

Copy me, brothers, one and all of you, and notice those who 17
live by the example you get from me. For many—as 18
I have often told you and tell you now with tears—many
live as enemies of the cross of Christ. Destruction is 19
their fate, the belly is their god, they glory in their shame,
these men of earthly mind !

In the last paragraph we found the Apostle declaring that no other conception of the life in Christ than his own was possible for those whose maturity made them competent to form a judgment. Now he addresses to his readers a direct injunction to copy him.

17 Once more he calls them **brothers,** perhaps in this instance in order to forestall any disposition that might arise to resent his seeming self-assertion. **Copy me, one and all of you,** he writes. His words may be literally rendered either ' become fellow-imitators *of* me,' or else ' become fellow-imitators *with* me ' ; and the injunction may be, and has been, interpreted in three different ways.

(*a*) Some understand the Apostle to mean : ' join with me in imitating Christ.' So Bengel, for example, interprets the words. In the *Expository Times*, vol. v, p. 287, W. F. McMichael bases upon an examination of the occurrences of compound nouns analogous to the one here used for fellow-imitator (which occurs here only in the New Testament) the conclusion that this is the only meaning the present clause can rightly bear. The context, however, makes no reference to the imitation of Christ, and we may reasonably suppose that if this had been Paul's meaning his words would have made it more evident. The name of Christ would surely have been introduced.

(*b*) Others interpret the injunction to mean : ' join with those who are already imitating me,' ' join the company of my imitators.' As this, however, is virtually what Paul says in the next clause, this interpretation introduces into his words a gratuitous tautology.

(*c*) The remaining interpretation makes the Apostle say : ' join with one another in imitating me,' or, as our translation well puts it, **Copy me, one and all of you.** This doubtless is the meaning intended. It is the only meaning that is not open to some evident objection, and it is adopted by Lightfoot, Ellicott, and the majority of interpreters.

It is no unusual thing for Paul to urge his readers to make him their pattern. ' Then imitate me, I beg of you,' he says to the Corinthians in 1 Cor. 4 : 16 ; and elsewhere in the same epistle he writes, ' Copy me, as I copy Christ ' (11 : 1). See also 1 Thess. 1 : 6, 2 Thess. 3 : 7–9, Acts 26 : 29, as well as 4 : 9 of our epistle.   How firm must have been his confidence in his own rectitude, how positive his certainty that he himself **was** copying Christ !   His self-assertion is not enfeebled by any consciousness of moral poverty.   It was laid to his charge by some of his opponents that his doctrine conduced to sin, but he betrays no uneasiness that his doctrine would suffer through any scrutiny of his own life.

The necessity of urging upon his converts the counsel to copy him was in large measure forced upon the Apostle.   ' In the seventh decade of the first Christian century, with the N.T. yet unwritten, the living ideal of the Christ-life was far from being stereotyped in words or habits.   Fluid and free, its appeal had to come largely through men's experience and observation of one another, and the inevitable reproduction of character.   The channel of education was chiefly the seen or remembered character of definite individuals, the advice and conduct of the best people (Heb. 13 : 7).   Probably for each community one or two, dead or living, absent or present, represented the ideal of the Christian spirit ' (Moffatt, in the *Expository Times*, vol. x, p. 446).   Nor even yet is the task of providing a pattern of the Christ-life unnecessary.   ' For all the popularization of the Christian ideal since the first century,' says Moffatt on the same page, ' this function has not yet become an anachronism.   According to the sincerity and richness of his character, each man still stands to some others authoritatively for a more or less large portion of the ideal.'

To the direct command to copy him the Apostle joins a further injunction :   **and notice,** he says, **those who live by the example you get from me.**   ' Notice,' says Beet, ' that the example of Paul did not supersede the need and value of the example of others who imitate him.   For a less example under our immediate observation is sometimes more effective than a greater one at a distance ' (p. 104).   The Greek word rendered **notice** connotes close observation.   In Rom. 16 : 17 the same verb is used in the sense of marking in order to shun ; **here** it means to observe with the object of imitating. The word used here for example is found in the same ethical sense also in 1 Thess. 1 : 7, 2 Thess. 3 : 9, 1 Tim. 4 : 12, Titus 2 : 7, 1 Pet. 5 : 3. Note the second person—*you* get—where the third person would have been naturally expected : by its use the Apostle seems to intimate that the example is available for those whom he is addressing as it is for those of whom he is speaking—those who are already turning it to account.

Literally the Greek says, not ' the example you get from *me*,' but ' the example you get from *us*.' In our translation the first person plural is interpreted of the Apostle alone. In Greek, as in English and other languages, the first person plural is often used for the singular. It is so used not seldom in the epistles of Paul. But is it so used here ? Ellicott would not object to the singular rendering, for he inclines to the view that the plural pronoun ' is the Apostle's designation of himself viewed less in his personal than his official relations.' Though why he should emphasize his official relations when urging others to imitate him is not evident. It may be said in favour of the singular rendering that a reference to others along with himself comes somewhat awkwardly in the absence of the slightest hint on the Apostle's part as to the identity of those whom he thus associates with himself. On the other hand, the use by Paul of both the singular and the plural pronouns in reference to himself in the same sentence would have been strange. It is sometimes said that he felt the me in the first part of the sentence to be too egotistical, and so finished the sentence with the plural pronoun ! But it may be questioned whether the Apostle would allow himself to be disturbed by a misgiving that was capable of being dispelled by a mere change of pronoun. On the whole, the view that the plural pronoun includes others besides the Apostle is to be preferred. But who these others are we can only guess. If the present paragraph belongs to the epistle to the Philippians, then the ' us ' would refer to Paul and those of his fellow-workers who were known to the Philippians, particularly those who were now with him in Ephesus, such as Timotheus and

Epaphroditus. In that case ' those who live by the example you get from us ' would be certain members of the Philippian Church whom the rest could copy to their profit. On the other hand, if, as we hold, this paragraph originally formed no part of the Philippian epistle, then it is a futile task to inquire minutely regarding the persons whom Paul here associates with himself.

Whatever may have been the exact circumstances under which this verse was written, it certainly suggests the precept that ' everything in a minister should be exemplary ' (Trapp). ' Take heed to yourselves,' said Baxter to the ministers of Worcester, ' lest you may unsay that with your lives which you say with your tongues, and be the greatest hinderers of the success of your own labours. It much hindereth our work when other men are, all the week long, contradicting to poor people in private that which we have been speaking to them from the Word of God in public ; because we cannot be at hand to manifest their folly ; but it will much more hinder if we contradict ourselves, and if your actions give your tongue the lie. . . . One proud, surly, lordly word, one needless contention, one covetous action, may cut the throat of many a sermon ' (quoted by Moffatt in the *Expositor* for November 1916, p. 349).

In this verse and the next Paul gives his reason for address- **18** ing to his readers the injunctions of ver. 17. The translators of the A.V., conscious no doubt that ver. 20, which they rightly introduce with ' for,' and not with ' but,' does not come naturally after ver. 19, make a parenthesis of vers. 18 and 19, enclosing them within brackets. But surely the connexion between ver. 17 and ver. 18 is too close to permit even the slight disjunction which is involved in the punctuation of the A.V.

For many—as I have often told you and tell you now with tears—many live as enemies of the cross of Christ : that is why the Apostle would have his readers copy him. He shudders at the thought of their being influenced to their hurt by men who live as enemies of the cross of Christ !

Who are these persons the mention of whom now brings

tears to the Apostle's eyes ? By some they have been identified
with the Judaizers of the second verse of this chapter. That
was the view of Hort. By others they are identified with the
persons whom we can discern behind the words of the Apostle
in ver. 13—those who claimed to have reached perfection.
There is, however, no compelling reason for identifying them
with either of these two classes. Neither Judaizers nor ' perfectionists ' as such would merit the reproachful strictures of
vers. 18 and 19. It is probable that the Apostle is now speaking of another class altogether.

One thing seems certain : these persons were within the
pale of the Christian Church. The grounds on which this conclusion is based are well stated by Kennedy. For one thing,
the word **live** in ver. 18 renders the same Greek word as does
the word ' live ' in ver. 17, and seeing that in ver. 17 it means
to live as Christians, it presumably bears the same meaning in
ver. 18. Again, the fact that the Apostle is moved to tears
as he speaks of them suggests that they bear the name of
Christ, for it is scarcely probable that his emotions would have
been thus deeply stirred had they been Jews or pagans.
Furthermore, the phrase **enemies of the cross of Christ** would
have been ' a mere platitude ' (as Kennedy puts it) if used of
persons outside the Christian pale. It was a perverted type of
Christian life that these men exhibited : that is why the
Apostle is so urgent that his readers should follow the example
set by his own life. They were Antinomian Christians—men
who distorted and misapplied Paul's own doctrine of God's
free grace. It was the fact that they perverted and travestied
his doctrine that above all else moved him to tears as he spoke
of them. They interpreted Christian liberty as licence to
gratify the lusts of the flesh. They presumed that inasmuch
as they were ' in Christ,' they were free from the control of the
moral law. They were free ! They were at liberty to indulge
any passion ! Their freedom was converted into ' an opening
for the flesh ' (Gal. 5 : 13). If we knew the circumstances
under which vers. 1*b*–19 of this chapter were written, we should
perhaps be able to identify these Antinomians with greater
precision On general grounds they are more likely to have

been Gentile than Jewish Christians. What exactly led Paul to utter this warning against their influence just at this point we can only surmise. Was he led to do so by the thought that the ' perfectionists ' of whom he was thinking when he wrote the last paragraph were in peculiar danger of drifting into Antinomianism ? They were perfect ! Surely nothing could harm *them* ! They could indulge any appetite with impunity ! Christians who cease to strive after a higher perfection are apt to slip back into places of peril.

It is difficult to believe—as has often been remarked by writers on our epistle—that Antinomian Christians of the type here spoken of formed part of the Philippian Church. How, for example, could the Apostle have written as he does in 1 : 3 ff. to a community that included such men in its membership ? And so recourse is sometimes had to the conjecture that Paul is uttering a warning against an evil that was threatening the Church from without. Indeed the impossibility of thinking that the Philippian Church harboured such persons has led some expositors to maintain that Paul must have had in mind the surrounding heathen population. The reasons, however, which have already been given for regarding those of whom he speaks as members of the Christian Church seem to us to be conclusive. The impression made upon us by the Apostle's words is that the Antinomians of whom he speaks are right among his readers. The words which form the parenthesis in our translation—as I have often told you and tell you now with tears—do not in the original Greek (as conceivably they might do in the English rendering) imply that the readers had no first-hand acquaintance with them. They show that the peril was of long standing ; and the readers' need of reiterated warning over a long period is best explained on the supposition that the persons who constituted the peril were on the spot. The analogy of ver. 17 also points in the same direction. Those who live by the example they get from Paul and his associates are, we may suppose, members of the community addressed by the Apostle ; and presumably therefore the persons whose example they are to shun are amongst them. It is obvious that all this gives strong support to the hypothesis that the present paragraph did not originally form part of the Epistle to the Philippians.

The warning often given in the past Paul now repeats—and he does so with tears. The words with tears represent a participle in the Greek, and the very choice of verb would seem to point to the intensity of his grief, for the verb is commonly used of loud expression of pain or sorrow. Paul was a man of strong and deep emotions. ' I wrote you,' he once said to the Corinthians, ' in sore distress and misery of heart, with many a tear ' (2 Cor. 2 : 4). He tells the Ephesian elders at Miletus how he had served the Lord among them ' with many a tear,' and bids them remember ' how for three whole years ' he had ' never ceased night and day to watch over each one ' of them ' with tears ' (Acts 20 : 19 and 31). Plummer quotes the words in which Newman describes the emotion under which he wrote his *Apologia* : ' I have been constantly in tears, and constantly crying out in distress.'

These Antinomian Christians live as enemies of the cross of Christ. The Greek has the definite article with the word enemies, and it is possible that the Apostle means that they are *the* enemies *par excellence* of the cross of Christ. Whether he means that or not, he certainly means more than that their conception of the cross is opposed to right doctrine. The description of them in ver. 19 makes it clear that the present clause means that their whole life is antagonistic to the cross. Their spirit is the reverse of the spirit of the cross. It tends to subvert the cross. Paul thinks of their lives as contradicting and obstructing the whole design of the death of Christ, neutralizing the influence of the cross as a renovating principle. The phrase enemies of the cross of Christ points markedly to the central place occupied by the cross in the thought of Paul.

19 Ver. 19 consists of a frightful description of these persons whose manner of life called forth the counsel of this paragraph. The first of its four clauses is a statement of their destiny, while the remaining three specify some of their characteristics. Bengel observes that the destiny is announced first in order that the succeeding clauses may be read with the greater horror.

174

Destruction is their fate—thus is their destiny set forth. The word here rendered **destruction** is used also in 1 : 28, where it is rendered ' ruin.' See the note there. The A.V. has ' perdition ' in 1 : 28 and ' destruction ' in the present verse ; the R.V. has ' perdition ' in both places. The noun is Paul's usual word to express the antithesis of salvation. And those whose destiny he describes by its means are within the Church of Christ ! The word translated **fate** is represented by ' end ' both in the A.V. and in the R.V. **Fate** is an excellent rendering, for the word here connotes the idea of inevitability ; it stands for the unescapable end or outcome of the life these persons are living. Paul has the same word in Rom. 6 : 21 in the saying ' the end of all that is death.' It is used also in 2 Cor. 11 : 15, Heb. 6 : 8, 1 Pet. 4 : 17. What but destruction can be the fate of the enemies of the cross of Christ—the cross which is God's means of salvation ?

Now come the three clauses which describe their characteristics. The first declares that **the belly is their god.** Whatever their profession or pretensions might be, the belly is the real object of their worship, the supreme interest of their life. This metaphorical use of **belly** covers seemingly more than mere gluttony. Kennedy remarks that it ' is probably used as a general term to include all that belongs most essentially to the bodily, fleshly life of man.' It stands for the satisfaction of the carnal nature. *Venter* in Latin is similarly used for the fleshly appetites in general. These Antinomians were ' men of coarse and unblushing indulgence ' (Rainy, p. 287).

The indictment proceeds in the words **they glory in their shame.** What they deem to be their glory is, when rightly viewed, a ground of shame. ' What they valued themselves upon, what they inwardly, at least, rejoiced in, and applauded themselves for, what they would, perhaps, have most cheerfully dwelt upon in congenial company, were things of which they had every reason to be ashamed ' (Rainy, p. 288). What precisely is it that Paul means by **their shame** ? The reference surely is not, as some have thought, to their circumcision. Nor is it the actual indulgence in which they glory ; nor yet, as Rainy thinks, the resources they have gathered for the worship of their god the belly. Paul is probably thinking of their perverted liberty. They would boast of their Christian liberty ; they would glory in their freedom ; but in their case it was a liberty debased and prostituted. Did they only know it, their glory was a reason for shame and humiliation.

The description closes with the words **these men of earthly mind !** The R.V., somewhat more literally, has ' who mind earthly things.' The verb whose participle is employed in the phrase is the verb, found twice in ver. 15 and often elsewhere in our epistle, of which more than once we have had occasion to state that it denotes much more than mere intellectual perception. The present phrase denotes that the whole trend and inclination of the life of these persons is towards the things of earth. The same verb is used in the injunction of Col. 3 : 2 : ' mind what is above, not what is on earth.' **These men of earthly mind** is a terrible indictment of men who profess to comprehend and live by the faith of Christ.

CHAPTERS III AND IV

iii. Joy and Steadfastness in the Lord (III. 1*a*, 20, 21 ; IV. 1)

1*a*, 20 **Well then, my brothers, rejoice in the Lord. But [For] we are a colony of heaven, and we wait for the Saviour who**

21 **comes from heaven, the Lord Jesus Christ, who will transform the body that belongs to our low estate till it resembles the body of his Glory, by the same power that**

iv. **enables him to make everything subject to himself.**

1 **So then, my brothers, for whom I cherish love and longing, my joy and crown, this is how you must stand firm in the Lord, O my beloved.**

The expression with which the Apostle introduces this paragraph appears in our translation as **well then.** Both the A.V. and the R.V. render it by ' finally.' In 4 : 8, where the same expression recurs, our translation agrees with the A.V. and the R.V. in the rendering ' finally.' The phrase consists of the Greek adjective meaning ' remaining ' preceded by the definite article, and may be rendered literally 'as for what remains.' The expression itself does not of necessity denote that when a writer employs it he is about to bring his writing to a close. It is, however, the kind of phrase that is more likely to be required towards the end of a writing, and is often correctly rendered by means of some such word as 'finally.' It is also a natural phrase to use in making a transition to a fresh subject, and Paul not seldom uses it when he passes to the more practical section of a letter. In its present occurrence the expression would seem to mark a transition. From this point on our epistle consists of a number of paragraphs, all save one quite brief, in which the Apostle appears to be replying to various specific points raised in a letter which he had received from Philippi. The present paragraph is the first of these.

So far our exposition of chap. 3 has proceeded on the supposition that vers. 1*b*–19 are a Pauline fragment which did not originally form part of the Epistle to the Philippians. We now return to the actual letter sent to Philippi, combining, to form the present paragraph, a clause that in the traditional text precedes the interpolation with three verses that follow it.

There does not seem to be much doubt that ver. 20 originally opened with the word 'for,' as in the A.V. and the R.V., and not with but, as in our translation. It is true that a considerable number of ancient authorities can be mustered in support of the reading but. Among all these, however, there is only one Greek manuscript—a cursive of the sixth century. All the rest are either versions or citations in early writers. This evidence for the reading but shows that 'for' was felt to be awkward; but it stops far short of proving that but was the original reading. 'For,' seemingly, was changed to but to enable ver. 20 to attach itself more easily to the interpolation.

Even with the true reading 'for,' it is not an impossible task to discover more or less satisfactory ways of attaching ver. 20 to the closing part of the interpolation. We may, for example, regard the verse as furnishing a reason for the injunction to copy the Apostle (vers. 17–19). Or we may connect ver. 20 more directly with the description of the

N   177

enemies of the cross of Christ in vers. 18, 19 (and in particular with the closing words of the description ' these men of earthly mind ') and regard it, with Vincent, as ' confirming the statement concerning the one party by showing the opposite course or character of the other.' Or, again, we may think that between ver. 19 and ver. 20 there passed through the Apostle's mind a thought that did not find actual expression in his words. That is Lightfoot's way of establishing the connexion, for he paraphrases thus : ' Their souls are mundane and grovelling. They have no fellowship with *us* ; for *we* are citizens of a heavenly commonwealth.'

Other points of possible contact or contrast between ver. 19 and ver. 20 have been noted by expositors, as for example by Bengel, who finds in **Saviour** (ver. 20) a designed contrast to ' destruction ' (ver. 19), and in **Lord** (ver. 20) a contrast to ' the belly is their god ' (ver. 19). But when all has been said that can be said, it must be conceded that ver. 20 in its true and original form does not follow ver. 19 with ease and naturalness. On the other hand, it will readily be admitted that it follows in a most natural manner after the injunction of 3 : 1*a* : **My brothers, rejoice in the Lord ; for we are a colony of heaven.**

Confirmation of the hypothesis that ver. 20 originally came directly after 1*a* may perhaps be found in the fact that the text as thus rearranged reminds us of the words of Jesus to the Seventy recorded in Luke 10 : 20, which may well have been in the Apostle's mind. ' Rejoice,' says Jesus to the Seventy, ' because your names are enrolled in heaven.' **Rejoice in the Lord,** says the Apostle to the Philippians, **for we are a colony of heaven.** The words of Jesus allude to the ' book of life ' which Paul actually mentions in 4 : 3 ; and it is significant that the mention of it leads him immediately (in 4 : 4) to repeat the injunction to rejoice. The thought in Phil. 3 : 20 is clearly the same as that in Luke 10 : 20. In his comment on the Lucan text Trapp remarks that to have their names written in heaven was to be ' enrolled burgesses of the New Jerusalem.' See the paper on ' The Philippian Interpolation : Where does it End ? ' in the *Expositor* for January 1920.

At this point in our epistle, as we have seen, the Apostle makes a transition. He now appears to be taking up one by one certain things which the Philippians had mentioned in a letter to him. It is easy by reading between the lines of the present paragraph (3 : 1a, 20, 21 ; 4 : 1) to discern what was taking place at Philippi, and to surmise what the Philippians had said in their letter. The Christian community was being persecuted by those who looked upon the new faith as something incompatible with Roman citizenship and as involving disloyalty to the Emperor. Such charges were frequently levelled against the Christians. The words of our paragraph suggest that the persecuted believers were tempted to lose heart. All this they had recorded in their letter. So the Apostle pleads with them to rejoice in the Lord and to stand firm in him. How natural against a background of persecution are the many terms of endearment which he employs in his effort to cheer them, as well as his mention of their citizenship, more august than that of Rome, and of their Saviour, more potent than the Emperor. Only against such a background does the present paragraph become intelligible. The same background lies behind 1 : 27–30.

Well then, my brothers, rejoice in the Lord. Note how the 1a expressions **my brothers** and **in the Lord** are taken up again in 4 : 1—another hint that 3 : 1a and 4 : 1 were not originally as far apart as they are in the traditional text.

The word rendered **rejoice** is translated 'farewell' in the margin of the R.V. It can, and often does, bear that meaning. In 2 Cor. 13 : 11, for example, it is suitably rendered 'goodbye' in our translation. But that meaning is not by any means as suitable as **rejoice** in the present verse. The margin of the R.V. has 'farewell' for the same word again in 4 : 4. It is **in the Lord** that Paul bids the Philippians rejoice. How easily this phrase, or some equivalent, comes to him ! Only 'in Christ' could the harassed Christians at Philippi triumphantly rejoice in the face of persecution.

For we are a colony of heaven—that is the ground on 20 which the Apostle bases the injunction of ver. 1a. The sudden change to the first person is quite in Paul's manner.

179

Frequently, when addressing his readers in the second person, he suddenly turns to the first person as if to avoid the exclusion of himself from some privilege or responsibility. Compare 1 Cor. 5 : 7. In the present clause the Apostle employs a noun (*politeuma*) of which this is the solitary New Testament occurrence. Literally rendered, what he says would run : ' for our *politeuma* is in heaven.' A kindred verb is used in the phrase ' do lead a life ' in 1 : 27, which helps to confirm the view that the same background lies behind 1 : 27–30 and the present passage. Now, what meaning are we to give to the word *politeuma* ? The A.V. has ' for our conversation is in heaven.' ' Conversation ' here of course bears its archaic meaning of ' manner or intercourse of life,' the sense intended by the A.V. being, seemingly, ' our manner of life belongs to heaven, is in harmony with heaven.'

The most natural and probable meaning of *politeuma* here, however, is either ' citizenship ' or ' state.' The R.V. has ' citizenship ' in its text, and ' commonwealth ' in its margin. Either ' citizenship ' or ' state ' gives excellent sense. Most modern expositors seem to favour ' state.' But would Paul have said that the Christian's state was *in* heaven ? Would he not rather have said that heaven *was* his state or city ? For this reason we take his meaning to be ' for our citizenship is in heaven,' that is, we are enrolled as burgesses in heaven. Seeing that Paul and those whom he is addressing are citizens of heaven while not actually in heaven, it follows that they are colonists of heaven. This is how the excellent rendering of our translation is arrived at. Souter, in his *Pocket Lexicon*, says that the word *politeuma* itself sometimes means a colony, adding that this meaning gives excellent sense in the present passage. We do not know what evidence there is for this meaning, but even if the word could mean a colony that would not here be a suitable meaning, for it would make the Apostle say ' our colony is in heaven,' which surely is not what he means.

The same conception of the august citizenship of the Christian believer is found in Eph. 2 : 19 and in Heb. 11 : 13 ff. With such passages as these should be compared the description of the Christians in the fifth chapter of the *Epistle to Diognetus*, where occurs the statement that 'they pass their time upon the earth, but they have their citizenship in heaven.'

Philippi was a Roman colony—a miniature Rome in distant Macedonia. Many of its inhabitants would be Roman citizens, and these would constitute the aristocracy of the city. How many Roman citizens were members of the Christian community we have no means of ascertaining. The Roman citizens at Philippi were intensely proud of their citizenship, as we may see from Acts 16 : 20, 21. If these proud Romans were charging the Christians with the crime of belonging to a fellowship that involved disloyalty to Rome and the Emperor, we can imagine how Paul's noble words would comfort and hearten his readers. It is not the common word 'is' from the ordinary verb 'to be' that the Apostle employs in the present sentence, but a verb which lays stress on the actual existence of the citizenship ; it is as if he were assuring them that their heavenly citizenship is no delusion, no mere dream of the fancy. There is emphasis, too, on the word 'our'— '*our* citizenship is in heaven'—which is intelligible only if Paul had some other citizenship in his mind as he wrote. This again corroborates our reading of the situation that occasioned the writing of this paragraph.

To the statement that he and his fellow-Christians are a colony of heaven the Apostle adds that they are possessed of a mighty expectation : and we wait for the Saviour who comes from heaven, the Lord Jesus Christ. In Greek (as in several other languages) the word for heaven is often plural. It is so in tᴸe opening clause of this verse—for we are a colony of heaven. The clause with which we are now dealing—the one that speaks of waiting for the Saviour—is in the Greek a relative clause in which the word heaven does not actually occur. As the relative pronoun is in the singular, some scholars (among whom are Bengel, Lipsius, and Kennedy) have contended that heaven cannot be its antecedent. The antecedent, they say, must be the *politeuma*, which must therefore here be used in a local sense, seeing that the Saviour

181

is to come from it. It is quite permissible, however, to regard the relative phrase as of the nature of an adverb (meaning ' whence ') and to take heaven as the antecedent. It is **from heaven,** as our translation rightly has it, that the Saviour is expected.

The Greek literally says ' *a* Saviour,' not ' *the* Saviour,' the absence of the definite article serving to draw attention to the character or capacity in which the Lord Jesus Christ was looked for. There is, too, some emphasis on the word ' Saviour,' which is not easy to explain. Some detect in the emphasis an implied contrast between his coming as Judge and his coming as Saviour. Can it be that the words of Jesus to the Seventy are still in Paul's mind ? Jesus tells them that he had watched Satan fall from heaven. From that same heaven Paul waits for a *Saviour* !

Our translation is at one with the R.V. in rendering the verb in this clause by **wait for.** The Greek verb denotes a waiting that is eager, intense. The A.V. renders by ' look for,' which perhaps has in it more of the idea of eager longing than has **wait for.** The verb implies a concentration on one object to the disregard of all else. It is used in Rom. 8 : 19, 23, 25, I Cor. 1 : 7, Gal. 5 : 5, Heb. 9 : 28, I Pet. 3 : 20, and seems to have been a favourite word to use of the expectation of the Parousia. That expectation was a cardinal element in the life of the early Church, and its moral power is well illustrated by our present passage.

Jesus is expected as **Saviour.** Apart from the Pastorals, the only other occurrence of the word ' Saviour ' in the Pauline epistles is in Eph. 5 : 23. In the New Testament as a whole the word occurs only twenty-four times, ten of these being in the Pastorals, and not one of the ten in those parts which appear to be genuine Pauline notes. In eight of the twenty-four occurrences the word refers to God. The Old Testament often speaks of God as a saving God, using for the most part a verbal participle to express the thought. In this the LXX generally follows the example of the Hebrew, though sometimes it employs the Greek noun, as for example in Isa. 45 : 21. The source of the Christian use of the term for God and Christ

was probably the Old Testament usage. It is true that the
Old Testament does not once speak of the Messiah as Saviour,
but it was inevitable that the term should be applied by the
Christians to the Christ who had saved them from evil spirits,
from the oppression of fatalism, from the bondage of the Law,
and from sin. The term was employed in the Cults for the
saviour-god. It was also applied to Zeus, Apollo, and others
of the gods ; and there exists an abundance of inscriptional
evidence to show that it was applied to the Roman Emperors
(see Deissmann, *Light from the Ancient East*, pp. 368, 369).
The Christians at Philippi would be charged by their opponents
with the criminal folly of putting themselves outside the pale
of the Saviour-Emperor's care and protection. Paul reminds
them that they also have their Saviour, that their state has
its Emperor. Notice the full name and title—**the Lord Jesus
Christ.**

Ver. 21 states what the Saviour will do at his coming : 21
**who will transform the body that belongs to our low estate
till it resembles the body of his Glory, by the same power that
enables him to make everything subject to himself.** Why
does Paul specifically mention the transformation of the body
as the work to be accomplished by the Saviour at his Parousia ?
Some think he introduces this thought as a contrast to the
thought of the desecration of the body by the Antinomians
spoken of in ver. 19 ; but there is nothing in ver. 21 that
naturally suggests the persons referred to in vers. 18, 19.
If vers. 1*b*–19 are an interpolation, then ver. 21 is brought
into close proximity to the latter part of chap. 2, and it is
possible that it was the thought of the all but mortal illness
of Epaphroditus that led Paul to think of the **body that belongs
to our low estate.**

But it may not be necessary to find in the context a **reason**
for the reference to the transformation of the body. At the
Parousia that is just what would remain to complete their
salvation. If any explanation is required of the mention of
the body, perhaps it may be found in the fact that the Philippian Christians were being subjected to bodily suffering and
torture. We remember that lashes and imprisonment were

the lot of Paul himself at Philippi, and the suggestion that the Philippians were now undergoing suffering in some ways similar is lifted out of the region of surmise by the words of 1 : 30. We remember also how his Roman citizenship had stood the Apostle in good stead at Philippi : would not the thought of the nobler citizenship which they shared with him put new spirit into the suffering Christians at Philippi ?

The body in its present state is described by the Apostle as **the body that belongs to our low estate.** The R.V. has 'the body of our humiliation,' while the A.V. renders 'our vile body.' There is not the least suggestion in the Greek of Stoic contempt for the body as the unhappy rendering of the A.V. might lead one to suppose. When Archbishop Whately in his last illness heard his chaplain read the words of Paul in the rendering of the A.V., he exclaimed, 'Read his own words ! ' **The body that belongs to our low estate** is just what the Apostle means. To him our present life is a state of humiliation as compared with the state of glory that awaits us. The body we now have is in keeping with our present low estate. It is subject to weakness, the home of fleshly lusts, the ready instrument of sin.

There are several points of contact between the present paragraph and vers. 5–11 of chap. 2. A verb cognate with the noun rendered **low estate** is used of Christ in 2 : 8—' he humbly stooped.' **Glory** in ver. 21 answers to the same word in 2 : 11. The verb rendered **transform** embodies the noun translated ' form ' in 2 : 8, while the adjective that underlies the words **till it resembles** embodies the noun rendered ' nature ' in 2 : 6. These points of contact go far towards justifying the inference that the passage in chap. 2 was in Paul's mind as he wrote the passage in chap. 3 ; and they make it difficult to believe that the present paragraph is not an original part of the Epistle to the Philippians. They tell strongly against Kirsopp Lake's theory that the interpolation extends as far as 4 : 3.

The transformed body will resemble **the body of his Glory.** This is also the rendering of the R.V., and is far superior to that of the A.V.—' his glorious body.' The phrase means ' the body which he now has in his state of exaltation '—' the form,' as Vincent puts it, ' in which his perfect spiritual being is manifest.' That is what the believer's body will resemble ! Paul's expectation climbs to dizzy heights. And if the believer's body is to be like his Lord's, it follows that his spirit also must be like his, for spirits that were not alike would not be thought of as inhabiting bodies of the same nature. ' We are children of God now, beloved ; what we are to be is not apparent yet, but we do know that when he appears, we are to be like him—for we are to see him as he is ' (1 John 3 : 2).

Paul does not picture the life to come apart from the body ; he has not cast off his Jewish mode of thought in order to replace it by the Greek doctrine of the immortality of the soul. ' Paul shrank, with Pharisaic dislike, from any Hellenic conception of the immortality of the soul apart from a body. His realism made him shudder at any idea of disembodiment. It is not possible to determine his exact view of the risen body, which he regarded as essential to the risen life ; sometimes he suggests that the present body will be transformed, sometimes that an entirely fresh body will be ours ; but he certainly believed in the creation of a new organism by the Spirit which should be adequate to the needs of the new spirit ' (Moffatt, *Paul and Paulinism*, pp. 37, 38). It may be that the idea of a transformed body and that of a body entirely fresh were not to him mutually exclusive. ' Niagara,' says Beet, ' remains the same while every drop of water is ever changing.'

The remainder of the verse tells that the Saviour will bring to pass this great transformation **by the same power that enables him to make everything subject to himself.** Literally the words might be rendered ' in accordance with the power,' etc. The transforming of the believer's body will be in keeping with his mighty power. There is a suggestion in the clause that great power will be needed to effect the transformation ; but the task will not be beyond the Saviour's power. Calvin remarks that the object of the clause is to remove every possible doubt. The Philippian Christians need have no fear lest his power should prove inadequate for the task. Was Paul led to speak of the power of the Lord by his recollection of the words of Jesus recorded in connexion with the return of the Seventy ? See Luke 10 : 19 and 22.

The word used by Paul for **power** is used only of superhuman power in the New Testament. In 2 Thess. 2 : 9 and 11 it refers to diabolical power, and in all its other occurrences (Eph. 1 : 19, 3 : 7, 4 : 16 ; Col. 1 : 29, 2 : 12, and the present passage) to divine power.

The Apostle was certain that ultimately Christ would subdue all things to himself. ' For he must reign,' he tells the Corinthians, ' until all his foes are put under his feet. (Death is the last foe to be put down.) For God has put everything under his feet ' (1 Cor. 15 : 25–27*a*). Of this universal victory the changing of the believer's body will form a part ; it is part of the subjection of all things to him. The object of the transformation is to make us more fit for his service.

iv. 1 Now comes the direct injunction to stand firm in spite of persecution and depression. Our translation is right in not beginning a fresh paragraph with this verse. **So then, my brothers, for** whom I cherish love and longing, **my joy and crown, this is how you must stand firm in the Lord, O my beloved.** So then, that is, seeing that you have such abundant reason for rejoicing in the Lord. The appellation **my brothers** is repeated from 3 : 1*a*. To it the Apostle now adds **for whom I cherish love and longing.** In the Greek this clause consists of two adjectives, which are translated ' beloved ' and ' longed for ' both in the A.V. and in the R.V. Not only does the Apostle love them : he also longs to have them near him. This is the only occurrence of the second of the two adjectives in the New Testament. The multiplication of terms of endearment in this verse is a sign of the Apostle's deep sympathy with his suffering readers.

He tells them that they are his **joy and crown.** Beet remarks that this joy is ' understood only by those who have children in the faith.' Cf. 1 Thess. 3 : 9. The word used by Paul for **crown** is sometimes employed, it is true, for a kingly crown, the sign of sovereignty, but it more commonly represents the festive garland, or the garland bestowed as a reward of victory in the games. The Philippians are the Apostle's reward or his token of victory. Jewish rabbis were wont to speak of their disciples as their crown. Many expositors hold that when Paul addresses the Philippians as his crown, he is thinking exclusively of the Day of the Lord. But there is nothing in his words to preclude the thought that they are now his crown as they are now his joy. At the same time we know from vers. 20 and 21 of chap. 3 that the Parousia is in his mind, and so probably the thought of their being his crown on the great day is not absent. We remember how he says to the Thessalonians : 'For who is our hope, our joy, our crown of pride (who but you?) in the presence of our Lord Jesus on his arrival? Why, you, you are our glory and joy!' (1 Thess. 2 : 19, 20).

This is how you must stand firm in the Lord. How? Surely as persons who rejoice in the Lord because of their privileges and prospects. Only by rejoicing in the Lord shall they be able to stand firm in the Lord. The joy of the Lord is to be their strength. Thus, and thus only, shall they be proof against the malevolence of their persecutors. Often—but not always because of identical perils—the Apostle urges his converts to stand firm. See 1 Cor. 15 : 58, 16 : 13, Gal. 3 : 1, 1 Thess. 3 : 8. Most impressive are the words O my beloved at the end of the verse. Paul ' seems to linger over this theme, as if unable to break away from it ' (Lightfoot).

CHAPTER IV

EUODIA AND SYNTYCHE (IV. 2, 3)

I entreat Euodia and I entreat Syntyche to agree in the Lord. 2
And you, my true comrade, lend a hand to these women, 3
I beg of you; they have fought at my side in the active
service of the gospel, along with Clement and the rest of
my fellow-workers, whose names are in *the book of life*.

This is the second of the series of paragraphs in which Paul seems to be dealing with specific matters mentioned by the Philippians in a letter addressed to him. It is tantalizing in its brevity, and raises many questions which it leaves un-answered.

2   I entreat Euodia and I entreat Syntyche to agree in the Lord. We mention at the outset, in order to set them aside, the fantastic attempts of critics from Baur to Hitzig to dis-cover in these two names allusions to two parties in the early Church. For a statement of these theories see Zahn's *Intro-duction*, vol. 1, pp. 561, 562, and Lightfoot's detached note on 'Clement my fellow-labourer' on pp. 168–71 of his *Philippians*. Small wonder that Ellicott should speak of such attempts as 'monstrous,' or that Moffatt (*Introduction to the Lit. of the N.T.*, p. 171) should describe them as 'perverse.'

Euodia and Syntyche are names of persons, not of parties. In the A.V. the former appears as the name of a man—'Euodias.' Theodore of Mopsuestia (*circa* 350–428) tells of some who took the second of the two to be a man's name—Syntyches. He also mentions the fact that some held that Syntyches was the husband of Euodia and that he was none other than the jailer who figures in the story of Acts 16. The versions of Tyndale and Cranmer also make the second a man's name. Grotius took both persons to be men. Neither Euodias nor Syntyches has been found as the name of a man, whereas Euodia and Syntyche, as names of women, are common in inscriptions, though neither, as it happens, occurs in any of the inscriptions that have been found in Philippi. That in the present passage they are the names of two women belonging to the Church at Philippi would seem to be put beyond reasonable doubt by the expression 'these women' in ver. 3, for it is almost impossible to think that these words do not look back to the persons spoken of in ver. 2.

Ramsay suggests that one or other of these two women was Lydia, but there is nothing to lift the suggestion out of the region of conjecture. A feature of the account of Paul's visits to the cities of Macedonia in Acts 16 and 17 is the prominence of women. Lightfoot (pp. 55–7) calls attention to the testimony of Macedonian inscriptions which 'seem to assign to the sex a higher social influence than is common among the civilized nations of antiquity' (p. 56).

It is possible that the estrangement of Euodia and Syntyche lay at the root of the dissensions which make their presence felt so frequently in our epistle. In his appeal to them the Apostle significantly repeats the verb **I entreat,** ' as if,' says Bengel, ' he were exhorting each separately face to face.' This is in keeping with his determination, manifest throughout the letter, not to countenance the divisions in the Church. The repetition implies that in this quarrel, as in most, there was blame on either side. It is strange that the Vulgate should here employ two different verbs—*rogo* and *deprecor*.

Paul entreats them **to agree in the Lord.** The expression here rendered **to agree** is used also in 2 : 2, where our translation has ' living in harmony.' See the note there, and also the note on the words ' to be thinking of you all ' in 1 : 7. Literally, the phrase may be rendered ' to think the same thing,' but it means much more than ' to agree in thought or opinion.' Paul urges the two women to strive after a unity of sentiment and feeling, a harmony of life. And he entreats them to agree **in the Lord.** Once again the familiar phrase occurs. In Christ would their differences disappear. Let them but realize their common relation to him and the estrangement would be at an end. Some see in the fact that Paul urges them to agree **in the Lord** an indication that the quarrel was a religious controversy ; but whatever the nature of the dispute may have been, we cannot think of his urging them to agree in any other way than in the Lord.

The direct appeal to Euodia and Syntyche Paul supplements **3** by an appeal on their behalf addressed to a third person who is asked to exercise a ministry of reconciliation. **And you, my true comrade, lend a hand to these women, I beg of you.** The request is in the Greek introduced by a particle which is represented in the R.V. by ' yea.' Lightfoot observes that it introduces ' an affectionate appeal.' Paul uses it also in the appeal of Philem. 20. In our translation in the present passage there is no actual English word representing the Greek particle, but its presence makes itself felt in the tone of affectionate urgency which marks the rendering of the appeal. When Paul says **I beg of you,** he employs a different verb from the one he has just used in his appeal to Euodia and Syntyche. The verb rendered **beg** occurs also in 1 Thess. 4 : 1, 5 : 12 ; 2 Thess. 2 : 1, and nowhere else in Paul's epistles. He uses it only in his letters to Macedonian Churches. In 1 Thess 4 : 1 the two verbs ' beg ' and ' entreat ' occur in the same sentence, and Moulton and Milligan give an example of the same combination from a papyrus (*Vocabulary*, p. 255). ' To entreat ' is a more authoritative word than ' to beg.' The latter is a more friendly word, used more naturally than the former in addressing one's equal. Findlay (on 1 Thess. 4 : 1) says of the verb ' to beg ' that it ' conceives the request in a question-form (" Will you do so and so ? ") and thus gives a personal urgency to it.'

This third person the Apostle addresses as **my true comrade.** The A.V. and the R.V. both render by ' true yokefellow,' which brings out the primary significance of the designation. Who is the person whom Paul addresses in this way ? In the attempt to find an answer to this question conjecture has been most assiduous. Every possible person has been suggested, and some that are impossible. Clement of Alexandria surmised that the ' true comrade ' was the Apostle's wife, and Renan appended to this surmise the further conjecture that his wife was none other than Lydia ! Trapp succinctly disposes of this view with the comment : ' Not Paul's wife, for he had none,' which would seem to be a legitimate deduction from 1 Cor. 7 : 7. If Paul had a wife at this time, one wonders why she should now be at Philippi ; and moreover, if he had been addressing a woman, the Greek would have been slightly different. Wieseler thought the appeal was addressed to Christ, the words being a prayer. But it is in the highest degree improbable that the Apostle would introduce into his letter the direct speech of his prayer. Nor is it probable that he would address Christ as his ' yokefellow ' ; though this last objection could be overcome by giving to the noun its other possible, but less probable, meaning of ' joiner-together.' Some have seen Barnabas in the **true comrade.** Others favour Luke (see Ramsay, *Paul the Traveller and Roman Citizen*, p. 358, and David Smith, *Life and Letters of St. Paul*, p. 519). Bengel, followed by Wesley, suggests Silas. Estius fixes upon Timotheus, and some who favour this suggestion call attention to the fact that the same adjective true is applied to Timotheus in 1 Tim. 1 : 2, while the cognate adverb is employed in 2 : 20 of our epistle, where Paul speaks of his 'genuine interest' in the welfare of the Philippians. Victorinus, Grotius, and Lightfoot regard Epaphroditus as the person addressed by Paul. Neither of these last two views, however, is at all probable, for both Timotheus and Epaphroditus were now with Paul, and it is hard to believe that words spoken in the first instance as an aside in the course of dictation would have found their way into the letter.

The interpretation that commends itself to the majority of recent English writers is the one that treats the Greek word rendered comrade as a proper name—'Synzygos.' The word is printed as a proper name in the margin of Westcott and Hort's Greek Testament ; and in his *Introduction to the Lit. of the N.T.* (p. 171) Moffatt strongly inclines to this view. If this be the correct interpretation, the adjective true (see the note on the word 'genuine' in 2 : 20) would seem to suggest that Paul is playing on the meaning of the name— 'you who are a Synzygos (comrade) not in name only, but in very deed.' Compare the play on the name Onesimus in Philem. 11. It may be urged against this hypothesis that 'Synzygos' is nowhere else found as a proper name ; but the objection is not fatal. It may have been a name assumed at baptism. Whether it be a proper name or not, the person addressed would be some prominent and influential member of the Christian community at Philippi, whose identity would be obvious to the readers of the letter. It is possible that they had made mention of him in their letter to Paul as standing in some sort of relation to the estrangement of Euodia and Syntyche. It may be that when he was at Philippi the Apostle had been wont to call him his comrade. Chrysostom suggested that he might have been the husband or the brother of one of the women. If the husband, then it is possible that the correct rendering is, not my true comrade, but 'true consort,' that is, the true consort of one of the women ; this is a legitimate rendering, for the word **my** is not actually represented in the Greek. Luther and Ellicott take the person addressed by Paul to be the chief of the bishops at Philippi; but this, of course, is mere conjecture; we do not even know that one of the bishops was chief. Clearly the data do not permit of certainty.

Whoever he may have been, he is asked to **lend a hand** to the women. The same verb is used in Luke 5 : 7. The manner of Paul's appeal to him suggests that the women were themselves endeavouring to adjust their differences, and perhaps finding the task none too easy. The plea on their behalf is reinforced by means of an argument based upon the services they had rendered to the cause of the gospel. They are worthy of all the sympathy and help that the **true comrade** can give to them. **They have fought**, says Paul, **at my side in the active service of the gospel.** Once again the Apostle derives his metaphor from the arena. See the note on ' fighting side by side ' in 1 : 27—the only other occurrence of the verb in the New Testament. It means to ' contend or strive along with someone else.' The rendering of the A.V. and the R.V. —' laboured with me '—fails to bring out adequately the ideas of opposition and strife involved in the word. Euodia and Syntyche had at one time been united in strenuous service in the face of opposition, and perhaps it was the persecution which the Philippian Church was now enduring that was prompting them to attempt to bring the estrangement to an end. Paul says they had fought at his side **in the active service of the gospel**, or, more literally, ' in the gospel,' the phrase denoting the sphere of their joint efforts. For the phrase compare Rom. 1 : 9 and 1 Thess. 3 : 2.

The Apostle adds **along with Clement and the rest of my fellow-workers, whose names are in** *the book of life*. For the hypothesis—which originated with Origen and became traditional in the Western Church—that the Clement to whom Paul alludes is to be identified with Clement of Rome, see Lightfoot's detached note (pp. 168–71) in which the theory is examined. It is only a conjecture, and a most improbable one at that.

These words regarding Clement and Paul's other fellow-workers are in our translation rightly taken in conjunction with **they have fought at my side in the active service of the gospel.** This is far more satisfactory than the view which would attach them to **lend a hand to these women.** Zahn, however, argues for the latter interpretation, and Lightfoot strongly inclines to it. But on *a priori* grounds it is not probable that Paul would desire a number of persons to engage in the delicate task of helping to reconcile two women who were at variance. Zahn contends that inasmuch as Paul is here emphasizing the claims of Euodia and Syntyche on the good offices of his **true comrade,** his argument would only be weakened by the mention of others who had been partners with them in the service they had rendered. The mention of Clement and the others may, however, be introduced to help the **true comrade** to recall some specific occasion which the Apostle has in mind. It may be that Clement and his unnamed companions had surrendered their lives on that occasion. The inference is often drawn from the words **whose names are in the book of life** that they were no longer living.

In the Apocalypse we read five or six times of the ' book of life ' (3 : 5, 13 : 8, 17 : 8, 20 : 12, 15 ; 21 : 27), but outside of the Apocalypse the expression occurs in the New Testament only in our present passage, although the idea embodied in the phrase appears in Luke 10 : 20 and in 3 : 20 of our epistle. The phrase or some equivalent is found several times in the Old Testament : that is why it is printed in italics in our translation. Charles maintains that originally to have one's name enrolled in the **book of life** implied participation in the *temporal* blessings of the Theocracy ; eventually the meaning of the expression was changed, and it came to refer to an immortality of blessedness (see his note on 1 Enoch 47 : 3). God will not forget His own, obscure and nameless though they be.

JOY AND PEACE (IV. 4-7)

Rejoice in the Lord always. I will say it again, ' rejoice.' 4
Let your forbearance be known to everyone; the Lord is 5
at hand. Never be anxious, but always make your 6

requests known to God in prayer and supplication with
7   thanksgiving; so shall God's peace, that surpasses all our
dreams, keep guard over your hearts and minds in Christ
Jesus.

It is the custom of expositors to interpret this paragraph
against the background suggested by the appeal addressed to
Euodia and Syntyche. On this view the Apostle is still dealing with the reciprocal relations of the members of the Christian community at Philippi. In harmony with this the word
rendered ' forbearance ' in ver. 5 is interpreted on the lines
of the definition given of it in Aristotle's *Nicomachean
Ethics,* where it is said to be the spirit that keeps a man from
insisting on his rights to the detriment of others, and makes
him willing to accept less than his just due.

The paragraph, however, as it seems to us, demands a different background. The Apostle now drops the internal
dissensions of the Church, and is led by his sympathy with
his harassed and persecuted readers to address to them some
further words of comfort and encouragement. The background of 4 : 4–7 is identical with that of 1 : 27–30 and 3 : 1*a*,
20, 21 ; 4 : 1. Note how in 4 : 5, as in 3 : 20, 21, appeal is made
to the great inspiriting fact of the approaching return of the
Lord. It may be that it was the mention of the ' book of life '
in 4 : 3 that induced the Apostle to renew the exhortation to
rejoice (see on 3 : 1*a* and 20).

4   **Rejoice in the Lord always**: the injunction of 3 : 1*a* is repeated, but now with the addition of **always.** Their joy is to
be uninterrupted and unbroken. No passing cloud is to
darken their serenity. ' Rejoice at all times ' is the Apostle's
injunction to another Macedonian Church (1 Thess. 5 : 17) ;
and in 2 Cor. 6 : 10 he speaks of himself as ' grieved but always
glad.' As in 3 : 1*a*, it is **in the Lord** that he again bids them
rejoice. ' As " the Lord " is to Paul Jesus risen and reigning,
to rejoice in him is simply to appropriate and rest upon the
Christian facts of freedom and redemption won by him for
men ' (Moffatt, in the *Expository Times,* vol. ix, p. 335).
Here as in 3 : 1*a* the margin of the R.V. has ' farewell ' for

rejoice. Lightfoot would include both meanings; but **rejoice** alone is adequate and preferable.

In the remainder of the verse the Apostle expresses his determination to repeat the exhortation : **I will say it again, 'rejoice.'** The R.V. also has the future ' I will say,' which is a more correct rendering than the present (' I say ') of the A.V. We can hardly think that Paul would have expressed himself in this way had not the conditions at Philippi been such as to make the injunction to rejoice seem almost unreasonable. In spite, however, of annoyance and persecution, unbroken joy is possible in the Lord. Kennedy aptly quotes George Herbert's comment on Paul's twice-repeated injunction : ' He doubles it to take away the scruple of those that might say, what, shall we rejoice in afflictions ? ' In the *Expository Times*, vol. xxxv, pp. 151 ff., Rendel Harris makes the interesting suggestion that in Paul's doubled exhortation we have an echo of certain words in the closing scene of the *Eumenides* of Aeschylus.

Paul now speaks of the spirit which his readers should **5** manifest in the face of persecution. **Let your forbearance be known to everyone.** The word rendered **forbearance** is in the Greek a neuter adjective doing duty as an abstract noun. The cognate noun is found in Acts 24 : 4 and 2 Cor. 10 : 1. There is no difference of meaning between the noun and the neuter adjective as used in our present passage. The adjective occurs also in 1 Tim. 3 : 3, Titus 3 : 2, Jas. 3 : 17, 1 Pet. 2 : 18. ' Forbearance ' is also the rendering of the text of the R.V. in our passage, the margin having ' gentleness.' The A.V. renders by ' moderation.' The Greek word, as Moulton and Milligan remark, is ' a very elusive term ' (*Vocabulary*, p. 238). In the present context it stands for the spirit that does not attempt to retaliate, but submissively endures persecution. It is used of Jesus in 2 Cor. 10 : 1. Compare 1 Pet. 2 : 23. Wesley renders ' yieldingness, sweetness of temper.' Trench (*Synonyms*, p. 151) includes courtesy, patience, patient mind, in his list of renderings of the word in various English translations, adding that ' gentleness ' commends itself to him as the best English equivalent. It may be that here (as seems to be the case in ver. 6) the Apostle has in mind the teaching of Jesus. See Matt. 5 : 38 ff.

In support of the interpretation which **we give to the word** we may note that in 2 Cor. 10 : 1 it is used in conjunction with the word which the R.V. renders by 'meekness,' and that the adjective is used in 1 Tim. 3 : 3 and Titus 3 : 2 side by side with the adjective meaning 'disinclined to fight.' So in Jas. 3 : 17 we find it in the company of such adjectives as 'peaceable' and 'conciliatory.' In one of Moulton and Milligan's examples (*Vocabulary*, p. 238) the noun stands in contrast to insolence and force. In his letter to the Ephesians (chap. 10) Ignatius employs the noun in just the sense which, as we contend, should be given to it in our present passage. The words of Ignatius make it clear that his readers were exposed to persecution. We quote Kirsopp Lake's rendering, in which 'gentleness' stands for the word we are discussing. 'Be yourselves gentle,' writes Ignatius, 'in answer to their wrath ; be humble-minded in answer to their proud speaking ; offer prayer for their blasphemy ; be steadfast in the faith for their error ; be gentle for their cruelty, and do not seek to retaliate. Let us be proved their brothers by our gentleness and let us be imitators of the Lord, and seek who may suffer the more wrong, be the more destitute, the more despised.' Paul and Ignatius are urging upon their respective readers the same behaviour.

The Philippian Christians are to let their **forbearance be known to everyone.** The expression suggests that Paul has in mind a wider circle than the Christian community. All the heathen inhabitants who came into any sort of contact with the Christians are to know their spirit of gentle forbearance by seeing it in action. The believers are to demonstrate it in all their intercourse with them. Compare Matt. 5 : 16.

It is no easy task for human nature to display this spirit with unbroken consistency under provocation. That is why the Apostle adds that **the Lord is** at hand, for the very thought of his nearness would prove a stimulus. Two interpretations of this clause are possible, both of which are allowed by the **Greek.** The clause has been taken to mean (*a*) 'the Lord is nigh unto you, present with you to aid and to bless.' This gives excellent sense. Analogous statements are numerous in the Old Testament. Moule thinks Ps. 119 : 151 makes this interpretation probable, for there the LXX employs the very word that Paul uses here for at hand. The clause has also been interpreted to mean (*b*) ' the Lord is coming soon.' This is the commonly accepted and the more probable interpretation. The expression ' Maran atha ' in 1 Cor. 16 : 22 is probably the same statement in Aramaic. The phrase in its Aramaic form may well have been used as a watchword in the early Church. If this second interpretation be accepted, we have here the fifth reference in our epistle to the return of Christ. The Philippian Christians could afford to be gentle and conciliatory, for the Lord at his coming would avenge them upon their oppressors. Cf. Rom. 12 : 19. The minatory tone of the clause points to the fact that Paul has the pagan persecutors in mind.

The hostile attitude of their pagan neighbours might well 6 cause anxiety to arise in the hearts of the Philippian Christians. That explains the counsel **never be anxious.** Here again the Apostle is echoing his Master's teaching. See Matt. 6 : 25-34. They must *never* be anxious, or ' in nothing,' as the R.V. more literally has it. Paul allows no exception. To the Corinthians he writes in a similar strain : ' I want you to be free from all anxieties ' (1 Cor. 7 : 32).

The Apostle points out a more excellent way than the path of anxiety. **Never be anxious,** *but* **always make your requests known to God in prayer and supplication with thanksgiving.** Always ! The A.V. and the R.V. both render more literally ' in everything.' There is an evident contrast with ' in nothing ' in the preceding clause. ' The way to be anxious about nothing is to be prayerful about everything ' (Rainy, p. 332). The word rendered 'request' occurs also in Luke 23 : 24 and 1 John 5 : 15, and means a particular petition or the definite object asked for. Prayer and supplication are combined also in Eph. 6 : 18, 1 Tim. 2 : 1, 5 : 5. This is the only occurrence in our epistle of the word here rendered **prayer** ; it is a more general term than supplication, standing as it does for man's approach to God in the widest sense. The narrower and more particular term **supplication** occurs also in 1 : 4 (twice) and 1 : 19. It means a specific appeal, a petition for the supply of a definite want. Though it is possible thus to distinguish between prayer and supplication, ' the two words thus linked together are meant less to be distinguished than to include and enforce the fullest and freest "speaking unto the Lord "' (Moule). Every possible cause of anxiety should be made known to God, or, more literally, ' in the presence of God,' even as the letter of Sennacherib was spread before Him by Hezekiah (2 Kings 19 : 14, Isa. 37 : 14). And every request is to be presented **with thanksgiving.** The spirit of gratitude is a necessary element in the prayer that is an antidote to anxiety. Prayer and thanksgiving are combined also in 1 Thess. 5 : 17, 18, Col. 4 : 2, 1 Tim. 2 : 1. Frequently does the Apostle enjoin upon his readers the duty of thanksgiving. Cf. Eph. 5 : 20 and Col. 4 : 2.

7 If the requests are always thus made known to God, a certain consequence inevitably follows : **so shall God's peace, that surpasses all our dreams, keep guard over your hearts and minds in Christ Jesus.** Here only in the New Testament do we find the expression **God's peace,** for in Col. 3 : 15 the true reading is ' the peace of Christ,' not ' the peace of God.' It is called **God's peace** because it is His gift and is akin to the peace that abides in Him. Wesley defines it as ' that calm, heavenly repose, that tranquillity of spirit, which God only can give.' In ver. 9 God is called ' the God of peace.' Cf. 2 Thess. 3 : 16.

The peace of God is described in the words **that surpasses all our dreams.** Both the A.V. and the R.V. have ' which passeth all understanding.' The verb occurs also in 2 : 3 and 3 : 8. The Greek of the clause is capable of a double interpretation. The meaning may be that God's peace accomplishes more than any forethought or scheming on our part can ever achieve. This is the interpretation adopted by Lightfoot, Vincent, Jones, Plummer, etc. On the other hand, the clause may mean that God's peace is beyond the power of man's mind to comprehend. This is the interpretation adopted in our translation, and it is also that of Ellicott, Moule, Kennedy, Beet, etc. Between the two interpretations it is by no means easy to decide. In favour of the former it is sometimes urged that the latter gives a sense which has no special relevancy. In favour of the latter is the fact that it is the interpretation of the Greek expositors. It is supported too by Eph. 3 : 20 : 'Now to him who by the action of his power within us can do all things, aye far more than we ever ask or imagine,' where the verb 'imagine' is cognate with the noun used in our clause. Lightfoot, though he rejects this interpretation, admits that it receives strong support from this Ephesian text. Either explanation gives good sense, and there is no compelling reason for accepting one rather than the other. Some interpreters would combine the two.

The verb **shall keep guard over** appears in the A.V. as ' shall keep ' and in the R.V. as ' shall guard,' on both of which the rendering of our translation is an improvement. The same verb occurs in 2 Cor. 11 : 32, Gal. 3 : 23, 1 Pet. 1 : 5. It is the natural and usual word to employ when speaking of a garrison keeping guard over a city, and it is more than possible that Paul had that metaphor in his mind. Philippi was guarded by a Roman garrison, and the figure would appeal with special force to the readers. It may be that their pagan persecutors were alleging that the adherents of the new faith had forfeited their right to the protection of the city garrison. Paul reminds them that they have an inward sentinel—none other than God's own peace.

This peace of God would keep guard over their **hearts and minds.** The same words are used in the A.V. to render the objects of the verb. The R.V. has ' your hearts and your thoughts.' The word rendered **heart** is found also in 1 : 7, where our translation has ' mind.' We there saw that it frequently denotes the seat of the intelligence. The word rendered **mind** in the present verse is beyond doubt used in 2 Cor. 3 : 14, 4 : 4 to denote the faculty of thought. Whether it is used in that sense here is doubtful. If it is so used, then Paul speaks of two faculties, in which case **heart** possibly stands for the seat of the affections and the will, and mind for the seat of the intelligence.

It is possible, however, that the second term means not mind but ' thought.' ' Thought ' is the more natural meaning of the word considered by itself. If we give it that meaning here, then the Apostle's promise is that God's peace will keep guard both over the minds of his readers and over the thoughts that arise out of them. It is not easy to reach a definite decision. It may perhaps be contended that the metaphor of keeping guard over suits the faculty of thought somewhat better than it suits the thoughts that are its product—a consideration which lends support to the rendering adopted in our translation.

Paul brings this noble sentence to a close with the great phrase **in Christ Jesus**. It is the third reference to Christ in this brief paragraph! Some interpreters speak of Christ Jesus as the citadel in which the believer is guarded by God's peace. But such a view only confuses the figure. If the metaphor of a garrison is in Paul's mind at all, it is man's inner being that is pictured as a citadel over which God's peace keeps guard. The phrase **in Christ Jesus** is introduced to remind the readers that outside of him there is no guardianship, no security, no peace, no joy. When God's peace leaves the citadel, it is a sign that peril is at hand ; the unclean spirits of vindictiveness and anxiety are claiming again their old habitation. Kennedy quotes Rendel Harris (*Memoranda Sacra*, p. 130) to the effect that ' this peace is like some magic mirror, by the dimness growing on which we may discern the breath of an unclean spirit that would work us ill.' The paragraph opened with joy : it ends with peace. If God's peace be not in the heart, then assuredly there is no joy. They alone whose hearts are guarded by His peace are able to sing His song.

PAGAN MORALITY AND CHRISTIAN TRUTH (IV. 8, 9)

8 Finally, brothers, keep in mind whatever is true, whatever is worthy, whatever is just, whatever is pure, whatever is attractive, whatever is high-toned, all excellence, all

merit. Practise also what you have learned and received 9 from me, what you heard me say and what you saw me do ; then the God of peace will be with you.

This paragraph may well have been written in answer to a question from Philippi. Often, however, it is supposed to have been added to prevent a possible misunderstanding of the paragraph that immediately precedes. Vers. 6 and 7, it is thought, might possibly have given the readers the impression that all that was required of them in order to secure the guardianship of God's peace was that they should make their requests known to God. Paul anticipates any such misconception—so the exponents of this view maintain—by declaring that if the peace of God is to be with them, they must keep in their minds all things good and noble, and put into practice the things they had learned from him, whether by direct instruction or through his example.

Vers. 8 and 9, however, when subjected to closer scrutiny, would seem to require some other explanation to account for their presence. In ver. 8 Paul seems to be thinking not of the specific virtues of the new faith, but rather of 'pagan' morality. Of the eight words employed in this great catalogue of virtues, two are found here only in the New Testament ; another occurs nowhere else in the Pauline epistles, and another still nowhere else except in the Pastorals. This suggests that some at least of the words were not everyday terms in the Christian vocabulary. The list reminds one of the catalogues of virtues to be found in the writings of the Greek moralists. Some of the terms, as we shall see when we examine them, suggest certain features of Roman life and institutions. The probability is strong that the Apostle is here commending what was good in pagan life and morality. Plummer quotes from von Soden's *Early Christian Literature*, p. 113, the statement that 'nowhere has the born Jew approached so closely to the moral ideal of the Greek philosophers as in the conceptions of honour and worth which he here strings together.'

Now, there must have been some special reason to account

for the penning of this elaborate injunction to keep in mind the virtues of pagan ethics. We cannot do much more than surmise what that reason may have been. The Philippian Christians, as we learn from other parts of our epistle, were being persecuted. Were their persecutors claiming superiority for their own virtues? Did the fact that they were being persecuted tend to blind the Christians to what was good in the heathen life by which they were surrounded? Did they regard pagan excellences as demonic caricatures of Christian virtues? Were they troubled by the problem of the relation of pagan to Christian morality? Had they inquired of the Apostle what should be their attitude to pagan ethics? It may be that there existed among them a difference of opinion on this question; that may explain the promise that if they give obedience to the Apostle's injunction, the God of peace will be with them. Is it because he is anxious to conciliate some of them that Paul once again introduces the word **brothers**?

8 **Finally** renders the same Greek expression that in 3 : 1a is rendered ' well then.' See the note there. The use of the expression in the present verse may be due to the consciousness on Paul's part that the letter is now drawing towards its close. But even so it is not probable that he intended to convey exactly the meaning that is conveyed by the English word ' finally,' seeing that the important paragraph dealing with the gift of the Philippians (vers. 10–20) is to follow. It may be that the phrase here, as often elsewhere, does little more than mark a transition from one subject to another.

In his catalogue of virtues the Apostle employs six adjectives and two nouns. In the Greek the adjectives are all in the plural. Both the A.V. and the R.V. render literally ' whatsoever things are true,' etc. The singular of our translation (**whatever is true**, etc.) expresses the meaning with equal exactness. Let us first look at the six adjectives in turn. The sixfold repetition of **whatever is** imparts to the verse a stately impressiveness.

True: so also the A.V. and the R.V. render the first of the adjectives. The reference must not be confined to truthfulness in speech, as Bengel's comment—*in sermone*—would restrict it. Veracity of course is included ; but Paul has in mind all that is true in thought, disposition, and deed. Sincerity is covered by the phrase. Moulton and Milligan remark that in the papyri the adjective ' seems always to bear the normal meaning of " true in fact " ' (*Vocabulary*, p. 21).

Worthy : the A.V. has ' honest ' in its text, with ' venerable ' in the margin ; the R.V. has ' honourable ' and ' reverend ' in its text and margin respectively. The adjective is found elsewhere in the New Testament only in 1 Tim. 3 : 8 and 11, Titus 2 : 2, and the cognate noun only in 1 Tim. 2 : 2, 3 : 4, Titus 2 : 7. Etymologically it is related to a verb which means to reverence or worship. It is frequently used in the Greek writers of the gods and goddesses—of Apollo, Demeter, Pallas Athena, and many more. It is used also to describe things associated with the gods and goddesses, such as temples and sacrifices. It is not restricted, however, to these uses, for it is applied to human beings and to things other than those we have just specified—more often to persons than to things. The natural words by which to render it into English are such as august, solemn, noble, majestic, dignified. **Worthy** scarcely does justice to the richness of its connotation. When the A.V. was produced, the word ' honest ' was nearer in meaning to the Latin *honestus* than it is to-day, signifying as it then did ' worthy of honour ' or ' regarded with honour.' Maurice Jones remarks that here the adjective ' would represent the " gravitas," the noble seriousness of the best Roman type.'

Just : so also the A.V. and the R.V. render. In the papyri the word is applied to such things as a ' just ' measure or a ' just ' rule (Moulton and Milligan, *Vocabulary*, p. 162). The widest possible significance must be given to the word in our passage ; it describes that which is in accordance with the loftiest conception of right. Paul was probably thinking of the estimable features of Roman law and government.

Pure : here again our translation agrees with the A.V. and the R.V. The cognate adverb is used in 1 : 17. Like the word rendered worthy, this word also is in the Greek writers ' frequently applied to heathen gods and goddesses '

(Trench, *Synonyms*, p. 333). Trench also observes that it is the adjective ' predominantly employed ' ' to express freedom from impurities of the flesh.' It should not, of course, be restricted to that meaning in the present passage. Moulton and Milligan (*Vocabulary*, p. 5), after giving examples of its various uses in the papyri, remark that ' the adjective and its derivatives may accordingly take a wide meaning, as wide as our *pure* in the ethical sense.' Jones observes that ' there would be associated with the word the thought of domestic purity which in the best Roman life reached a high standard.'

Attractive : both the A.V. and the R.V. have ' lovely.' This is the solitary occurrence of the word in the New Testament. It can be used both of persons and of things. Its primary meaning is ' love-inspiring.' When the A.V. was first issued, the English word ' lovely ' still retained a sense of its derivation and meant ' worthy of being loved.' When used of *things*, the adjective here employed means pleasing, grateful, attractive. There are in Sirach two interesting examples of its use as applied to persons. One is in 4 : 7 : ' Make thyself attractive to the congregation,' or, as the R.V. renders, ' Get thyself the love of the congregation.' The other occurs in 20 : 13 : ' He that is wise in words shall make himself beloved ' (R.V.). In the next section of our epistle we shall find several words or expressions that are used in Sirach. One wonders whether Paul had been reading Sirach just before writing to the Philippians, and whether this word **attractive** was suggested to him by the passages we have quoted.

High-toned : both the A.V. and the R.V. have ' of good report,' the latter also having ' gracious ' in its margin. Like the preceding adjective, this one also is in the New Testament confined to this single occurrence. In 2 Cor. 6 : 8 our translation agrees with the A.V. and the R.V. in rendering the cognate noun by ' good report.' In our present passage the rendering ' of good report ' is based on the assumption that the root-meaning of the adjective is ' well-spoken of.' The more probable primary meaning, however, is ' well-speaking.' From this are derived such meanings as uttering-

sounds-of-good-omen, fair-sounding, auspicious. The adjective
would apply to anything that had a good ring. ' High-
toned ' is an exact English equivalent. Moulton and Milligan
observe that ' a suggestion of the earlier associations of this
word may perhaps be found in Phil. 4 : 8, where it recalls
Greek ethical teaching, and " signifies the delicacy which guards
the lips, that nothing may be expressed in public worship that
could disturb devotion or give rise to scandal " ' (*Vocabulary,*
p. 267 ; the quotation in the extract is from a work by
E. Curtius).

Lest any virtue should perchance have been omitted the
Apostle appends the words **all excellence, all merit.** The more
literal rendering of the A.V. and the R.V. runs : ' if there
be any virtue, and if there be any praise.' Nowhere else
in the Pauline epistles is the word rendered **excellence** to be
found ; and elsewhere in the New Testament it occurs only in
1 Pet. 2 : 9 and 2 Pet. 1 : 3 and 5. The English word ' virtue,'
as Moulton and Milligan (p. 75) observe, ' is too narrow for a
word which had nearly all the forces of our adjective " good." '
Excellence is a more satisfactory, because a more inclusive,
rendering ; and it is interesting to note that in the later papyri
the Greek word is used like our ' Excellency ' as a title of
courtesy (see Moulton and Milligan, p. 76). Lightfoot's
explanation of the word—' whatever value may reside in your
old heathen conception of virtue '—suits our view of the
passage as a whole. The word is one of the great terms of
heathen ethics, and to explain its rarity in the New Testament
we draw once more on Moulton and Milligan : ' The limitation
of this word to four occurrences in N.T. may possibly be
connected with the very width of its significance in non-
Christian ethics : it had not precision enough for large use
in Christian language ' (p. 75).

For **merit** both the A.V. and the R.V. have ' praise.' Praise
is the common meaning of the word. In 1 : 11 it is used of
the **praise** of God. Nine out of its eleven New Testament
occurrences are in Paul. Here the word evidently stands for
that which deserves praise. Hort (on 1 Pet. 1 : 7) observes
that whenever the Greeks use the word carefully ' they

THE EPISTLE OF PAUL TO THE PHILIPPIANS

include in it moral approbation.' **Merit** brings out the meaning well.

According to our translation, Paul urges his readers to **keep in mind** the things to which these great and noble terms apply. The A.V. and the text of the R.V. have ' think on these things,' while the margin of the latter has ' take account of.' The verb is common in the New Testament, particularly in the epistles of Paul. It occurs in 3 : 13 of our epistle, where the Apostle says : ' I for one do not *consider* myself to have appropriated this.' In the papyri, too, the verb ' is common in the sense of " reckon," " put down to one's account " ' (Moulton and Milligan, p. 377). **Keep in mind** is scarcely adequate. Paul tells his readers to ' take into account ' or ' not to leave out of account ' the virtues he has enumerated. The Philippian Christians cannot afford to ignore the great virtues of pagan morality. Let them reflect upon them and endeavour to form a true judgment regarding them, so as to give them their rightful place in their lives.

9 Not only must the Philippian Christians take into account all that is of worth in pagan morality : they must also put into practice the things they have learned from the Apostle himself. No contrast is intended between thinking in the one case and practising in the other ; for the ' thinking ' in ver. 8 has, as Ellicott says, ' a distinctly practical reference.' A distinction, however, is intended—and our translation makes this clear—between the things which Paul in ver. 8 urges his readers to take into account and the things which in ver. 9 he urges them to practise.

They are to practise ' the things which you learned and received and heard and saw in me.' So the words run when literally rendered. The first pair of these four verbs refer to the definite Christian instruction which the Philippians had received from the Apostle ; the second pair to the example he had set them. In our translation these clauses are thus rendered : **what you have learned and received from me, what you heard me say and what you saw me do.** The words **from me** are not actually represented in the Greek, but must be understood from the ' in me ' of the next clause. To learn

206

and to receive are by some expositors distinguished as mental apprehension and moral approbation respectively, and the distinction may well be intended, for the verb rendered ' to receive ' seems at times to mean ' to accept, to approve.'

There is room for doubt whether the rendering **what you heard me say** correctly interprets the clause ' the things which you heard in me.' Unless we are to think that Paul makes a distinction between his formal instruction and his informal talk—which is scarcely probable—this rendering makes the clause identical in meaning with the words which immediately precede. What the Apostle means, as we think, is ' what you heard of as being in me and what you have actually seen in me,' or in other words, ' my demeanour as you heard of it and as you saw it.' When he speaks of their ' hearing ' of his demeanour, we are not forced to conclude that he is thinking only of his behaviour when he was away from Philippi, for even when he was in their city the whole body of Philippian Christians could not possibly see and observe him all the time. They would tell each other of what they had individually seen of his demeanour. Their knowledge of his life even when at Philippi would be dependent in part on hearsay. The jailer, for example, would tell of his behaviour in the prison. It is possible, however, that Paul has in mind the reports which had reached Philippi of his demeanour in other places.

The paragraph ends with a promise of the blessing that will be theirs if obedience be given to the double injunction. **Then the God of peace will be with you.** Then is an improvement on the ' and ' of the A.V. and the R.V., for the clause describes a result that will follow if heed be given to the commands. God is called the God of peace also in Rom. 15 : 33, 16 : 20, 1 Thess. 5 : 23, Heb. 13 : 20. In 2 Cor. 13 : 11 He is called ' the God of love and peace.' In 2 Thess. 3 : 16 Christ is ' the Lord of peace.' Cf. also 1 Cor. 14 : 33. The promise of ver. 9 is greater and more wonderful even than that of ver. 7 ; for it is now declared not merely that God's peace will be with them, but God Himself, the author and fountain of peace. Divine peace in all the varieties of its manifestations will abound if the God of peace be with them.

GRATITUDE AND SELF-SUFFICIENCY (IV. 10-20)

10 It was a great joy to me in the Lord that your care for me could revive again; for what you lacked was never the care but
11 the chance of showing it. Not that I complain of want,
12 for I have learned how to be content wherever I am. I know how to live humbly ; I also know how to live in prosperity. I have been initiated into the secret for all sorts and conditions of life, for plenty and for hunger, for
13 prosperity and for privations. In him who strengthens
14 me I am able for anything. But you were kind enough
15 to take your share in my trouble. You Philippians are well aware that in the early days of the gospel, when I had left Macedonia, no church but yourselves had any financial
16 dealings with me ; even when I was in Thessalonica, you
17 sent money more than once for my needs. It is not the money I am anxious for ; what I am anxious for is the interest that accumulates in this way to your divine credit !
18 Your debt to me is fully paid and more than paid ! I am amply supplied with what you have sent by Epaphroditus, *a fragrant perfume*, the sort of sacrifice that God approves
19 and welcomes. My God will supply all your own needs
20 from his wealth in Glory in Christ Jesus. Glory to God our Father for ever and ever : Amen.

Now at last Paul speaks specifically of the gift which the Philippians had sent to him. The particle with which this paragraph is introduced is not actually represented in our translation. In the A.V. and the R.V. it appears as ' but.' According to Lightfoot, the particle here ' arrests a subject which is in danger of escaping.' ' It is,' he adds, ' as if the Apostle said " I must not forget to thank you for your gift." ' The particle, however, affords no justification whatsoever for the suggestion that the epistle came near to being sent off without the present paragraph. It is frequently used when transition is made to a fresh subject, and may well be omitted in an English translation.

It is the fashion to assume that the present paragraph is Paul's first expression of thanks for the gift ; but the assumption seems to us to contradict all the available evidence. We learn from 2 : 25–30 that in the interval that had passed since the coming of the gift, news had passed from Ephesus (where Paul now is) to Philippi and again from Philippi to Ephesus. That in itself almost amounts to a proof that in the course of that interval letters had passed between Paul and the Philippians. Of this conclusion ample corroboration is furnished by the present paragraph, for it permits us to deduce by fair inference that a letter had come from Philippi along with the gift, that Paul had already replied to that letter, and that the Philippians had written to him a second time complaining of what appeared to them to be a lack of adequate appreciation of their kindness. It is to this second letter from Philippi that the Apostle makes reply in our epistle. See the paper on ' The First and Second Epistles to the Philippians' in the *Expository Times* for December 1922.

The position of the paragraph at the very close of the epistle lends some slight support to the contention that this is not Paul's first expression of thanks. It is possible that passing allusions to the gift are to be detected earlier in the letter, as, for example, in 1 : 5. But the Apostle, as Kennedy puts it, ' has not, up till now, *expressly* thanked them for their generous gift.' Had the present letter been the first to go to Philippi with his thanks, he would surely not have deferred his reference to their gift until he had said everything else that he had to say. There is, too, a certain indirectness in his manner of expressing his thanks which accords with the view that he had already written to thank the Philippians.

The Apostle's extraordinary emphasis on his independence in this paragraph points to the same conclusion ; for such emphatic insistence on his own self-sufficiency is neither natural nor seemly unless it be an expansion in self-defence of some earlier statement which had been misconstrued by his correspondents. A passing allusion to his independence might conceivably have been introduced into an initial expression of thanks, but scarcely so pronounced a declaration as meets us in this paragraph.

Furthermore, a note of rebuke can be clearly detected in the Apostle's words. It is true that he rebukes with gentleness and delicacy ; none the less the presence of the rebuke is unmistakable (see the notes on vers. 15 and 18). The censure becomes more intelligible if Paul is defending himself against a misinterpretation of something he had previously said about the gift or about his own attitude thereto. As we shall see, the phraseology of ver. 15 suggests that it was the Philippians themselves who first introduced into the correspondence the mention of their previous acts of kindness ; and as we may safely assume that they would not have done this in the letter that accompanied the gift, we can only conclude that their doing so was the outcome of resentment caused by something that had been said by Paul in his first letter of thanks.

The very structure of the present paragraph makes plausible a surmise regarding the statement made in Paul's first letter and resented by the Philippians ; for the passage exhibits a seemingly nervous alternation between gratitude and appreciation on the one hand, and insistence on his independence and self-sufficiency on the other. Gratitude or appreciation is expressed in ver. 10, vers. 14–16, and vers. 18–20, whereas the intervening verses (namely, vers. 11–13, and ver. 17) set forth the Apostle's independence. The very manner in which the change is made from gratitude to independence or back from independence to gratitude shows that the Apostle is somewhat anxiously endeavouring to strike the balance between the two—to avoid on the one side the Scylla of seeming to lose his independence when he is appreciative, and on the other side the Charybdis of appearing to be lacking in appreciation when insisting on his independence. We seem to be driven to the conclusion that he was conscious of some constraint. He does not write as one who is free to express his thanks in a straightforward, natural way. The method he adopts is intelligible only on the supposition that he is expanding in self-defence some previous statement which his readers had misconstrued. If our reasoning is sound, it follows that in his first letter the Apostle had said (*a*) that he was thankful for the gift, but (*b*) that he was not in actual need of it. The latter statement it was that gave offence to the Philippians, for to them it appeared to point to a want of appreciation ; and in their chagrin they remind the Apostle of the occasions on which he had been glad to receive their help. Paul, however, does not recant ; on the contrary, he repeats his earlier declarations, though not in the brief form in which they were originally made. He expands, enlarges, and explains. The present paragraph is but a fuller statement of his gratitude and his independence, and the strange alternation that marks it is intelligible only when seen against some such background as we have sketched.

What was it that led the Apostle to say in his first letter that he was not in actual need of the help that the Philippians had sent to him ? The answer to this question is suggested by ver. 10. There Paul tells of his great joy that (as the R.V. literally renders) ' now at length ye have revived your thought for me.' It is often said with truth that the words rendered ' now at length ' do not of necessity involve reproach, and it is also true that the Apostle adds a clause—**for what you lacked was never the care but the chance of showing it**—which makes it clear that he was fully aware that the Philippians were not responsible for the delay. But even so the words ' now at length ' might easily have conveyed to the readers the impression that Paul was annoyed and aggrieved because of the delay. They would probably have read in them a rebuke of their tardiness. The only reasonable explanation of the choice by Paul of words capable of being thus construed is that he is quoting words that had first been used by the Philippians themselves. The phrase ' now at length ' must have occurred in an apology for delay which they had sent to Paul, and the natural place for such an apology would be in the letter that accompanied the gift. Desiring to assuage their regret at the delay, the Apostle—so we surmise—told them that he was not actually in need of the help they had sent.

His disavowal of need, however, though made with kindly intent, was read as evidence of want of appreciation, provoking the reply to which Paul makes answer in our epistle. Instead of mitigating their remorse, it evoked a recital of the occasions on which the Apostle had been glad to receive their assistance. Paul's reply is the noble passage we are now examining.

It is doubtful whether there is in the passage as much pleasantry as some writers think. The use of financial terms is unmistakable and sheds a certain glow of playfulness over the paragraph ; but the tone of the passage is too serious to admit of much pleasantry, for there quivers through it an anxious desire to banish misunderstanding from the minds of the readers and disappointment from their hearts.

Whether this be the Apostle's first acknowledgment of the gift, or, as we have argued, the second, no other acknowledgment comparable with it in sublimity has survived in the letters of the past. ' The passage,' says von Soden, ' presents as tactful a treatment of a delicate matter as can well be found in the whole range of high literature ' (quoted by Plummer, p. 99).

10 **It was a great joy to me in the Lord that your care for me could revive again.** The past tense—' it *was* a great joy '—is commonly interpreted as an epistolary past. According to this interpretation, the joy is that which the Apostle feels as he writes but which would be in the past when the letter was read at Philippi. This interpretation underlies and explains the present tense of the R.V. If, however, our reading of the situation is correct, the past tense admits of a more probable explanation. It describes the Apostle's feeling when he received the gift. So far from being indifferent or ungrateful Paul experienced **a great joy.** And it was a great joy **in the Lord.** In 3 : 1 and 4 : 4 he enjoins the Philippians to rejoice ' in the Lord.' In the present verse the phrase signifies that his joy was in keeping with his relation to his Lord ; it was free from any tincture of ingratitude or resentment such as would be unworthy of that relation.

The ground of his joy is expressed in the words that **your** care for me could revive again. This rendering has no adequate equivalent for the ' now at length ' of the R.V. which we have already discussed. The very same expression is used in Rom. 1 : 10, where our translation has ' at last.' We must not place any emphasis on the word **could** in the rendering of the present clause, as if Paul were surprised that their care for him should revive. There is no hint in his words that he had given up hope of witnessing its revival. The next clause shows that he was aware that the possibility of its revival was present **all** along. **Could revive again** in our rendering means ' was enabled to revive again.'

Paul uses a rare word for **revive**, this being its only occurrence in the New Testament. It suggests the picture of a tree putting on fresh foliage after the winter. The verb is found in Sirach 50 : 10. As was observed in the note on the word ' attractive ' in ver. 8, the present context exhibits some words or phrases found in Sirach ; and it is not impossible that Paul had just been reading that book. It is a Greek *verb* that underlies the word **care** in the present clause—the verb that is used in the phrase ' to be thinking of you ' in 1 : 7, and frequently elsewhere in our epistle. See on 1 : 7. It is not because the gift of the Philippians has come to him that Paul rejoices, but rather because their care for him has revived.

To avert the possibility of their reading into his words a censure of their tardiness, the Apostle adds : **for what you lacked was never the care but the chance of showing it.** Here again he employs a verb (' to be without opportunity ') which occurs nowhere else in the New Testament. What precisely was it that robbed the Philippians of the chance of showing their care ? Various answers have been given to this question. Ramsay has suggested that towards the end of his career family property came to Paul which enabled him to meet the expenses incident to an appeal to the Emperor (see *St. Paul the Traveller and the Roman Citizen*, pp. 310–13) ; and some scholars have maintained that it was the coming of this property that deprived the Philippians of the chance of helping him. Ramsay indeed is of the opinion that the Apostle was still provided with ample means when he wrote our epistle.

'It is plain,' he says, ' that he did not actually need the help that they now sent ' (*op. cit.*, p. 359). The impression left on our mind by the present passage is utterly opposed to this. And even if it were possible to demonstrate that Ramsay's suggestion that property came to the Apostle is in accordance with the facts, the Ephesian origin of our epistle would lessen the likelihood that the coming of the patrimony had anything whatsoever to do with the Philippians' lack of opportunity to manifest their care. The lack is more likely to have been due to some disability on their part than to the absence of need on the Apostle's part. Chrysostom surmised that it was their poverty that made it impossible for them to send help. Or perhaps no messenger was available to take the gift. In 2 Cor. 8 : 2 Paul speaks of the ' deep poverty ' of the Churches of Macedonia.

11   Vers. 11–13 contain Paul's first statement of his independence. The words **not that,** with which it is introduced, show that its object is to keep the readers from drawing an erroneous conclusion from the declaration of his joy in ver. 10. The words **not that I complain of want** may be literally rendered (as in the A.V. and the R.V.) ' not that I speak in respect of want,' that is, ' it is not the fact that you have relieved my want that makes me say what I have just said.' He disclaims an attitude to want that would make its removal a ground for joy. In itself this clause does not decide whether or not Paul was now provided with means. The context, however, seems to us to show unmistakably that he was not. The word here used for **want** occurs elsewhere in the New Testament only in Mark 12 : 44.

Paul proceeds to justify the assertion that the relief of his want was not the cause of his joy. **For I have learned,** he says, **how to be content wherever I am.** The pronoun is emphatic : *I* have learned. However rare an achievement it might be to reach this state, *he* had reached it. The adjective rendered **content** occurs here only in the New Testament, though the cognate noun is found in 2 Cor. 9 : 8 and 1 Tim. 6 : 6. ' Content ' is also the rendering of the A.V. and the R.V., but it scarcely does justice to Paul's adjective, which means ' self-sufficient ' or ' independent.' The adjective was common with the Stoics to describe the man who was self-sufficient for all circumstances. Paul's self-sufficiency, however, as ver. 13 shows differed *toto caelo* from that of the Stoics. ' The syllable *self-* states not the source, but the inwardness, of this sufficiency ' (Beet). The clause **wherever I am**, if literally rendered would be ' in the circumstances in which I am,' and might, taken alone, mean simply ' in my present circumstances '; but the context shows that the meaning here must be ' in whatever circumstances I find myself.'

This verse expands and explains the second half of ver. 11. **12 I know how to live humbly; I also know how to live in prosperity.** The main idea in Paul's mind when he speaks of living humbly is that of being in want. The verb rendered **to live humbly** is employed in classical Greek, as Moule points out, of the falling of a river in drought, and it is not impossible that the figure was present to the Apostle's mind. The same verb is used in 2 : 8 (' he humbly stooped ') and also in 2 Cor. 11 : 7 and 12 : 21. For Paul's own account of his privations see 1 Cor. 4 : 11–13 and 2 Cor. 11 : 23–27. Privations, however, could do him no harm. And he was equally immune from harm when fortune smiled : **I also know how to live in prosperity.** Very impressive is the repetition of **I know**—he knew the one secret as thoroughly as he knew the other. ' Sound bodies,' says Trapp, ' can bear sudden alternations of heat and cold.' ' For one man,' says Carlyle, ' who can stand prosperity, there are a hundred that will stand adversity ' (*Heroes*, 5).

The remainder of the verse consists of a more elaborate statement of Paul's self-sufficiency and his consequent adaptability to varied circumstances. **I have been initiated into the secret for all sorts and conditions of life, for plenty and for hunger, for prosperity and for privations.** The word ' initiate ' was the technical term for initiating into the Mystery Cults, and as such would be familiar to the readers. It came to be used without this technical connotation, but it is by no means improbable that the original meaning was in Paul's mind as he wrote. The present participle of the verb was used in later

Greek to denote a candidate for baptism (see Moulton and Milligan, *Vocabulary*, p. 418). This is the solitary occurrence of the word in the New Testament. The A.V. has ' I am instructed,' and the R.V. ' I have learned the secret.' It may be that its use implies (as Kennedy suggests) ' a difficult process to be gone through.'

The words **for all sorts and conditions of life** represent certain Greek words which may be literally rendered, as in the R.V., ' in everything and in all things.' The A.V. wrongly takes the former half of the expression to mean ' everywhere.' It is not easy to differentiate with precision between ' in everything ' and ' in all things.' The distinction commonly drawn is that the former means ' in each particular circumstance,' and the latter ' in all circumstances collectively '; but the whole phrase is probably nothing but a vague general expression, analogous to the English ' all and every,' bearing just such a meaning as is given to it in our translation. The four expressions **for plenty, for hunger, for prosperity, for privations** represent four infinitives in the Greek. **For prosperity** renders the same verb that is used earlier in this verse (**to live in prosperity**), and comes again in ver. 18. **For privations** renders a verb cognate with the word ' want ' in ver. 11.

13 This verse is a general statement of the Apostle's self-sufficiency, and sets forth its source and inspiration. **In him who strengthens me I am able for anything.** Paul's independence is the outcome of his dependence upon Another. Maurice Jones appositely quotes G. G. Findlay, who in his *Christian Doctrine and Morals* says: ' The self-sufficiency of the Christian is relative: an independence of the world through dependence upon God. The Stoic self-sufficiency pretends to be absolute. One is the contentment of faith, the other of pride.' The name of Christ which appears in this verse in the A.V. is rightly omitted in our translation, as in the R.V., for the support which it receives from ancient authorities is but meagre. It is not ' through ' Christ (as the A.V. has it) that Paul is able for anything, but in him—in vital union with him. The verb strengthens, or (as it may be rendered) ' infuses

power into,' speaks of the bestowal of a power that is inward
and hidden. The same verb is found in Acts 9 : 22, Rom.
4 : 20, Eph. 6 : 10, 1 Tim. 1 : 12, 2 Tim. 2 : 1, 4 : 17. This
inward strength which Christ supplies is described in Col.
1 : 29 as ' the divine energy which is a power within me.'
The verb **I am able** has reference to the outward manifestation
of this hidden power. The comprehensiveness of Paul's statement is arresting. There is no conceivable condition of life
that he cannot face, no fortune or misfortune that he cannot
stand. Cf. 2 Cor. 12 : 9, 10.

The part of the present paragraph that ends here has
become inseparably linked with Oliver Cromwell. Carlyle
quotes Harvey as follows : ' At Hampton Court, a few days
after the death of the Lady Elizabeth, which touched him
nearly,—being then himself under bodily distempers, fore-
runners of that Sickness which was to death, and in his bed-
chamber,—he called for his Bible, and desired an honourable
and godly person there, with others, present, To read unto
him that passage in *Philippians* Fourth : " *Not that I speak
in respect of want ; . . . which strengtheneth me.*" Which read,
—said he, to use his own words as near as I can remember
them : " This Scripture did once save my life ; when my
eldest Son died ; which went as a dagger to my heart, indeed
it did." And then repeating the words of the text himself,
and reading the tenth and eleventh verses, of Paul's contenta-
tion, and submission to the will of God in all conditions,—
said he : " It's true, Paul, *you* have learned this, and attained
to this measure of grace : but what shall *I* do ? Ah poor
creature, it is a hard lesson for me to take out ! I find it so ! "
But reading on to the thirteenth verse, where Paul saith,
" *I can do all things through Christ that strengtheneth me,*"—
then faith began to work, and his heart to find support and
comfort, and he said thus to himself, " He that was Paul's
Christ is my Christ too ! " And so drew waters out of the
well of Salvation ' (Carlyle's *Letters and Speeches of Oliver
Cromwell*, vol. iv, pp. 198, 199).

In vers. 14–16 Paul turns from his independence to speak 14
again of his appreciation of the kindness of the Philippians.

Some measure of rebuke, as we shall see, is mingled with the appreciation.

But you were kind enough to take your share in my trouble. Instead of **but**, the A.V. has 'notwithstanding,' and the R.V. 'howbeit,' either of which comes nearer to the meaning of the particle used by Paul than does the weaker **but**, for the particle brings into relief his desire to prevent his readers from drawing from the immediately preceding words the inference that he was lacking in appreciation. The words rendered **you were kind enough** represent Greek words which literally mean 'you did well,' or 'you did nobly.' The very same phrase is used in Acts 10 : 33. With the verb in the future tense the phrase is common in the papyri forming part of a request with the meaning 'please' or 'pray.' This exact use is found in 3 John 6 : 'Pray speed them on their journey worthily of God.' It is quite possible that in our present passage the phrase should be given a meaning more akin to its literal significance than the meaning given to it in our translation, and expressing a more generous commendation of the action of the Philippians than does the rendering **you were kind enough**. 'You did nobly,' says the Apostle 'in taking your share in my trouble.'

Trouble here is wider and more inclusive than poverty ; and when the Apostle commends his readers for sharing his trouble he is thinking not merely of the pecuniary help they had sent, but also of the sympathy that had prompted the gift, and especially of the vicarious ministry of Epaphroditus their envoy. Still, the sending of the money was a part of their participation in his trouble. A gift of money may be a means of fellowship.

15 Here, we think, is one of the points at which the note of rebuke can be detected—and that notwithstanding the fact that the verse has to do with acts of generosity to the Apostle performed by the Philippians. Why does Paul introduce the word **Philippians** ? He addresses his readers after the same manner in 2 Cor. 6 : 11 and Gal. 3 : 1. In the three passages, as it seems to us, the name is introduced in order to soften or tone down a rebuke, lest perchance it might seem too severe.

But are we justified in finding a rebuke in the present verse? Its opening words, when literally rendered, run thus: 'And ye yourselves also know, ye Philippians.' Paul says that they, as well as he, are acquainted with their past generosity to him. The verb which he employs is the ordinary verb 'to know.' Now, Rendel Harris has pointed out—in the *Expositor* for September 1898—that in 1 Thessalonians this verb in several of its occurrences bears the special meaning 'you have admitted in your letter,' or 'your letter shows that you are aware.' That, we suggest, is the meaning it bears in our present passage. The Apostle, it seems, is not alone in remembering the past kindnesses of the Philippians! A letter from Philippi has made it clear that the Philippians themselves also remembered them. Paul was not pleased that they should remind him of their former gifts. 'He who receives a kindness,' says Cicero, 'should never forget it; he who bestows a kindness should never mention it' (*Laelius*, 71). The Philippians had not scrupled to make mention of their past kindnesses.

If we are right in the surmise that the mention of the former gifts was in the first instance made by the Philippians, it follows that their feelings must have been hurt by something that Paul had said after he had received the gift brought by Epaphroditus, for we cannot think that the reminder formed part of the letter that accompanied the gift. The action of the Philippians becomes intelligible only if in his reply to that letter the Apostle had said something that brought disappointment to them and aroused their displeasure. We may be sure that they would detect the note of rebuke in Paul's present reference to their reminder, but the word **Philippians** would show that the reproof came from a heart that was full of tenderness even when it was rebuking.

Paul employs the Greek form of the Latin name *Philippenses*, and the very choice of this form may perhaps imply that as he wrote he had in mind the fact that Philippi was a Roman colony. He respects the natural pride of the Philippians in their Roman citizenship. See Ramsay in the *Journal of Theological Studies*, vol. i, p. 116. The choice of name does not,

however, justify the inference that his readers were all of
them Roman citizens. What proportion of them possessed
the Roman citizenship it is impossible to say. Some of them,
we may be sure, would possess it ; but in everyday speech all
the inhabitants of the city could be described and addressed
as *Philippenses*.

You are well aware, says the Apostle, that in the early days
of the gospel, when I had left Macedonia, no church but yourselves had any financial dealings with me. In the early days of
the gospel can only mean at the time when Paul first preached
the gospel in Macedonia. The clause rendered when I had
left Macedonia admits also of being rendered 'when I left
Macedonia,' that is, 'at the time of my departure from Macedonia.' It does not of necessity refer to the time after Paul
had left Macedonia, and we do not think that it does as a
matter of fact refer to that time. The most natural way to
take the next verse—ver. 16—is, we think, to regard the gifts
sent to Thessalonica as having been sent within the time
specified in the clause which we are now discussing. It is not
probable that Paul, who is here disclaiming lack of appreciation of the kindness of the Philippians, would first, in ver. 15,
refer to gifts sent to him after he had left Macedonia, and then
refer to earlier gifts sent to Macedonia just as if the mention of
them were an afterthought. Moreover, the words in the early
days of the gospel suggest that we should give to the immediately succeeding clause as early a reference as the Greek
permits. So, with Ellicott, we believe that in ver. 15 Paul has
in mind the dealings which the Philippians had had with him
' previously to, or possibly at, his departure ' from Macedonia.
If, however, our translation is right in giving to the clause the
meaning when I had left Macedonia, the reference will be to
the supplying of the Apostle's wants by ' the brothers who
came from Macedonia ' of which he speaks in 2 Cor. 11 : 9.
If, on the other hand, the clause means ' at the time of my
departure from Macedonia,' Paul may be thinking of all the
gifts that came from Philippi about that time, including those
that came to Thessalonica and are mentioned in ver. 16, as
well as the gift or gifts sent to Corinth and spoken of in

2 Cor. 11 : 9. For all we know to the contrary the Philippians may have sent gifts to Beroea, the last place Paul visited in Macedonia, and to Athens, the place first visited by him after his departure from Macedonia. If, as is possible, his stay in Beroea (Acts 17 : 10–13) was relatively brief as compared with his stay in Thessalonica (17 : 1–12), the help sent to Thessalonica might well have been thought of as coming at the time of his departure from Macedonia.

No church but yourselves had any financial dealings with me. It is with some hesitation that we question the precise accuracy of this rendering. It fails, as it seems to us, to do justice to a certain nuance that is discernible in the Greek. In the most deft and delicate manner possible Paul contrives in these words to rebuke the Philippians for reminding him of their past acts of generosity. The words are literally rendered in the R.V. : ' no church had fellowship with me in the matter of giving and receiving, but ye only.' The expression ' giving and receiving ' occurs in Sirach 41 : 9 and 42 : 7, and its use by Paul is another indication (see on ver. 8 and ver. 10) that he may have been reading Sirach just before writing this chapter. The phrase is taken from the language of commerce, in which it is used of the credit and debit sides of an account. Whether in the present passage its reference should be limited, as in our translation, to the giving of financial help by the Philippians and the receiving of it by the Apostle is, to say the least, debatable. So far as the literal meaning of the words goes, there is a sense in which the phrase could be applied to all the Pauline Churches, for in the case of each and all of them there was a giving and a receiving—a giving of spiritual gifts on the part of the Apostle, and a receiving of them on the part of the Churches. In its ordinary commercial use the phrase would seem to embrace both sides of a transaction—the giving of the wares and the receiving of the payment. So here it embraces, as we think, the passing of spiritual gifts from Paul to the Philippians as well as the passing from them to him of financial help. The Philippian Church stood in a class by itself because in its case a double transaction had been effected : the things of the Spirit had passed in one direction and gifts of money in the other. This is the interpretation of Chrysostom, Augustine, and most of the earlier expositors. It is also that of Calvin, and is adopted by Ellicott and Lipsius in modern times. The use of the phrase is a gentle reminder that the gifts of the Philippians had been matched and more than matched by the greater gifts that had come to them through the ministrations of the Apostle. The same thought is more openly expressed in 1 Cor. 9 : 11 : ' If we sowed you the seeds of spiritual good, is it a great matter if we reap your worldly goods ? ' Cf. also Philem. 19.

16   **Even when I was in Thessalonica,** continues the Apostle, **you sent money more than once for my needs.** In the Greek this verse is introduced by a particle which is not actually represented in our translation. This particle is capable of being rendered in two ways : it may mean ' that,' introducing an object clause (which in the present case would be parallel with the clause introduced by ' that ' in ver. 15), or it may mean ' for ' or ' because.' Both the A.V. and the R.V. have ' for.' If in ver. 15 we render ' when I had left Macedonia ' and understand Paul to be speaking in that verse of gifts sent to him after his departure from Macedonia, then the introductory particle in ver. 16 must be rendered by ' that,' inasmuch as gifts sent to Thessalonica cannot be an instance of gifts sent after he had left Macedonia. In that case ver. 16 calls attention to an even more signal example of the kindness of the Philippians than was in Paul's mind when he was writing ver. 15. Why, even before he had left Thessalonica they had sent help to him ! If, on the other hand, in ver. 15 Paul is thinking of gifts received by him before he had left Macedonia, it may be that those gifts are none other than the gifts sent to Thessalonica. In that case ver. 15 and ver. 16 both refer to the same gifts, the latter verse corroborating the statement made in the former. Either ' that ' or ' for ' would then suitably introduce ver. 16, the latter, perhaps, being a somewhat more natural introduction than the former. This second method of interpreting vers. 15 and 16 is, we think, the more probable. The word ' even ' points to the fact that they had sent help so soon after the Apostle's departure from Philippi—even at so

early a date—rather than (as some maintain) to the fact that Thessalonica was a much larger and wealthier city than Philippi ; for the relative wealth of the two cities would have no bearing at all on the relative wealth of the two Churches.

The Greek words rendered **more than once** occur also in I Thess. 2 : 18 and literally mean ' both once and twice.' It is not possible to decide whether this means just twice and no more, or whether it should be given a vaguer meaning as in our translation. The A.V. and the R.V. both have ' once and again.' Whichever meaning we give to the phrase, this verse implies (as does also the tenor of certain parts of the Thessalonian epistles) that the length of Paul's stay in Thessalonica was more than three weeks, which is the duration suggested by the narrative of the Acts of the Apostles.

The word **money** is not actually represented in the Greek. Paul appears scrupulously to avoid the direct mention of money throughout the paragraph. The phrase ' for my needs ' has some financial colouring, the preposition being common in the papyri to denote the object for which money is provided or exacted.

The Thessalonian epistles contain no allusion to the gifts from Philippi. In I Thess. 2 : 9 and 2 Thess. 3 : 8 the Apostle speaks of his strenuous toil at Thessalonica which made him independent of the Thessalonians. Clearly, then, the gifts of the Philippians did not render toil on his part unnecessary.

Now comes Paul's last statement of his independence. This **17** verse opens with the words rendered ' not that ' in ver. 11 : Paul is eager to dissipate any tendency on the part of the Philippians to imagine that it was the mere receiving of the money that gave him joy. **It is not the money,** he says, **I am anxious for.** What he actually says is ' the gift,' not **the money,** for he still seems to be deliberately avoiding the use of the word ' money.' Still, his meaning is that it is not the mere money he is anxious for. He uses the definite article, because he means the gift in any particular case— whatever gift they might from time to time send to him. The force of the present tense is that he is describing his habitual attitude.

What I am anxious for, he adds, is the interest that accumulates in this way to your divine credit. The repetition of I am anxious for is impressive. The word rendered interest is the ordinary Greek word for ' fruit,' and so it is translated in the A.V. and the R.V. But in the present context, as Chrysostom seems to have recognized, it naturally means interest, in harmony with the financial tone of the passage as a whole. Moulton and Milligan, *Vocabulary*, p. 321, remark that no example of the word used in this sense has been found in the papyri, but they quote the corresponding use of a kindred word ' as showing how easily this sense might arise.' The epithet divine is not actually in the Greek, but its introduction is suggested and justified by the character of the verse as a whole. The gifts of the Philippians are an investment, and each adds to the amount of the interest that God places to their credit. The time for which the interest accumulates is the Day of the Lord, and the verb used for ' accumulate ' suggests the abundance of the divine reward. It is the advantage that comes to his helpers, not the benefit accruing to himself, that the Apostle values and seeks. We are reminded of his words to the Corinthians : ' I want yourselves and not your money ' (2 Cor. 12 : 14).

18   Once again the note of gratitude is sounded. On that note the paragraph opened, and on that note it closes. Your debt to me is fully paid and more than paid ! The first half of this statement appears in the R.V. as ' I have all things.' Now the verb rendered ' I have ' is found in the papyri and on ostraca as ' a technical expression regularly employed in drawing up a receipt' (Deissmann, *Light from the Ancient East*, p. 111), and this usage has given to the *present* tense—which is the tense employed in our passage—the meaning ' I have received.' That is the rendering given in the margin of the A.V. Similarly the present tense is rendered by ' they have received ' in Matt. 6 : 2, 5, 16 (R.V.), and by ' ye have received' in Luke 6 : 24 (A.V. and R.V.). The verb is another of the financial terms used in this paragraph. The Apostle is giving his readers a receipt for their payment. Your debt to me is fully paid expresses his meaning exactly. Here again, as in

ver. 15, there is a delicate hint that the gifts of the **Philippians** are after all but the payment of a debt.

Not only is their debt fully paid, it is **more than paid.** Literally, what the Apostle says is ' I abound.' It is the verb which occurs twice in ver. 12 with the meaning ' to live in prosperity.' How could he be wanting in appreciation of a gift that more than paid any debt they owed to him ? **I am amply supplied,** he proceeds, **with what you have sent by Epaphroditus.** Now that their gift has come, no single need of his remains unsupplied. He piles statement upon statement to bring home to his readers the absurdity of imagining that he was not grateful. How could he be ungrateful when their gift made it possible for him to say that all his needs were amply supplied ?

In the remainder of the verse Paul speaks of the gift in terms that set forth its value in the sight of God. This is the climax of his refutation of the charge of ingratitude. If the gift is pleasing to God, how can the Apostle harbour any dissatisfaction ? To God it is **a fragrant perfume.** As the italic type reminds us, the phrase is quoted from the Old Testament, where it is frequently employed to describe an offering that is pleasing to God. See, for example, Gen. 8 : 21, Exod. 29 : 18, Lev. 1 : 9, 13, 17, Ezek. 20 : 41. It occurs also in Sirach 50 : 15 (17), and furnishes yet another point of contact between that work and the present paragraph. The phrase is used in Eph. 5 : 2, while the two nouns that compose it in the Greek both occur in 2 Cor. 2 : 14–16. Paul adds that the gift is **the sort of sacrifice that God approves and welcomes.**

The God who values the gift as a sacrifice offered unto 19 Himself will not be regardless of the needs of the givers. Cf. Prov. 19 : 17, Matt. 10 : 42, Heb. 6 : 10. **My God,** says Paul, **will supply all your own needs from his wealth in Glory in Christ Jesus.** My God occurs also in 1 : 3, where see the note. Does the Apostle here use the expression to suggest that his intimate relation with God gives him authority to declare what God will do ? Or does its use suggest the thought that God will not overlook or leave unrewarded a kindness done

Q   225

to one so intimately related to Himself ? Paul cannot himself reward his readers ; nevertheless they shall not go without reward. The repetition in this verse of the verb ' to supply,' which has just been used in ver. 18, is doubtless intentional and significant : the Philippians have supplied the Apostle's needs ; his God will supply *their* needs. Whether the Apostle has in mind material needs or spiritual needs or both classes of needs is matter of dispute among expositors. It is difficult to think that spiritual needs are not included, but, on the other hand, 2 Cor. 9 : 8 makes it possible, if not probable, that Paul is thinking of material needs as well, for there he says : ' God is able to bless you with ample means, so that you may always have quite enough for any emergency of your own and ample besides for any kind act to others.' This comprehensive interpretation is confirmed by the fact that Paul says *all* your own needs.

It is from his wealth **in Glory in Christ Jesus** that God will supply their needs ; or rather, more literally, ' *in accordance with* His wealth.' The rewarding will be not merely *from* His wealth, but also in a manner that befits His wealth—on a scale worthy of His wealth. God's wealth is a frequent theme in the epistles of Paul. See, for example, Rom. 2 : 4, 9 : 23. The words **in Glory** are not easy to interpret in the present context. By some they are taken to mean ' in a glorious manner ' or ' gloriously,' as though they described the mode of the divine rewarding. Others take them to mean ' in the glorious life of the coming age.' If this be the meaning, then the needs of which Paul speaks will be spiritual needs ; and it may be argued that the reference to the interest accumulating (ver. 17) is favourable to this interpretation. There are others, again, who take the words **in Glory** closely with wealth, as if Paul meant that God's wealth had its abode in His Glory or power (for ' glory ' is sometimes all but synonymous with ' power ' : see Sanday and Headlam on Rom. 6 : 4). This very variety of exposition shows that the words do not take their place easily and naturally in their context. Is it possible that through some accident the word ' glory ' has slipped in from the next verse ? Its removal from

226

the present verse would leave the much more simple and intelligible expression his wealth in Christ Jesus. It is possible, however, that in Christ Jesus should be taken closely with will supply and not with wealth. In him, ' the ever-blessed sphere in which alone all is realised ' (Ellicott), will the needs of the Philippians be supplied.

The great passage ends with a doxology in which glory is 20 ascribed **to God our Father for ever and ever.** As in Gal. 1 : 5, the doxology is called forth by the thought of the goodness of God. Nor is it out of harmony with this to suggest that its introduction in our passage may be due, at least in part, to Paul's desire to lift his readers up into the very presence of God in order that any disaffection or ill-will that still remained in their hearts might be removed, for in His presence all ill-feelings wither and die. ' Lift up your heart to God,' writes Wesley to one of his correspondents, ' or you will be angry with me ' (*Letters*, p. 205). As is usual in doxologies, the **word glory** has the definite article in the Greek : the glory ascribed to God is the glory that is due to Him.

FINAL SALUTATIONS AND BENEDICTION (IV. 21–23)

Salute every saint in Christ Jesus. The brothers beside me 21 salute you. All the saints salute you, especially the 22 Imperial slaves. The grace of the Lord Jesus Christ be 23 with your spirit. Amen.

A few brief salutations and a benediction bring the letter to its close. These would probably be written in the Apostle's own hand, for he tells us in 2 Thess. 3 : 17 that a salutation in his own hand was a mark in every letter of his. Compare also 1 Cor. 16 : 21, Gal. 6 : 11, Col. 4 : 18.

Why no individual Philippians are mentioned we can only surmise. Why is there no greeting for Lydia and the jailer ? Some special greetings may have been sent by Epaphroditus. Or perhaps the Apostle, in view of the dissensions in the Church, omitted all personal salutations so as not to give his readers any possible ground for questioning his impartiality.

21   **Salute every saint in Christ Jesus.**   So also the A.V. and the
R.V. render.   To whom is this injunction addressed ?   Perhaps
to the bishops whom the Apostle greets in the opening salutation (1 : 2), for to them the epistle would be delivered, and to
one of them would be assigned the duty of reading it to the
assembled Church.   Beet does not think the injunction is
addressed to any small group, for he says : ' To the Church
collectively is committed a greeting for every member of it.'

The Apostle sends his greeting to **every saint**—to every
member of the Church individually.   Compare the greeting
in 3 John 15 : ' salute the friends one by one.'   Trapp remarks
that it would be ' a great encouragement to the meaner to be
so respected.'   In his parting word, as throughout the epistle,
Paul makes it plain that he does not countenance their differences.   For the word **saints** see on 1 : 1.

The word **salute** is common in the New Testament ; and
the papyri have shown that it was the regular word used for
conveying a greeting at the end of a letter (see Moulton and
Milligan, *Vocabulary*, p. 85).

Grammatically the words **in Christ Jesus** may go either with
salute or with **every saint**.   Kennedy, Beet, Jones, Plummer,
Dibelius, connect them with **salute,** and to this view Lightfoot
inclines.   Lipsius and Moule connect them with **every saint,**
and Ellicott regards this construction as ' perhaps slightly
the more probable.'   It is no argument in favour of connect-
ing the words with **salute** to say that **saints** is sufficiently
defined without the addition of **in Christ Jesus,** for in 1 : 1 Paul
speaks of the ' saints in Christ Jesus.'   It gives ' spiritual
emphasis to the greeting,' as Beet observes, to take the words
with **salute.**   The only New Testament passages that have any
bearing on the question are Rom. 16 : 22 and 1 Cor. 16 : 19,
in both of which ' in the Lord ' goes with **salute.**

The brothers beside me salute you, continues the Apostle.
So in Gal. 1 : 2 he mentions ' all the brothers who are beside
me.'   For the term ' brother ' see on 1 : 12.   Some scholars
have felt that the present clause and the censure of 2 : 21 are
so incompatible that they cannot possibly belong to the same
letter.   In so far as there is justification for this feeling it helps

to confirm our suspicions regarding the right of 2 : 19-24 to form part of our epistle (see the notes on the paragraph) ; but the one text is not necessarily incompatible with the other (see Moffatt, *Introduction to the Lit. of the N.T.*, p. 175).

Who the brothers are it is not easy to say. The Philippians would understand. Epaphroditus can scarcely be included, since he would be at Philippi when the letter was read. We think of Prisca and Aquila, of Timotheus and Apollos who were at Ephesus when Paul was there. Some of those named in Rom. 16—if that chapter was sent to Ephesus—may well be among the brothers who send their greetings to Philippi.

There follows the greeting of the whole Church at Ephesus 22 —all the saints salute you. Compare the similar greeting in 2 Cor. 13 : 13. Of one group in the Church the Apostle emphasizes the greeting—especially, he says, the Imperial slaves. This rendering might conceivably give the impression that all the Imperial slaves in the place from which Paul was writing were saints. It would be a more exact rendering of the Greek to say ' especially those who are of the number of the Imperial slaves.'

Both the A.V. and the R.V. have the literal rendering ' they that are of Caesar's household.' Our translation correctly interprets ' Caesar's household ' as the Imperial slaves ; the term, of course, would include freedmen as well as slaves. The word ' household ' could refer to the Emperor's *family*, but the reference here is certainly to the Imperial servants. It has been pointed out in the *Introduction* that these slaves were to be found elsewhere than in Rome, and that there exists inscriptional evidence that there were at Ephesus associations of Imperial freedmen and slaves. In Paul's time, as Kennedy says, ' most of the Emperor's household servants came from the East.' It may be that those whose greetings the Apostle sends to Philippi belonged to Ephesus before they entered the Imperial household and were now living in retirement in their native city. Lightfoot, who regards our epistle as sent from Rome, and assumes that Rom. 16 was sent to Rome, argues in a special note (pp. 171–8) that the salutations in Romans include the names of some members of the Imperial household who sent their greetings to Philippi. He calls attention to the fact that many of the names found in Rom. 16 are to be met with in inscriptions, chiefly sepulchral, relating to the household of the Emperor found in the neighbourhood of Rome. If Rom. 16 was sent to Ephesus, it is still possible—inasmuch as our epistle was probably sent from Ephesus—to think that among the names in Rom. 16 are some of the Imperial slaves whose greetings are sent to Philippi.

As to the reason for the special emphasis on the greeting of the Imperial slaves we can only guess. Apparently the Philippians were acquainted with them. They may have visited Philippi on some Imperial mission ; or perhaps when they retired from Rome they had returned to Ephesus by way of Macedonia and had been hospitably entertained by the Philippian Christians.

23 Last of all comes the benediction : **The grace of the Lord Jesus Christ be with your spirit.** All Paul's letters have a benediction at or near their close, and in every benediction he invokes the **grace** of the Lord Jesus Christ upon his readers. For the word grace see on 1 : 2. It is ' peace ' that is invoked in the benedictions of 1 Pet. 5 : 14 and 3 John 14. Col. 4 : 18 has the simple form ' Grace be with you.' Compare also the benedictions in 1 Timotheus, 2 Timotheus, Titus, and Hebrews. The most elaborate of the Pauline benedictions is that in 2 Cor. 13 : 14.

The Apostle prays that the grace may be with the **spirit** of his readers. So in Gal. 6 : 18 and Philem. 25. Cf. 2 Tim. 4 : 22. In our verse the A.V. has ' with you all ' instead of **with your spirit**, but the authority for its reading is weak. Paul uses the singular **spirit**, although a number of persons are addressed. Plummer compares Rom. 8 : 16 and 1 Thess. 5 : 23. Spirit is here used, seemingly, not, as so often in Paul's letters, for the regenerate nature of those who are in Christ, but for the inner nature of man.

Our translation agrees with the A.V. in reading **Amen.** Westcott and Hort and the R.V. omit it, but the evidence for it is strong.

INDEX

231

INDEX

Love, 19-21, 26, 38-40, 76, 78 f.,
150
Luther, 28, 38, 192
Lydia, ix, 48, 190

MACKENZIE, 46
Mackintosh, 84, 86 f.
McMichael, W. F., 168
McNeile, A. H., xiii, xvi
Merit, 205 f.
Meyer, 64, 93, 153
Milligan, 6, 8, 10, 105, 113
Mind, 16, 199 f.
Moffatt, xiii f., xx, 15, 23, 43, 83,
107, 115, 124 f., 131-3, 138, 141,
148, 164 f., 169, 171, 185, 188,
191, 194, 229
Morality, pagan, 201 f., 205 f.,
215 f.
Moses, 48, 68, 99-101, 104, 122,
164
Moule, 25, 32, 42, 68, 73, 78-80,
93 f., 119, 121, 124, 130, 148,
155, 197 f., 215
Moulton, J. H., 75, 150, 152
Moulton & Milligan, 6, 10, 12,
16, 20, 23 f., 27, 41, 50, 56 f., 86,
96, 105, 108, 114 f., 190, 195 f.,
203-6, 216, 224, 228
Mystery Cults, 152-4, 161, 165

NAME, 94-6
Nature, 86, 91, 152, 164-7
Newman, 48, 174

OMEN, 70 f.
Opponents, 68-70
Origen, 192

PAGET, 167
Parousia, 13, 25, 58, 108, 183,
187
Peace, 7, 198-202, 207 f., 230
Peake, 149
Perfect (or Perfection), 155-61,
164, 172 f.
Philippi, ix f., xix f., 4, 69, 181
Plummer, 81, 86, 174, 201, 212,
230
Polycarp, 6, 63
Praetorium, 28-31
Praise (of God), 26
Prayer, 8, 10 f., 19-21, 48 f.,
197 f., 201

Preachers, 36-44, 79, 133
Preaching (Christ), 37, 40
Pride, to (or to exult), 138
Privilege, 138-44
Prize, 163 f.
Proclaiming (Christ), 37, 40 f.
Progress, 28, 60, 155 f.
Prove, to, 22 f.
Pure, 203 f.
Purpose (of God), 12, 40, 95

RAINY, 21, 36, 67, 164, 166, 175 f.,
197
Ramsay, 188, 190, 213 f., 219
Randolph, B. W., 63
Remembrance, 10
Renan, 190
Resurrection, 154, 156 f., 185
Resurrection (of Christ), 150-3
Return (of Christ), 194, 197
Revive, to, 213
Ridley, Bishop, 32, 34
Righteousness, 25 f., 149 f., 158
Robertson, F. W., 156, 160 f.
Robertson & Plummer, 20
Robinson, Armitage, 20
Robinson, B. W., xiv
Romanes, 167
Rome, xii-xiv, xvi-xxi, 29, 229 f.
Ruin, 175

SACRIFICE, 109-11
Saints, 1, 3 f., 228 f.
Salvation, 42, 48, 70 f., 98-104
Sanday & Headlam, 22
Savonarola, 62 f., 72, 109
Scare, to, 68 f.
Self-sufficiency (of Paul), 209 f.,
211 f., 214-17, 223
Servants, 1-3, 116, 229 f.
Silas, ix
Sirach, 204, 213, 221
Smith, David, 190
Soul, 65 f., 79, 113
Souter, 42, 180
Spirit, 65, 230
Spirit (of Jesus), 49, 59, 85
Stevenson, R. L., 167
Stimulus, 76
Suffering(s), 71-3, 151-3
Supplication. See Prayer
Syntyche, 188-94
Synzygos, 191

233

INDEX